PHILOSOPHY AND SCIENCE IN PHENOMENOLOGICAL PERSPECTIVE

PHAENOMENOLOGICA
COLLECTION FONDÉE PAR H.L. VAN BREDA ET PUBLIÉE
SOUS LE PATRONAGE DES CENTRES D'ARCHIVES-HUSSERL

95

PHILOSOPHY AND SCIENCE IN PHENOMENOLOGICAL PERSPECTIVE

edited by

KAH KYUNG CHO

PHILOSOPHY AND SCIENCE IN PHENOMENOLOGICAL PERSPECTIVE

edited by

KAH KYUNG CHO

1984 **MARTINUS NIJHOFF PUBLISHERS**
a member of the KLUWER ACADEMIC PUBLISHERS GROUP
DORDRECHT / BOSTON / LANCASTER

Distributors

for the United States and Canada: Kluwer Academic Publishers, 190 Old Derby Street, Hingham, MA 02043, USA

for the UK and Ireland: Kluwer Academic Publishers, MTP Press Limited, Falcon House, Queen Square, Lancaster LA1 1RN, England

for all other countries: Kluwer Academic Publishers Group, Distribution Center, P.O. Box 322, 3300 AH Dordrecht, The Netherlands

Library of Congress Cataloging in Publication Data

Philosophy and science in phenomenological perspective.

(Phaenomenologica ; 95)
"Articles included in this volume originate from contributions to the International Conference on Philosophy and Science in Phenomenological Perspective, held in Buffalo in March 1982"--Pref.
Includes bibliographical references and index.
1. Phenomenology--Congresses. I. Cho, Kah Kyung.
II. International Conference on Philosophy and Science in Phenomenological Perspective (1982 : Buffalo, N.Y.)
III. Series.
B829.5.P49 1984 142'.7 84-1463

ISBN-13: 978-94-009-6115-9 e-ISBN-13: 978-94-009-6113-5
DOI: 10.1007/978-94-009-6113-5

Copyright

CONTENTS

To the Memory of Marvin Farber

PREFACE

The articles included in this volume originate from contributions to the *International Conference on Philosophy and Science in Phenomenological Perspective*, held in Buffalo in March 1982. The occasion had been to honor the late Professor Marvin Farber, a long time distinguished member of the Department of Philosophy, State University of New York at Buffalo, and the Founding Editor of the journal, *Philosophy and Phenomenological Research.*

Many of the papers were subsequently rewritten, expanded or otherwise edited to be published in the series *Phaenomenologica*. The articles by Professor Frings and Professor Rotenstreich had not been presented at the conference, although they were originally invited papers. We regret that not all papers submitted to the conference, including comments, could be accommodated in this volume. Nonetheless, our sincere gratitude is due to all participants who have made the conference a memorable and worthy event.

The Department of Philosophy, State University of New York at Buffalo, as the sponsor of the conference, wishes to acknowledge the grants from the *Conferences in the Disciplines Program, Conversations in the Disciplines Program,* and the *International Studies* of the State University of New York at Buffalo, as well as for a grant from the National Endowment for the Humanities.

The International Phenomenological Society, with Professor Roderick Chisholm succeeding Marvin Farber as its president, co-sponsored the conference.

Special thanks are due to Professor Jorge Gracia, who helped mobilize the resources in Buffalo for the conference, and to Professor Samuel IJsseling of the Husserl-Archives at Louvain for his support in making this publication possible. We also wish to express our gratitude to Mr. A.W. Schimmelpenninck of the Martinus Nijhoff Publishing Co., for his kind cooperation.

June, 1984 Buffalo

Cho, K.K. (ed.) Philosophy and Science in Phenomenological Perspective.

ISBN 978-94-009-6115-9

INTRODUCTION: PHENOMENOLOGY AS RIGOROUS PHILOSOPHY IN THEORY AND PRACTICE

KAH KYUNG CHO (BUFFALO)

In a letter to Dorion Cairns dated March 21, 1930, Husserl spoke of his project of "Philosophy as Rigorous Science" as an attempt to "secure an infinitely progressive co-operative work," and lamented that "nearly all of his former disciples were stuck in half-heartedness and shunned the radicalism which is so essential and necessary for phenomenology."[1]

Today, a little over half a century later, the philosophical movement that Husserl brought into being cannot complain of a dearth of proof regarding the progress of its research. Nor is the congenial spirit of cooperation among its followers, often defying the distance between continents, lacking. For all practical purposes, the movement has provided a global forum for young and established scholars alike to try their skill at freely varying the "essential" ways to look at "phenomena". That as a result Husserl's own demonstrations were less than rigorously adopted was seen even as a sign of fidelity to the very spirit of phenomenology.[2] The upshot of this is the bewildering array of interpretive and creative works that now fill the annual catalogue of phenomenology-related publications. Many of these Husserl would have regarded just as half-hearted, oblivious to the call for a radical reflection which to him was the only way to continue the work that began with the promise of a thoroughgoing scientific rigor.

It was the rise of "existentially" or "anthropologically" oriented philosophers from among the foremost ranks of his "school" that Husserl eyed with increasing suspicion. The "realism and anthropologism" mentioned in his letter were no doubt a reference to the thoughts of Heidegger and Scheler, who had already established divergent interpretations of phenomenology and thus directly or indirectly undermined the influence of Husserl. If the undiscriminating eyes

1. Dorion Cairns, "A Letter from Husserl," in *Edmund Husserl 1859-1959 Recueil Commémoratif (Phaenomenologica 4)*, The Hague 1959, p. 285.
2. See Marvin Farber, *Phenomenology and Existence*, New York 1967, p. 19.

Cho, K.K. (ed.) Philosophy and Science in Phenomenological Perspective.

ISBN 978-94-009-6115-9

of the wider public saw in Heidegger and Scheler contributors to the common cause of phenomenology, Husserl certainly did not share such a view. In fact, by the time he wrote to Cairns, he had given up whatever hopes he had of his more famous "followers", and was now confiding his inner worries to a man who seemed free of biases, as if by so doing he would get some consolation. In 1938, Husserl died a very lonely man, his work unfinished, his once numerous students scattered.

When, some twenty years later, the publication of his manuscripts revived the interest in Husserl's philosophy, this renewal was not to serve, at least not primarily, the cause of phenomenology as a rigorous scientific philosophy. For the "renaissance" of phenomenology has been inspired to a great extent by the directional signal of the *life-worldly* turn, and the "life-world" had been understood to represent a "counter-concept to the world of science."[3] How was it possible that Husserl's original design to ground the science more concretely and radically in the life-worldly experience, had in all appearance propelled the phenomenological movement into an opposite direction? Did not Husserl conceive of the life-world as the roots, as the matrix and source of all "norms" and "categories" that are valid for science?

Three factors may have contributed to this unintended turn. The first is the historically associative connotation of "life". Since Dilthey and Nietzsche, but also since Bergson, life had become closely associated with a dynamic force that is unfathomable and fluid, with the irrational will and with the vital "*élan*" that is opposed to scientific reason and understanding. Husserl's reference to the life-world as the source of "subjective-relative" evidence whose authority rests on "immediate seeing" was hardly calculated to enhance the stature of an absolute, rigorous philosophy. The second is the internal development of phenomenology in a wider circle. Although Heidegger had spearheaded the trend to "finitude", which not only focused on the finite, temporal structure of man's existence, but also frontally challenged Husserl's ambition to establish a "definitive" and finally valid philosophical science, it was the French wing of existentialized phenomenology that gave currency to a *lived experience*, as if the phenomenology of perception and bodily comportment was the logical extention of Husserl's own life-worldly problematic. The third and more grave factor may be the inherent difficulty and weakness of Husserl's *Crisis*-work in presenting his case before the jury of science. The principle of intuition, no matter how constructively its role in vindicating the right of man's "sensuous" nature may be viewed within the recent history of philosophy dominated by abstract reason, could not

3. Hans-Georg Gadamer, "The Phenomenological Movement," in *Philosophical Hermeneutics*, Los Angeles 1976, p. 152.

be overextended to cover the territory of science. For modern sciences, theoretical physics in particular, have gone a long way toward a methodically refined formalization which made it possible, nay, even necessary, to "give up the intuitive understanding,"[4] something that Husserl felt indispensable for all levels of theoretical abstractions.

But the real hindrance to a "co-operative" work in unfolding the problem of life-world was the "transcendental turn" that Husserl gave to his phenomenology. It was precisely by applying the method of *reduction* to the utmost that Husserl had hoped to radicalize his program of philosophy as a rigorous science. Life-world was not meant as the irreducible residue that must be recognized in its "facticity". On the contrary, this one grand domain of facts and factual experience also had to be subjected to reduction, had to be constituted in the transcendental consciousness. The procedure would be the same as with all other objects, leaving only the transcendental ego as the absolute pole, with the rest of the world, including the empirical ego, its body and perceptions, completely bracketed. Even when the phenomena to be described were no longer the abstract, higher-level logical entities as in *Logical Investigations*, but the so-called "subjective-relative" and individually intuitable experiences, Husserl would demand the same "aerified" reflective approach, which presupposes abstraction from the "existence" of the given objects as well as complete detachment of the observer from worldly involvement.

Merleau-Ponty, however, has taken issue with this purely "theoretiical," impartial, spectator's stance. In the living flow of ordinary life, man primarily loses himself in actions, and only secondarily and inadequately reflects. A philosopher's life is no exception. Even his transcendental reflection must leave an unilluminated and unexplained "shadow", or the "unconscious" in life which indeed constitutes the conditions for the possibility of thought, but which could not possibly be retrieved by thought in full clarity. "The most important lesson," claimed Merleau-Ponty defiantly, "that the (theory of) reduction gives us is the impossibility of a complete reduction."[5] Instead of an after-the-fact re-tracing of a lived experience, Merleau-Ponty would settle for a basically "positivistic" method of description, conceding the "spectator-subject" no more margin of reflection than that realized by an "actor-subject" in an everyday situation. The acting ego can no more perform the act of pure seeing than the seeing ego can double as an

4. Rudolf Carnap, "Foundations of Logic and Mathematics," in *The Encyclopedia of Unified Science*, Vol. III, Chicago 1937, (Section 24, 25). See also Kah Kyung Cho, "Anschauung und Abstraktion im Lichte der modernen Wissenschaftstheorie," in *9. Deutscher Kongress für Philosophie*, Meisenheim am Glan 1969, pp. 131-158.

5. Maurice Merleau-Ponty, *Phénoménologie de la Perception*, Paris 1945, p. VIII.

acting ego. The task of phenomenological description, in order to be faithful to this restricted reality in which one lives primarily, must now be carried out with the eyes of the acting self who is absorbed in action and thus sees himself no differently from seeing a third person, unable to penetrate the inner workings of his consciousness. This slipping back from the first person to the third person turns the omni-present first person transcendental subject of Husserl into a "quasi-object" in the sense that the human body (*Leib*), not pure consciousness, is recognized as the origin of world orientation. Now perception, not reflection, becomes the primary way in which man encounters the world.

The living human body perceives itself and the world around it in a state in which the epistemological separation of the subject from the object has not yet taken place. Perception is still submerged, so to speak, in the body, which, in turn, is "engaged" with the world. This engaged behavior in response to the environment is called "comportment." Situated somewhere between pure conceptual spontaneity and dull involuntary passivity, man exists primarily as body and in terms of bodily reaction to the world. Here even the speech act, which is usually considered a higher level conscious activity than the ordinary sense perception, can be seen as a way man comports himself meaningfully within the world. Merleau-Ponty adhered strictly to the model of an executing or performing self and maintained that the speaker is simply unconscious of the complex operations going on in his psyche. Speaking is analogous to the act of eating, when one does not "know" what one's digestive organs are doing to the food. When a person speaks, the mastery of grammatical laws and phonological rules just happen to be there, intimately interwoven with the function of speech organs. Speaking for the most part unfolds itself like a natural event, beyond the reach of reflective awareness.[6] The kinesthetic control of speech organs and their coordination may be transcendentally reconstructed and described, which was exactly what Husserl demanded. But Merleau-Ponty refused to place the concrete, living human being on such an abstract level of pure spectatorship. The cue of a life-worldly turn found its echo in an "existentialized turn," and Merleau-Ponty was conviced that Husserl's phenomenology could be consistently put into practice only as "existentialism."

The refusal – and in this refusal Merleau-Ponty was by no means alone – to consistently perform the transcendental reduction and to eliminate the corporeal and perceptual residues of the mundane ego presented, in Husserl's view, the largest roadblock to his cherished goal, the rigorous science. The rigor Husserl demanded was not the same as

6. *Op. cit.* Merleau-Ponty compares speaking to an electrical bulb that lights up spontaneously. See R. Boehm's German translation, Berlin 1966, p. 208.

"accuracy" or "exactness" required in the empirical sciences. Such standard "virtues" or disciplined techniques in the observation of data or in the use of logical instruments for correct reasoning and inference were certainly not spurned, but they were inevitably muffled by the constant cry for rigor. The latter presented a more general, more basic criterion for the scientific character of philosophy as such, with the greatest possible emphasis placed on the question of *beginning*. In Husserl's phenomenology, more than in Kant's critical philosophy with which it shared many essential features, the *de jure* question of how the thought must proceed had become such an overriding issue that indeed the "issues themselves" alluded to in the famous slogan should be interpreted in the sense of the *origin* and *genesis* of "meaning" and in no case as the objects understood by realism. The "half-heartedness" Husserl spoke of was a reference to the inability, or the unwillingness, of philosophers to show that all objectivities, including the "unconscious" functions of one's own body and soul, derive their meaning from the constitutive achievements of the transcendental ego. In a strict sense, therefore, there would be no "pre-given" objects, not even "passively" pre-given ones. For as long as things are *meant* to be what they are, – and only certain determinately meant objects are present to our consciousness, the "whatness" of the pre-given objects must be dissolved, according to Husserl, into the question of "how" they have become to mean what they mean. The rigor is the persistency in dissolving the "what" into "how", tracing the latter all the way back to its origin.

Of course, Husserl respected other familiar requirements pertaining to the practice of a scientific philosophy. In his article, *Philosophy as Rigorous Science*, first published in 1911 in *Logos*, he formulated several such requirements in general terms. Besides the well-known precept of presuppositionlessness, he identified the following criteria: 1. Suspension of judgment with regard to the question of existence; 2. Strict adherence to the method of pure description (of essence); 3. Neutrality toward the issues of *Weltanschauung*; 4. Disavowel of any metaphysical commitments; 5. Critique of naturalism, philosophical anthropology, psychologism and historicism. Most of these features could have been taken from a textbook glossary on scientific positivism. Husserl seemed to have felt at times that it was to his advantage to claim the title of "positivist" for himself.[7] By upholding the ideal of a purely descriptive science, refraining from any commitment to metaphysics and maintaining a critical distance to hybrid and relativistic forms of knowledge associated with philosophical anthropology and

7. *Ideen zu einer reinen Phänomenologie und phänomenologischen Philosophie*, Husserliana IV, The Hague 1950, p. 46.

historicism, Husserl would have made a respectable member in the family of positivists. But no sooner had he laid claim to the title of a "genuine" positivist than he proposed to qualify the meaning of the "positive" in his own sense, namely, as the "originary" and self-evident in the context of transcendental reflection, and thus he parted company forthwith with the positivists of any and every persuasion. For it is because "we disavow reflection"[8] that we are entitled us to be positivists. When Husserl, on the other hand, introduced the transcendental reflection as the highest authority to judge the pedigrees of positivism, not only was he stretching the well-defined meaning of positivism beyond its tolerance, but he was also transforming the character of his own phenomenological description. In the case of a strictly descriptive procedure to which he was committed initially, it had been assumed that between an act of consciousness and its "object" there was a one-to-one correlation. To a perceiving act, a perceived "object", and, similarly, to an imagining act, an imagined "object" was correlated.

A more intense reflection on the modality of givenness of an "object", however, led Husserl to the recognition that even in a straightforward "thing-experience," the structure of consciousness contained more elements of awareness than were assumed to be given immediately to the perception. The perceptual act takes on the quality of "co-awareness," as the perceived physical object tends to *imply* that there is more to be perceived; for example that there is the backside to be seen if the observer turns around the object, etc. The thematic treatment of this theory of implications marked the transition from the simple phenomenological description to the phenomenological *analysis*, which would lay bare the "horizon"-structure of consciousness, including both the spatial and temporal aspects of the wider "fringes" of our intentional experience. And it was with the formulation of this seminal idea of temporal horizon that a bridgehead was laid down for a transcendental constitution of "historicity," a dimension that at first seemed incompatible with the method of transcendental reduction that held in abeyance everything that belonged to the natural world and history. Such a reflective intensification of the analysis, in ever widening circles, of the manner in which "objects" are given to consciousness could hardly be in keeping with a positivist's conception of the straightforward description of data.

To a strictly positivistically trained philosopher, Husserl's method might appear rather undisciplined for its failure to clearly mark the region of objects, the positive data. Transcendental reflection, furthermore, would appear to him a subjectivist introspection having no real bearing on the progress of positive sciences. Such reflection could yield

8. Jürgen Habermas, *Knowledge and Human Interests*, Boston 1968, p. vii.

a better result if consigned to an empirical psychology or even to sociology, since Husserl's theory of "horizon" pointed to socio-cultural and historical background, without, of course, admitting its own indebtedness to concrete conditions obtaining in such background. It was, however, Husserl himself who subjected all historical varieties of positivism to a sharp criticism. All positive sciences turned out to be "inadequate in principle," and the first task of his "Primary Philosophy" had been to show that "it is in principle impossible to ground a philosophy on a positivist spirit."[9] For half-heartedness, lack of clarity and inconsistency were equally apparent here as among the followers of phenomenology. The thrust to the first-given, to the absolute beginning, had never been consistently carried out, although such promises were there. He could not find, in the past history of philosophy, "any such philosophy of final form, one having the form of *rigorous* science unconditionally required of philosophy." Then he went on to declare: "Without a strict scientific *beginning* there cannot be a rigorous scientific progress. It is only with a strict *First Philosophy* that a rigorous philosophy as such, a *philosophia perennis*, can emerge, – to be sure as a philosophy that is always becoming, so long as the infinity belongs to the essence of all science, – and yet in the essential form of *final* validity."[10]

"First Philosophy," "universal science," "absolute and definitively valid (*endgültig*) justification of knowledge," – to these and some other synonyms for "rigorous science" Husserl added another, a more graphical title, "archaeology of consciousness."[11] This obsession with the question of the beginning, understood here as the question of how to begin philosophy, was in itself not novel. There was the more recent precedence of Descartes. But both in name and substance, the affinity between Kant's transcendental philosophy and Husserl's transcendental phenomenology has often been noted. The most significant difference between the two, however, consisted, once again, in the way transcendental reduction was performed or neglected respectively. Unlike Kant, Husserl did not attempt simply to "deduce" propositions from *a priori* concepts presumed to be first principles. Such pre-given concepts, however evident by virtue of the established authority of rational or positive sciences, could not provide any essential knowledge for Husserl. True knowledge must be gained by seeking "to attain the beginning in a free dedication to the problems themselves and to the demands stemming from them."[12] Even when the absolute transcendental region of

9. *Erste Philosophie (1923/24), Zweiter Teil, Husserliana VIII*, The Hague 1958, p. 28.
10. *Erste Philosophie (1923/1924), Erster Teil, Husserliana VII*, 1956, p. 6.
11. *Erste Philosophie, Zweiter Teil*, p. 29.
12. "Philosophy as Rigorous Science," in *Husserl, Shorter Works*, ed. by P. McCormick & F. Elliston, Notre Dame 1981, p. 195.

subjectivity with its meaning-bestowing functions has become illuminated, it did not promise automatically that essential knowledges would follow from it. Rather, the quest for the origin, the grounding of knowledge, has to go through the laborious process of *dismantling* the prejudices and accretions of unessential meanings each and every time we confront an "object." There was no "inventory" to be taken of the transcendental phenomenological reason as if such reason had a certain fixed magnitude and inherent properties. Husserl's transcendental phenomenology understood itself in all seriousness to be a philosophy of "bottomlessness" (*Bodenlosigkeit*), for its "method" had to "first create its ground for itself."[13]

In the tradition of speculative idealism for which Husserl had no great respect, Fichte once found himself in a similar situation. There is even a slight irony that Fichte dubbed his philosophy "Doctrine of Science." Apart from the substance of the scientific claim for his thought, Fichte presented a striking figure because for him, too, the problem of beginning decided the status of philosophy. For both Fichte and Husserl, the absolute beginning had to be anchored in the pure, thinking ego. For both, again, world was something eventually *created* by this ego. Obviously sensing a difficulty here, the young Helmut Plessner had once drawn Husserl's attention to the fact that in spite of the apparent resemblance, Fichte's ego was essentially a practical and moral principle, whereas "the question of the primacy of moral, aesthetic or religious principles over against the theoretical had been closed off to him (Husserl)."[14] Thus it is only with a view to realizing a universal moral order that Fichte could speak of the "creation" of the world through ego. Before him, Kant had similar reservations about the competence and reaches of pure theoretical reason and had in effect curtailed its power "to make room for practical reason." Husserl, however, never felt himself obliged to follow such conventions. Concepts and theories are just as good as they allow themselves to be intuitively fulfilled or as they do full justice to given phenomena. On this ground, Husserl rejected much of Kant's taxonomy that sprang out from purely conceptual or architectonic deliberations. In Descartes' "ego cogito", therefore, Husserl saw the *volitional* factor already fully at work, "a *will* to absolutely and radically ground the science." "A fully conscious will" has always been behind the drive toward a "rigorous science" in other periods of history as well.[15] A pure thinking reason unaccompanied by an impetus or a "practical interest" would be an abstraction.

13. Gadamer, *op. cit.*, p. 160.
14. Helmut Plessner, "Bei Husserl in Göttingen," in *Edmund Husserl 1859-1959*, p. 37.
15. "Philosophy as Rigorous Science," *op. cit.*, p. 168.

Husserl converged also on this point with Fichte, who stressed the role of free will in his principle of ego against Kant's concept of ego as the "unity of self-consciousness." In a rare reference to Fichte's name, Husserl admitted that such impulse "still dominates Fichte's philosophizing."[16] But Husserl had actually reversed the primacy of practical reason without sacrificing the practical element. By so doing, he surpassed the speculative idealism and entitled his transcendental ego to a "world-creating" role.

Since the humanity had come of age, according to Husserl, *theory* meant the basic attitude of *life* as such. Theory was not just a partial aspect of life, to be distinguished from other, practical concerns. Theoretical life included self-examination, responsibility and guidance by a mature reason. No one exemplified this life style so well as Socrates, in whom "contemplation" or "intuition" (*Anschauung*) and rationally guided moral and social actions were totally integrated.[17] By subsuming the practical interest under the concept of "theoretical life," which he occasionally also called "transcendental life," Husserl literally universalized the scope of his transcendental constitution. Thus not only the world of science, but also the "pre-scientific" life-world itself was drawn into the sphere of constitutive analysis. Needless to say, the structures of such life could not be taken naively as pre-given, as historically preceding and conditioning the mundane existence of an empirical ego. These structures have to be interrogated as to their origin, and their progressive genesis as well as their invarient, essential frameworks have to be made visible. The transcendental ego, to whose "performance" these structures owe their being, was exalted as the "creative" origin, insofar as it critically differentiates senses from nonsenses and puts its own stamp of approval on adequately exhibited senses.

"Adequate exhibition"? But what are its criteria? It is too easy to say the transcendental ego is the ultimate source of justification. While Husserl held that "*I am*" is "the true principle of all principles" and "the first proposition of all true philosophy,"[18] it is also well known that he declared in *Ideas* (§ 24) that "*Intuition*" is "the principle of all principles." Was he having two different, even contradictory principles? Though he never brought those two principles together under one definitive headline, it should be possible, even necessary, to reformulate his principle and say that it is "*I intuit.*" It is not that the critically reflective function of "I think" should be simply replaced by an intu-

16. *Ibid.*
17. Cf. "Philosophy as Rigorous Science," *op. cit.*, p. 166. See also "Die Idee einer philosophischen Kultur," in *Japanisch-deutsche Zeitschrift für Wissenschaft und Technik*, Lübeck 1923, pp. 45-51.
18. *Erste Philosophie, Zweiter Teil*, p. 48.

ition. One does a great injustice to Husserl if one fails to appreciate his genuine concern to establish philosophy as "an infinitely progressive co-operative work," as quoted from his letter to Cairns. He was bent on consolidating philosophy as a modern, specialized research that is capable of producing firm results, and those results, like any that are achieved by positive sciences, call for a cumulative, cooperative enterprise. Geometry, therefore, provided for him the model of such cooperative and progressive science. In "The Origin of Geometry," he defined the search for origin as "the inquiry back into the most original sense in which geometry once rose, was present as the tradition of millennia, is still present for us, and is still being worked on in a lively forward development."[19]

This passage illustrates admirably Husserl's sense of "origin" and, indirectly, what he meant by intuition. The historically primary and the a-temporal essence co-exist here together with the currently progressive work which a living geometrician is contributing to his science. Which one of these three modes of temporality is the true "origin"? It is neither one of these in particular, but the common meaning that underlies them all. And such meaning must of course be directly linked to the source, the transcendental subjectivity. Strictly speaking, only the latter is the true origin. For even the so-called timeless essence actually presupposes the open-ended possibility of being infinitely verified in its meaning and identified as such by everyone, any time. Least concerned with the first meaning of historical origin in his earlier years, Husserl gradually wove this dimension into the modality of the given at the present, notably in his concept of life-world. No doubt he had become more conscious of the frailty and contingency of all human enterprises that rise and fall in history. But to him this was never to be the reason to relativize or "finitize" the essentially idealized character of science. Scientific knowledge may be shown to be idealizations of the "subjective and relative" forms of ordinary experience, but Husserl was convinced that, if proper methods were followed, definitively secure foundations can be laid once and for all, and that an infinitely forward moving and cumulative body of knowledge can be added to such foundations. A cumulatively attained knowledge of the past, like that of geometry, is handed down to us as "sedimentations," which we for the most part take over as "passive" acquisitions. However, it is the positive sense of Husserl's "intuition" that one as a beginning philosopher is called upon to relate himself to such passive possessions *actively*, namely by activating or reactivating the slumbering experience in those possessions and to verify their meaning originarily. To the extent that someone today re-enacts the mental operations leading to the "insight" of a geometrical proposition that may have been first

19. "The Origin of Geometry," in *Husserl, Shorter Works*, p. 256.

discovered by Euclid over two thousand years ago, he is said to be *seeing* originarily. That he can do so is attributed to his assuming the transcendental posture.

It may strike us as strange that Husserl, who so emphatically pleaded for cooperation among his students in order to bring about the progress of philosophical science, had lost so little time on other methodological deliberations more suitable for a group type of research. "Communicative" methods designed to facilitate exchange and critique of ideas, but also to control perceptions and other subjective experiences, appear severely underrated or not present at all in his work. Instead, his transcendental method appeared as if it was deliberately calculated to nullify dialogical and discursive interactions, although the problem of language and of "intersubjectivity" did occupy a certain central place in his total work plan. A possible answer to this charge may be found in Husserl's Cartesian point of departure, to start, so to speak, from ground "zero." This is where there is only "I am." Other persons, before they enter into communicative interactions with me, will have to be "constituted" in *my* very own perception. Whatever else comes in addition to the "living bodies" (Leiber) of other human beings, such as voice and gesture, other more complex thoughts and ideas expressed by them, – all these belong in the final analysis to the "universal stream of my own world perception,"[20] and thus Husserl would imply that the mode of the givenness of others as communicative partners will have to be justified first, in my perception.

But between pure perceptual experiences and geometrical knowledge, there is a vast field of objects of which the phenomenological analysis may not always be as lucky to summon the origin. If philosophy had to bracket nothing less than the whole world and then reintroduce selectively a group of phenomena here and another group of phenomena there, who could guarantee that eventually world itself will be restored instead of some piecemeal fragments of it? Was it not what had actually happened already during the early history of phenomenological movement? And was not the methodological appeal to "direct seeing," the inspection of objects freely reintroduced after the reduction, and freely subjected to "essential variations", the license given to phenomenologists to scramble, rather than cooperate? To be sure, there were certain lasting contributions Husserl himself, and others in other areas, have made: intentional analysis of consciousness, its application to logic and psychology, method of phenomenological reduction, free variation and exemplification. But it is an irony that some of the most influential figures that came out of the phenomenological "school" have attained their stature by contradicting Husserl's basic doctrines. Merleau-Ponty

20. See *Erste Philosophie, Zweiter Teil*, p. 60.

not only abandoned transcendental reduction, but he "finitized" or rendered finite Husserl's rather "intellectualistic" intuition[21] by anchoring it in the human body. The sense of continuity and the promise of infinite progress for phenomenology as science were sharply censured by Heidegger's existential-ontological interpretation in which the theme of Dasein's finitude replaced the infinite reflections of transcendental ego. Another irony is that Gilbert Ryle, in his scant compliments made to Husserl, recognized, of all things, "elucidation of concepts" as "sometimes original and illuminating," while decrying the method claimed for phenomenology as a "sham."[22] It is an irony because such original and illuminating conceptual elucidations were made possible, after all, because Husserl did not trust the traditional philosophical praxis of conceptual analysis, and went on to devise his own method of *seeing* directly, rather than talking indirectly, about the phenomena, by way of conceptual analysis.

Though this principle of intuition had proved to be fruitful as shown in many of Husserl's own demonstrations, the ideal of philosophy as rigorous science remained a promise not even halfway substantiated. In the deeper layers of Husserl's complex philosophical enterprise, moreover, there are promises that are not yet clearly identified as to their idealistic, critical or even "realistic" imports. He had imposed more tasks on those who even superficially "practice" some of his ways of looking at the world than he could actually resolve, and thus more close examination will be needed to separate the dead from the living elements of his philosophy.

The articles collected now in this volume will first be noted for the diversity of their topics. Such diversity is at once testimony to the enormous proliferation that research in phenomenology has undergone during the past several decades. By the same token, the internationality of contributing scholars may be taken as an index of the variety of philosophical traditions, of their styles and idioms that have widened, but also merged the horizons of phenomenological research. However, the main focus of the volume remained the classical, and thus in a sense perennial, problems which engaged Husserl's early attention. These are: intentionality, the idea of scientific rigor, critique of psychologism, the method of reduction, phenomenological concept of the "thing itself," time and time consciousness. Thus it is hoped that this volume brings an up-dated cross sectional view of the more lasting issues of Husserl's

21. E. Levinas spoke of "deeply intellectualist character of Husserl's intuitionism," in *The Theory of Intuition in Husserl's Phenomenology*, translated by A. Orianne, Evanston 1973, p. 155.
22. See Gilbert Ryle, "Review of M. Farber, The Foundation of Phenomenology," in *Philosophy*, Vol. 21, 1946, p. 267.

phenomenology, while integrating several important topics from nearby and applied fields.

THE INTENTIONAL APPROACH TO ONTOLOGY

RODERICK CHISHOLM (Providence)

FOREWORD

I am deeply honored to take part in this philosophical colloquium in honor of Marvin Farber. As philosophers we all know his work and we are thankful to him for his lasting contributions to our subject. Many of us have had the privilege of knowing him personally and of working with him. We cherish the memory of our association with this outstanding philosopher and genuine human being.

I will pay tribute to him in the best way that I know how – not just by talking about philosophy but by doing philosophy and trying to do it rigorously.

I will address myself to one of the central themes of the philosophical tradition that was founded by Franz Brentano and carried on by his immediate followers, Husserl, Meinong, Marty, and Twardowski. It was as a part of this tradition that Husserl founded the *Jahrbuch für Philosophie und phänomenologische Forschung* in 1913 and that Farber revived the journal in 1940 as *Philosophy and Phenomenological Research*.

I would propose "intentionalism" as the best term for this way of looking at philosophy.

One of the fundamental theses of intentionalism is this: that the phenomena of intentionality provide us with the means of understanding the general nature of reality. I will discuss this thesis today and try to say how it may be applied to two philosophical questions. The questions are: What is the nature of properties or attributes? And what is the distinction between those properties that are *psychological*, or *mental*, and those that are not? In answering the latter question, we may be said to be describing the nature of the psychological.

I will discuss these entities, not by reference to the *language* we use to represent them, but by reference to the kinds of *thoughts* we can have about them. That is to say, I will consider properties or attributes

Cho, K.K. (ed.) Philosophy and Science in Phenomenological Perspective.

ISBN 978-94-009-6115-9

as possible intentional objects and, in particular, as possible objects of attribution and conception. By taking this point of view, we are able to understand the *structure* of properties in a way we could not otherwise do. Thus we can distinguish between properties that are affirmative and properties that are negative; we can single out certain properties as being conjunctive and certain other properties as being disjunctive; we can, therefore, distinguish between properties that are compound and those that are noncompound. We are able to formulate a nontrivial criterion of property identity. And, as I have said, we are able to distinguish those properties that are *psychological* from those that are not.

My paper may be somewhat difficult to follow. I will compensate for this fact by making it relatively brief.

WHAT IS A PROPERTY?

Every philosopher must take some philosophical expressions as undefined. I will make use of four such expressions, all of them familiar. One is the concept of *exemplification* – as in "Socrates exemplifies humanity" and "Nothing exemplifies unicornicity." A second is that of *de re* necessity – as in "Socrates is necessarily such that he is self-identical." A third is the intentional concept of *considering* – as in "He considers what it is for a thing to be red" (more accurately, "The property of being red is such that he considers what it is for a thing to have it"). And the fourth is the intentional concept of *attributing* – as in "We attribute to him the motive of being altruistic." The two intentional concepts – considering and attributing – correspond in fundamental respects to what Brentano called *Vorstellen* and *Urteilen*, or presentation and judgment. The second implies the first but includes an element of commitment that is not present in the first.

What, then, is a property?

We could consider defining a *property* as that which is capable of being exemplified. We would then be saying that a property is a thing which is possibly such that there is something that exemplifies it. But there are properties that cannot possibly be exemplified. There is, for example, the property of being able to square the circle, a property Thomas Hobbes is said to have attributed to himself. And so we will not define the concept of a property in terms of exemplification.

Instead we will define it *intentionally*, in terms of attribution. A property is that which is capable of being attributed. In other words, a property is anything which is possibly such that there is someone who attributes it to something.

We have an answer, then, to the question "What is a property?"

The sense of "attribution" that is here presupposed is that of so-called *de re* believing. Recent studies of intentionality have shown, I think, that philosophers during the present century have made a fundamental mistake about the *objects* of believing. They have assumed that, in the first instance, believing is a matter of the acceptance of propositions. But I would say that this is wrong. In the first instance, believing is a matter, not of the acceptance of propositions, but of the attribution of properties.[1] For example, I am such that you attribute to me the property of standing, just as you are such that I attribute to you the property of sitting. So-called *de dicto* believing – the acceptance of propositions – is simply a subspecies of attributing: just as I may attribute to you the property of sitting, so may I attribute to the proposition that all men are mortal the property of being true.

Clearly whatever is attributable is also capable of being considered. We may put this point by saying what we have said implies that every property is conceivable.

If, in contemporary philosophy, one discusses a type of entity that is not an individual thing, one is confronted with the question: "What *criteria of identity* are there for the type of entity you are discussing?" We are now in a position to formulate an *intentional* criterion of property identity.

We have defined the concept of property by reference to attribution. And so let us also formulate our criterion of property identity by reference to attribution: A property P is identical with a property Q, if and only if: P and Q are necessarily such that, for every x, whoever attributes P to x attributes Q to x, and conversely.

BASIC RELATIONS BETWEEN PROPERTIES

Let us now look still further into the nature of properties or attributes. I will single out three different ways in which properties may be related to each other. I first consider two familiar relations which I will call property *implication* and property *inclusion*, respectively, and then I will contrast these concepts with the intentional concept of property *involvement*.

The property of being a man both implies and includes the property of being an animal. The property of rowing a boat implies but does not include the property of being a boat. We may say that one property thus *implies* another property if the first property is necessarily such that, if anything has it, then something has the second property. And

1. I have defended this view in detail in *The First Person: An Essay on Reference and Intentionality* (Brighton and Minneapolis: Harvester Press and University of Minnesota Press, 1981).

we may say that one property *includes* another property if the first property is necessarily such that whatever has it also has the second. You cannot have the property of being a man without also having the property of being an animal; therefore the property of being a man both implies and includes the property of being an animal. You cannot have the property of rowing a boat unless something has the property of being a boat; therefore the property of rowing a boat implies the property of being a boat. But you can have the property of rowing a boat without being a boat; therefore the property of rowing a boat does not include the property of being a boat.

Let us now contrast the relations of implication and inclusion with a further relation which I will call property *involvement*. This further relation is an intentional relation.

Consider these four properties: (1) being either red or round; (2) being nonred; (3) being possibly red; and (4) wanting something that is red. All these properties are intimately related to the property *being red*, yet they neither include nor imply it. They *involve* the property red in the following sense: each is necessarily such that it is impossible for anyone to consider something as having it without also considering something as having the property red.

One property may be said, then, to *involve* another property if the first is necessarily such that whoever considers something as having it also considers something as having the second.

The conjunctive property of being *both* red *and* round implies and involves the property of being round and it also implies and involves the property of being red. The *disjunctive* property of being *either* red *or* round also involves the property of being round (for you can't conceive the property of being either red or round without conceiving the property of being round), but it does *not* imply the property of being round. So, too, for the *negative* property of being nonround: it involves but does not imply the property of being round. Again, the *intentional* property of wanting to walk involves but does not imply the property of walking. The *dispositional* property of being intoxicating involves but does not imply the property of being intoxicated. And, finally, the *causal* property, preventing malaria, involves but does not imply the property of having malaria. Thus, many properties involve properties they do not imply.

And many properties imply properties they do not involve. Being red, for example, implies – but does not involve – being either red or round; it also implies but does not involve the property of being either red and round or red and nonround, as well as the property of being self-identical and that of being such that 7 and 5 are 12.

We may now use the intentional concept of involvement in order to explicate the internal structure of properties.

The property of being red may be said to be an *affirmative* property and that of being nonred may be said to be *negative*. The distinction is not a function of the fact that we use negative expressions such as "non" or "not" in connection with just one of the two expressions; it is not a linguistic distinction at all. It has to do, rather, with the structure or inner nature of the properties themselves.

We should note, first, that red and nonred are *contradictory* properties: each is necessarily such that whatever has it fails to have the other. And we should note, secondly, that nonred involves red and that red does not involve nonred. That is to say, one cannot conceive the property nonred without also conceiving the property red, but one can conceive the property red without conceiving the property nonred. This fact may be put briefly by saying: nonred *properly involves* red.

We could say, then, that a *negative property* is a property that properly involves its contradictory.[2]

Frege professed to see no difference whatever between affirmative and negative *Gedanken*, or states of affairs. I suspect he would have said the same thing about properties. But this intentional approach to properties shows us that, if he were to say such a thing about properties, he would be mistaken.

What is a *conjunctive* property? We may say that a conjunctive property is a property which bears a special relation to two further properties: it both implies and involves those further properties; it is implied by everything that implies both of those two properties; and neither of these properties involves the other. The two properties are the *conjuncts* of the conjunction. The property *red and round* will thus be a conjunction of the properties *red* and *round*. But it will not be a conjunction of *red* and *both round and self-identical*, for the property *red* does not involve the latter property.

A *disjunctive* property is a property that is related in the following way to two other properties: it is necessarily such that it is exemplified by a thing only if the thing has one or the other of the two properties; it involves each of the two properties but does not imply them; and neither one of the two properties involves the other. The two properties are its *disjuncts*. The expression "(red and round) or colored" will not

2. This definition has the consequence that the property expressed by "being both self-identical and nonred" is a negative property. We could avoid this consequence by defining "P is a negative property" this way: "There is a property Q such that P contradicts and properly involves Q; and P does not properly involve anything that contradicts and properly involves Q."

have a disjunctive property as its sense, for the sense of "red and round" involves that of "red."

A property may be said to be *compound* if it is either a negative property or a conjunction of properties or a disjunction of properties.

PSYCHOLOGICAL PROPERTIES

We are now able to make precise a distinction that is of first importance to philosophy – namely, the distinction between those properties that are *psychological*, or *mental*, and those that are not.

I shall interpret "psychological," or "mental," in such a way that a psychological or mental property can only be a property that implies *thinking* or *consciousness.*[3] But I will not *define* the psychological in terms of thinking or consciousness; instead, I will define the psychological in such a way that we will be in a position to define thinking or consciousness in terms of the psychological.

The simplest way of formulating the distinction is to restrict ourselves to a certain type of property – to what we may call, arbitrarily, *restricted properties*. In this way, we will be able to avoid a considerable amount of circumlocution. A "restricted property" will be a property having three different features: (1) only individual things can have it; (2) any individual that can have it can have it or fail to have it at any period during which the individual exists; and (3) it is possible that there are many individuals that have it and many individuals that do not have it. These three conditions may be illustrated by noting certain properties that *fail* to exemplify them. The properties of being an even number and being believed about fail to satisfy the first condition (for abstract objects may have them); the properties of being 27 years old, of being a thing such that it did walk, and of being a thing such that it will walk fail to satisfy the second condition (the first two cannot be had at the first moment of a thing's existence and the third cannot be had at the last); and the properties of being an individual thing and of being the tallest man do not satisfy the third condition (it is not possible that there are many individuals that have them and many that do not). It is obvious that most of the properties we have been discussing are "restricted" in the present sense of the term.

Let us now consider three different groups of psychological property. They are all "restricted."

Those of the first group are such that they both imply and involve

3. Compare C.I. Lewis, "Some Logical Considerations Concerning the Mental," in *Readings in Philosophical Analysis*, ed. H. Feigl and W.S. Sellars (New York: Appleton Century Crofts, 1949), pp. 385-92.

certain (restricted) properties they do not include. Examples are: (1) judging truly that there are nine planets; (2) perceiving that there is a cat on the roof; and (3) successfully endeavoring to raise one's arm. Judging truly that there are nine planets implies and involves but does not include the property of being a planet; perceiving that there is a cat on the roof implies and involves but does not include the property of being a cat; and successfully endeavoring to raise one's arm implies and involves but does not include the property of being an arm.

The second type of psychological property may be derived by generalizing upon those of the first type. The resulting property is implied and involved by the corresponding property of the first type, but it does not imply everything that the first type of property implies. Corresponding to our examples of the first type of psychological property, we have the following: (1) judging that there are nine planets; (2) taking there to be a cat; and (3) endeavoring to raise one's arm. These properties involve certain properties they do not include but they do not imply those properties. Thus, believing that there are nine planets involves the property of being a planet but does not imply it. And analogously for the other examples.

The properties of the third group may be arrived at by generalizing upon those in the second. But unlike those in the second, they do not even involve any properties they do not include. They are: (1) judging; (2) taking; and (3) endeavoring.

With these examples in mind we are now in a position to characterize the distinction between those properties that are psychological and those that are not.

There is one logical characteristic – I will call it the property of being "purely qualitative" – which, I suggest, is peculiar to what is psychological or mental. The members of the third set of properties that we have just singled out are all thus purely qualitative: judging, taking, and endeavoring. So, too, for believing, being pleased, wishing, wanting, hoping, sensing, feeling. Each of these properties is *purely qualitative* in the following sense: (1) it is possibly such that only *one* thing has it; and (2) it is a restricted property that includes every restricted property it implies or involves.[4] These two features provide us with a sufficient condition of the psychological.

Although the property of judging is purely qualitative, the property of judging that there are nine planets is not purely qualitative. For the

4. We should modify this definition if we wish to say that the disjunctive property, being pleased or displeased, is a purely qualitative property. We could replace clause (2) by "a purely qualitative property is a property that is logically equivalent to a disjunction of two restricted properties, each of which includes every property it implies or involves."

latter property involves but does not include the property of being a planet.

Some psychological properties, then, are purely qualitative and some are not. But every psychological property *includes* a property that is purely qualitative. And indeed we may take this fact as the defining mark of the psychological: a *psychological property* is a property that includes a purely qualitative property.

The members of each of our three groups of psychological properties all satisfy this description, for each such property includes a property that is purely qualitative. But the members of the second and third groups, unlike the members of the first group, are *purely psychological*. What, then, is the relevant sense of "purely psychological property"? We may say that a purely psychological property is a psychological property which is such that every restricted property it implies involves a property that is purely qualitative.

We could also characterize the *mental* in terms of the purely psychological. The properties in our first group are mental but we may be hesitant to call them psychological. The properties in the second and third groups, however, are quite clearly mental properties.

Purely psychological properties are those properties to which we have privileged access. Every such property is necessarily such that, if a person has it and if he attributes it to himself, then his attribution is *evident* in the strongest sense of the term.

Here, then, we have some of the consequences of viewing philosophical questions intentionally. This approach to philosophy seems to me to be of fundamental importance and I will do what I can to continue it.

THE QUESTION OF THE RATIONALITY OF SOCIAL INTERACTION

KARL-OTTO APEL (Frankfurt)

I

The topic of my paper could have its place in the context of analytical theory of action. But within the framework of a post-behavioristic approach, this type of action-theory seems to converge broadly with that of a phenomenology of action. Viewed this way, the question under discussion could hold a twofold cognitive interest. Relating the concept of *action* to the concept of *rationality* may, on the one hand, serve to explicate the concept of action (for example, in the sense of a typology of actions according to the criteria of their specific rationality or degree of rationalization). On the other hand, using the concept of rationality or rationalization in order to characterize types of action provides a method of explicating the concept of rationality or reason (for example, in the sense of a distinction between different concepts or types of rationality).[1]

The second direction corresponds to an old concern in philosophy: from Plato's distinction between *nous* and *dianoia*, through Kant's and Hegel's critical distinction between *Vernunft* and *Verstand*, up to the Frankfurt School's critique of a purely "instrumental reason." But it is obvious that these traditional attempts at explication and differentiation of the concept of rationality represent a style of thought other than that of modern action-theory. It could be, indeed, that a mutual explication and differentiation of the concepts of action and rationality may be more fruitful than the traditional attempts at distinguishing (for

1. Cf. Karl-Otto Apel, "Types of Rationality Today: The Continuum of Reason Between Science and Ethics," in *Rationality To-Day*, ed. Théodore F. Geraets (Ottawa: University of Ottawa Press, 1969), pp. 301-39; Apel, "The Common Presuppositions of Hermeneutics and Ethics: Types of Rationality Beyond Science and Technology," in *Phenomenology and the Human Sciences*, ed. John Sallis, vol. 9, Research in Phenomenology (Atlantic Highlands, N.J.: Humanities Press, 1979), pp. 35-53.

Cho, K.K. (ed.) Philosophy and Science in Phenomenological Perspective.

ISBN 978-94-009-6115-9

example, by reflection on one's consciousness) different faculties of the soul as faculties of rationality.

It is from this point of view that I shall pose and try to answer the question as to the relationship between *rationality* and *social interaction*. One may rephrase this question in the following way: Is there a special rationality of social interaction (say, of communication) that could not be reduced to the means-ends-rationality of the intentional actions of singular subjects of action? In order to explicate this question, I shall first draw a historical line from Weber's concept of an "understanding sociology" (*verstehende Soziologie*) to modern action-theory.

II

Max Weber posed the question of the rationality of social action within the framework of his foundation of a *verstehende Soziologie*. For him, asking for rationality always meant (and simultaneously) asking for the progressive realization of rationality within the context of the "occidental rationalization-process."[2]

Weber's paradigm of rationality in general was constituted by his concept of "purposive rationality" (*Zweckrationalität*). Roughly explicated, this concept covers both technical-instrumental rationality and what today is called rationality of choice in the sense of decision-theory. Besides that, Weber also used the concept "value-rationality" in order to designate a pre-condition for the selection of ends. It is remarkable that value-rationality for him did not figure as a higher or more comprehensive concept of rationality; rather, the opposite was the case. As a sociologist, Weber adopted the following typology of kinds of action with respect to their decreasing rationality.[3]

1. The highest stage of rationality is represented by *purposive ration-*

2. See Wolfgang Schluchter, *Die Entwicklung des kontinentalen Rationalismus: Eine Analyse von Max Webers Gesellschaftsgeschichte* (Tübingen: J.C.B. Mohr, 1979); and, more recently, Jürgen Habermas, *Theorie des kommunikativen Handelns*, vol. 1 (Frankfurt: Suhrkamp, 1981), chap. 2.

3. Cf. Jürgen Habermas, "Aspects of the Rationality of Action," in *Rationality To-Day*, ed. Th.F. Geraets. In what follows I neglect the further differentiation of types of rationality that has been distilled from Max Weber's works by Habermas (see note 2), where he tries to think with Weber against Weber, so to speak, in order to show the possibility and necessity – even on Weber's premises – of supposing higher and more comprehensive forms of rationality in sociology. In contrast to this strategy of argument, I shall in this paper follow a strategy of confrontation between Weber's self-understanding (according to which no rational choice of values may be conceived of) and those rationality-presuppositions we must call on, at least implicitly, when we are arguing about rationality.

ality. It prevails, according to Weber, if the agent chooses his aims or purposes against the background of a clearly articulated horizon of values and, further, if he chooses means suitable for reaching his aims by taking into account possible side effects of their application.

2. The second highest stage is represented by *value-rationality*. It prevails if the agent chooses ends and suitable means without considering possible side effects; that is to say, he makes choices simply because he is convinced of the unconditional, internal value of a certain mode of action, such that it *ought* to be performed, irrespective of possible side effects.

This specific concept of value-rationality becomes intelligible, in my opinion, upon accepting two presuppositions.

1. Behind the idea of an action to be performed without considering possible side effects because it is unconditionally or internally valuable, we may uncover Kant's concept of an unconditional duty to be derived from the "categorical imperative." (Actually the idea of the *internal value* of an action is a neo-Kantian transformation of the Kantian standpoint and, in this sense, refers not only to moral values but also to religious and aesthetic ones.)

2. There is a special reason why Weber considers "value-rational actions" as less rational than "purpose-rational actions." It obviously goes along with his conviction that the last axioms of valuing of different persons are necessarily incommensurable and hence must be a matter of prerational of irrational decisions of conscience. ("Everybody has to choose his gods," Weber's famous dictum states.[4]) Hence, to Weber value-rationality does not mean supplementing for "purposive-rationality" a higher principle of rational choice but rather relying on an irrational act of faith up to the point of disregarding the possible consequences of concrete actions.

It is on these Weberian presuppositions that value-rationality – that is, orientation towards the unconditional value of a mode of action (as, for example, the value of nonviolent pacifism) – becomes the basis for *Gesinnungsethik*. (I translate this "ethics of the right will or mentality," thinking of the spirit of the Sermon on the Mount or of Kant.)

Opposing this, purposive-rationality (that is, an orientation toward means and ends that from the outset considers the possible side effects of any concrete action) becomes the basis for an "ethics of responsibility" (*Verantwortungsethik*), such as we should hope to find in politicians. Hence, it is quite obvious that Weber ascribes a higher degree of rationality to the "ethics of responsibility" than to *Gesinnungsethik*,

4. See Max Weber's addresses "Politik als Beruf," reprinted in *Gesammelte politische Schriften*, 2d ed. (Tübingen, 1958) and "Wissenschaft als Beruf," reprinted in *Gesammelte Aufsätze zur Wissenschaftstheorie*, 3d ed. (Tübingen, 1968).

although he considers the latter to be indispensable existentially.

Historically, according to Weber, it was a specific connection of value-rationality and purposive rationality that made it possible for the first time to overcome the "affectual" and "traditional" type of prerational life-praxis by what he called a "methodical conduct of life" (*methodische Lebensführung*). This is what Weber found to be realized in the vocational ethic of ascetic Protestantism, which he analyzed in *The Protestant Ethic and the Spirit of Capitalism.*[5] Weber assumed, however, that throughout the development of capitalism the main tendency of the "occidental rationalization process" consists in the fact that a purposive rational orientation becomes predominant in all sectors of cultural and social life, whereas at the same time the traditional presuppositions of value-rationality (namely, religious world-views) are bound to dissolve. Hence, value-orientation becomes increasingly a matter of subjective decisions by individuals.[6] This is at least part of what Weber called the "process of disenchantment" (*Entzauberungsprozess*), which he thought was necessarily connected with the Western "rationalization process."

We may resume Weber's conception of rationality and rationalization by the following schema of a typology of action, which at the same time expresses degrees of rationality and historical stages in the rationalization of actions.[7]

Table. Rationally reflected elements of the frame of action

Types of action	Means	Ends	Values	Side effects
Purposive-rational	+	+	+	+
Value-rational	+	+	+	-
Affectual	+	+	-	-
Traditional	+	-	-	-

Weber's explication of rationality or rationalization is especially significant in our present context by its also comprehending explicitly "social actions." This is claimed, notwithstanding the fact that Weber supposes a special structure of interaction between agents. For, on the one hand, he defines the term "social relationship" with regard to

5. Weber, *The Protestant Ethic and the Spirit of Capitalism*, trans. Talcott Parsons (London and New York: Scribner, 1930).

6. A similar assessment was expressed by Robert Musil in his novel, *The Man Without Qualities* (1930-43; Eng. trans. 1953-60). The hero, Ulrich, is a pure *Möglichkeitsmensch*, for whom no value-orientations are made self-evident by the cultural tradition.

7. Cf. Habermas, "Aspects of the Rationality of Action," p. 194.

actions as being used "to denote the behavior of a plurality of actors insofar as, in its meaningful context, the action of each takes account of others and is thereby oriented."[8]

Thus far Weber seems to envisage the modern concept of social interactions by reciprocal expectations.

At the same time, however, he asserts: "Like every action, social action too can be determined first *purposive-rationally* and second *value-rationally*." To be determined "purposive-rationally" means, in this case, to be determined "through expectation as to the behavior of objects in the external world and of other men, using these expectations as 'conditions' or as 'means' for one's own ends; weighed and pursued rationally in terms of success."[9]

It becomes clear at this point that Weber understands the highest form of the rationality of social action as being an expansion of instrumental or means-ends rationality by reciprocity. This has indeed become a standard conception of rationality and rationalization of social action that has been developed to the present day, for example, by the mathematical theory of decision or rational choice and especially by the theory of strategic games as formulated by Von Neumann and Morgenstern.[10] In the light of the latter theory, Weber's conception of the rationality of social interaction may be understood as that of *strategical rationality*. In its simplest form it means that the agents as subjects of purposive-rational actions apply their means-ends-rationality to objects that, as subjects of purposive-rational actions, are expected to do the same with regard to the first-mentioned subjects of actions.

In somewhat more technical terms, the essence of strategical rationality may be expressed as follows:[11] Within the frame of a strategic game the utility-calculation of each actor is dependent upon those of every other actor, that is, upon using the calculations of the co-actors as means and conditions of one's own calculations. Hence, maximization of profit and minimization of loss that make up the rationality of rational choice from the viewpoint of elementary decision-theory are complicated by the fact that they can conflict with the corresponding calculations of the other actors. More precisely, control over the results of the actors' actions is restricted not only by lack of information about the environment (as is the case in elementary decision-theory) but also by the competing self-interest of the other decision-

8. Weber, *Wirtschaft und Gesellschaft*, 3d ed. (Cologne, 1964), p. 19.
9. Ibid., p. 17.
10. See John Von Neumann and Oskar Morgenstern, *Theory of Games and Economic Behavior* (Princeton, N.J.: Princeton University Press, 1944).
11. Cf. O. Höffe's critical overview in *Strategien der Humanität: Zur Ethik öffentlicher Entscheidungsprozesse* (Freiburg and Munich, 1975), pt. 1.

bearers. There is an ambivalent relationship, in principle, between one's own interest and competing interests. For the success of one's actions is dependent upon others who may be expected to support partially, at best, one's striving for success but who can also be expected partly to thwart it. Hence one's interests may be pursued partly by supporting and partly by thwarting the plans of the other actors. It is in accordance with this situation that strategic games-theory makes a distinction between two types of games: *competitive games* with regard to situations of pure conflict and *noncompetitive* games with regard to situations that offer opportunities for cooperation.

At this point in my explication of *strategical rationality of interaction*, let us call to mind our question as to whether there is a need for a special type of rationality for social action that may not be reduced to the means-ends-rationality of the intentional actions of singular subjects of action. A negative answer to this question, along the line of Weber's approach, seems indeed to be provided by the strategic games-theory. The rationality of social interaction, that is to say, the rationality of competition and of cooperation, seems to be nothing but a more complicated version of means-ends-rationality.

I have introduced the games-theory of strategical rationality of social action in order to expose the challenge to reason provided by the standard theory of possible rationality of action. But why and to what extent is there a challenge to reason bound up with this theory?

One hint of uneasiness may be suggested by Kant's second version of the "categorical imperative," which goes: "Act only in such a way that you may use humanity in your own person as well as in everybody else's person always as purpose and never merely as a means."[12]

It seems clear that there is no place for such an unconditional norm of ethical reason within the theory of strategical rationality of social interaction. Indeed, if the rationality of social interaction should be sufficiently defined by strategical rationality, then Kant obviously has not proposed an ethics of reason, as he claims, but rather an arational (or irrational) principle, a dogma that may only be understood as a secularized form of the Christian belief in man's being made in God's image.

Further, it seems clear that such a view would be in accordance with Weber's theory of "rationalization" and "disenchantment." In this light, ethics must be considered to be either an implication of religious belief (this would mean an ethics *before* the process of disenchantment) or a matter of conscious, but also irrational choice of one's ultimate axiom of valuing. This would mean ethics after the process of disenchantment.

12. Immanuel Kant, *Grundlegung zur Metaphysik der Sitten*, vol. 4 (Akademie-Textausgabe), pp. 428-29.

This view, it seems to me, has become the predominant ideology in Western industrial society. So far as the public domain is concerned (that is, the sphere of politics, economy, and even of positive law), the value-neutral forms of rationality – that is, scientific, technological, and strategical rationality – appear to be acknowledged as the only conceivable forms of rationality. Morals, on the other hand, are widely regarded as a private affair along with religion. Many people consider this to be a necessary and sufficient condition of liberal democracy. I have fallen into the habit of calling this ideology the Western complementarity-system of scienticism and instrumentalism on the one hand, and irrationalistic existentialism on the other.[13]

However, let us return to our problem: What may be said from the viewpoint of philosophical action-theory with regard to the monopoly-claim of strategical rationality of social action in view of the tension between this claim and Kantian ethics?

First, we should examine whether, contrary to Kant's claim, ethics might be conceivable on the basis of people's well-understood self-interest – That is to say, on the basis of strategical rationality in the sense of modern games-theory, for example, an ethics of negotiation and compromise under the standard of common life interests. In the present world situation one might perhaps even assume that a strategically grounded ethics of agreement about the preservation of the conditions for survival is forced upon humankind, for example, by the ecological crisis and the threat of nuclear war. Thus, one might think it a consequence of a long-range strategic calculation to reach an agreement about the total rate of annual consumption of energy, that is, at a rate compatible with a restriction of environmental destruction and a new ecological equilibrium.

I think, however, that the first problem of a macroethics in the age of ecological crisis cannot be solved on the basis of strategic rationality alone. For the required state of ecological equilibrium may be realized in different ways. More precisely, the problem of fixing a rate of energy consumption implies a problem of distribution that may be solved in different ways. Strategic rationality alone would never motivate rich and developed industrial nations to share planetary resources with poor and underdeveloped countries in a way that could be called just. Thus it becomes clear that the strategic problem of preserving an *ecological equilibrium* is by no means identical with the ethical problem of preserving a *humane equilibrium* of justice based on generalized reciprocity of claims and duties.

13. Cf. Apel, *Towards a Transformation of Philosophy* (London: Routledge and Kegal Paul, 1980), pp. 233 ff.; also, Apel, "The Conflicts of Our Time and the Problem of Political Ethics," in *From Contract to Community* (New York and Basel: Marcel Dekker, 1978), pp. 81-102.

The same dilemma exists with regard to the distribution of food in the face of imminent starvation in the Third World. With regard to this problem, the purely strategical ratio of the Western world seems to be represented by a remark made by the economist Friedrich von Hayek. The Nobel-prizewinner is reported to have pleaded for the starvation of Third World peoples who cannot help themselves, in case there is a further sharpening of the crisis of resources. (Presumably, he only expressed the tacit reasoning of many people in the rich countries, since there is also the alternative of restricting one's own standard of living. This may be called the reaction of *strategical ratio* to the Pope's irrational attempts at preventing the people of Mexico, the Philippines, and Nigeria from practicing birth control.)

In my opinion, it is conceivable in respect to the threat of nuclear war that the strategically calculated self-interest of the world powers may suffice to preserve a state of equilibrium that guarantees peace and thus secures the life interests of those who might be affected by such a war. But such an achievement of strategical rationality would be one brought about by fear of death, as is the transition from the state of nature to the state of law, according to Thomas Hobbes. Hence, it would function only as long as the equilibrium of military power is not disturbed. Thus one might suppose that maintenance of a power equilibrium is the number-one problem of strategic thinking in our day.

By showing that strategical rationality does not warrant a satisfactory ethics we have not, of course, delivered a decisive argument against the monopoly-claim of this type of rationality for social action. For, as I have suggested, it may be that ethics cannot be grounded rationally.[14] It is well-known that Kant's ethics of "morally legislative reason" has been criticized not only for its formalism but also for its deficiency with regard to its ultimate foundation. (In fact, Kant did not solve the problem of "deducing transcendentally" the "reality" of an autonomous legislative reason and hence the validity of the "categorical imperative," a problem he himself designated as one still to be solved, in his *Groundwork of the Metaphysics of Morals.*[15] Kant rejected the task of grounding the "moral law" and instead pointed rather dogmatically

14. A rational foundation of ethics is considered impossible, not only by Max Weber and positivists of all stripes but also by Popperians and (for other reasons) representatives of historism and post-Wittgensteinian paradigm-relativism. With respect to this problem, see Apel, "The Problem of Philosophical Ultimate Grounding in Light of a Transcendental Pragmatic of Language," *Man and World* 8, no. 3 (1975), pp. 239-75. See also my writings cited in n. 13.

15. See Kant, *Grundlegung zur Metaphysik der Sitten*, pp. 392, 425, 444-45, 447-48, 449-50.

to the "fact of reason."[16]) If ethics cannot be grounded rationally, this circumstance could support the suspicion that reason is in fact only an instrumental faculty of calculating in the service of self-interest, as was supposed by Luther, Hobbes, and Nietzsche; in other words, it is a faculty of value-neutral instrumental-technological or strategical rationality in the sense of Weber's paradigm of "purposive rationality." This could be the last word of scientific philosophy as well as of theology.

III

In the face of this situation, I would now like to approach the problem from another viewpoint. I shall not directly play off the point of ethics against that of strategical rationality, but rather the point of consensual communication by arguments. In doing so, I suppose that this essay is a social action in the sense of consensual communication. By taking this position I shall follow another strategy of argument in order to reach the purpose of my essay.

At this point the question is: What is a strategy of argumentation? What is the purpose of such a strategy? Since this paper is about "strategy" and "purpose," one could assume that a strategy of argumentation is just a piece of strategical means-ends-rationality. In this case, the purpose of my essay is to persuade my readers to believe in the existence of a nonstrategical rationality of consensual communication. But if this is true, my project would be hopeless from the beginning, for it would involve a pragmatic self-contradiction. In order to show that consensual communication by arguments represents an example of nonstrategical rationality, I actually would have to perform acts of *strategical* rationality. For acts of persuasion must be conceived of as acts of using other people's thoughts and feelings as means in the service of one's own purposes. Thus it seems that the need for following a strategy of persuasion would in itself be an argument in favor of the monopoly of strategical rationality of social action.

However, would it really be an argument? I do not think so. For to the extent that it were to be successful as a strategy of persuasion, it would fail to reach a consensus about the validity or nonvalidity of an argument, and thereby about the truth or falsehood of a statement. In this case it would not function as a strategy of argument at all but at best as a rhetorical strategy. This difference, which appears to have

16. Kant, *Kritik der praktischen Vernunft*, vol. 5 (Akademie-Textausgabe), pp. 46-7. Cf. K.-H. Ilting, "Der naturalistische Fehlschluss bei Kant," in *Rehabilitierung der praktischen Vernunft*, ed. M. Riedel (Freiburg: Rombach, 1972), pp. 113-32.

been first recognized by Socrates in his argument with the Sophists, may be elucidated, I think, with the aid of modern *speech-act theory.*[17]

The point of the difference, it seems to me, is the following: Within strategical rhetoric,[18] speech-acts are merely conceived of as a special case of purposive-rational actions, namely, as *perlocutionary* realizations of purposes of actions in relation to other persons. The "perlocutionary effect," which is the purpose of the speech-act (say, a certain reaction or merely a certain belief or feeling to be produced in the hearer), is then mediated strategically by the "illocutionary effect" of the speech-act, that is, by the understanding of the meaning of the sign by the hearer. However, the perlocutionary effect is not made dependent on the illocutionary effect in such a way that the possibility of an alternative (that is, positive or negative) judgment of the validity (truth or practical liability) of the message be included in the purpose of the speech-act.

It is precisely this change in the relationship between the illocutionary and the perlocutionary effect of speech-acts that makes up the function of argumentative speech and, in its context, of a strategy of argument. For the latter is a strategy (and thus far a case of means-ends-rationality) only insofar as it serves to convince the partner of the validity of arguments, and thereby of the truth of argumentatively grounded statements or of the practical liability of argumentatively justified demands or norms.

In contradictinction to the perlocutionary purpose of a persuasive act, the perlocutionary effect of an argumentative act has been subordinated a priori to the possibility and risk of a rationally grounded assent or dissent of the hearer on the basis of the illocutionary effect of the speech-act. Thus far, the proper purpose of argumentative speech does not consist in the perlocutionary realization of a private or subjective purpose or intention that has been fixed precommunicatively by an agent. Neither does it consist in a perlocutionary realization of a consensus qua compromise between the subjective purposes or intentions that were fixed precommunicatively by different agents.

17. Cf. John Langshaw Austin, *How to Do Things with Words* (Cambridge, Mass.: Harvard University Press, 1962) and John R. Searle, *Speech Acts: An Essay in the Philosophy of Language* (London: Cambridge University Press, 1969).

18. This is indeed a narrow concept of rhetoric that often has been called into question by philosophically minded rhetoricians from Isocrates to Cicero to the Italian Humanists. Cf. Apel, *Die Idee der Sprache in der Tradition des Humanismus von Dante bis Vico*, 3d ed. (Bonn: Bouvier, 1980). In our day a philosophically positive concept of rhetoric has been defended by Chaïm Perelman and Lucie Olbrechts-Tyteca in *Traité de l'argumentation. La nouvelle rhétorique*, 2d ed. (Brussels: Éditions de l'Institut de Sociologie de l'Université Libre, 1970).

The purpose consists rather in reaching a consensus about the intersubjective validity (or invalidity) of those validity-claims that are bound up with the message of the illocutionary acts. In other words, the purpose of argumentation is constituted by the possibility of sharing the meaning, the truth, and the practical liability of norms that are connected with the message to be understood and thus to make up the illocutionary effect of speech. The one who argues, that is to say, must suppose that it is possible to reach a consensus that is indefinitely expansible, not by openly or covertly strategical means that stand in the service of subjective aims, but by aiming at ends that are a priori common ends and by ways that are a priori liable methods for all. These suppositions seem to define the peculiar means-ends-rationality of a strategy of argument. The purpose of this strategy is not subjective, as is the interest of a single agent or even that of a community that comes to an agreement by sacrificing conflicting purposes to a common superpurpose,[19] but it is essentially *transsubjective* as is the interest of reason itself. Thus, in contradistinction to all other strategies, a strategy of argument does not stand in the service of the life interest of a confined social system (an individual or group) but in the service of an interest of reason, namely redemption of validity-claims, which is a priori the interest of an indefinite community.[20]

Hence, one may say that a strategy of argument puts strategical rationality in the service of another type of rationality which is no longer instrumental but defines an end in itself, at least for the social action of arguing. This fact seems to provide an answer to my question

19. The model for dissolving conflicts by the conflicting parties' taking recourse to common superpurposes has been proposed as a device for a rational procedure of grounding moral norms in our day. But the concept, which could not serve as a method of reaching a consensus about truth-claims, cannot pass as a model of an ethical procedure of consensus-formation either; for it might also be used by opposing gangs taking recourse to a common criminal superpurpose, as, for example, profiting from the drug trade. Its character as a model of strategical, rather than ethical, rationality is constituted by its lack of a genuine principle of generalized reciprocity, which from the outset would prevent an agreement among the conflicting parties, at the cost of others who might be affected by the agreement.

20. It was Charles S. Peirce, the so-called founder of pragmatism, who explicitly claimed that consensus-formation by arguments is related, in principle, to an "indefinite community." This stand up against modern attempts at reducing the "function" of arguments – or even of truth – to a quasi-strategical function within the self-maintenance of a confined social system, as, for example, to the function of a transfer of achievements of a "reduction of meaning-complexity" within a community (as was claimed by Niklas Luhmann). Cf. the controversy between Luhmann and Habermas, in Habermas and Luhmann, *Theorie der Gesellschaft oder Socialtechnologie – Was leistet die Systemforschung?* (Frankfurt: Suhrkamp, 1971).

as to the possibility of a nonstrategical rationality of social interaction. For the possibility of a nonstrategical rationality of consensual communication obviously is the condition of the possibility of meaningful argumentation.

If by successful argumentation only a perlocutionary effect were to be reached without its being mediated by a sharing of meaning, truth, and intersubjective liability of norms, then arguing makes no sense. But arguments having sense is a necessary condition of our asking the question as to whether there is a nonstrategical rationality of social action. In short, arguing is nontranscendible by arguments.[21]

Thus, it is by a sense-critical or a transcendental pragmatic reflection on the conditions of the possibility of arguing that we arrive at the following result of our inquiry. If the question as to whether there is a nonstrategical rationality of social interaction is to be asked seriously and discussed meaningfully, then the possibility of an affirmative answer to this question must be supposed. There must be a nonstrategical rationality of social action at least on the level of communication by arguments. But communication by arguments is nothing more than an institutionalized means of redeeming the validity-claims of all communication by speech. Hence, we may state that the nonstrategical rationality of argumentative discourse makes explicit the rationality of consensual-communication between human beings. And since there is no valid thinking without the presupposition of an internalized communication by speech, one may say that the nonstrategical rationality of social interaction is the rationale of human thought, and as such it is even presupposed by human self-understanding of instrumental-technical and strategical rationality.[22]

Through further explication of the conditions of the possibility of argumentative discourse, we may also show in what the possibility of a progressive rationalization of consensual communication consists. It

21. This nonempirical "fact of reason" (Kant) may indeed become the vantage point for a strategy of "philosophical fundamental grounding" by transcendental-pragmatic reflection on the normative presuppositions of any meaningful arguments. Cf. my pertinent papers (see note 14) and, most recently, Kuhlmann, "Reflexive Letztbegründung: Zur These von der Unhintergehbarkeit der Argumentationssituation," in which the transcendental-pragmatic approach is defended against the objection that even the presupposition of a meaningful argument (and hence of theories) must be theory-impregnated and hence fallible.

22. According to the most recent biological theories of the evolution of behavior, in the interest of survival all animals must follow an "evolutionary stabilized strategy" of behavior that may be defined in terms of a maximal proliferation of their genes. But they cannot follow this strategy consciously or by intention. Human beings however who, due to their capacity for language, can have a concept of acting strategically seem to have this concept only on the condition that they never act merely strategically – as Thomas Hobbes supposed with regard to the natural state – but always by way of consensual communication as well.

may thus be shown, I think, that (contrary to Weber's assumption) the scope of the "occidental rationalization process" cannot be exhausted by the dimension of means-ends-rationality, although one may admit that an emancipation of the latter type of rationality (say, in economics and politics) has been characteristic of modern times. Beyond this rationalization-process, however, the occidental tradition from the Greeks onward has been characterized by the progress of normative discourse-sciences (in Greek, *technai logicai*; in Latin, *artes sermonicales*), namely, grammar, logic, and rhetoric.[23] In our day the scope of these discourse-sciences may be characterized by the dimensions of syntactics, semantics, and pragmatics, which are encompassed by (transcendental) semiotics.[24]

In the light of transcendental semiotics, the progressive development of human communication may be tentatively reconstructed as follows. On the level of human interaction prior to the invention of argumentative discourse we must suppose that intentions of strategical rationality in the service of self-maintenance and intentions in the sense of universal validity claims that can only be redeemed by the discursive rationality of consensual communication were unseparated in ordinary communication. However, one may assume that the scope of strategical rationality of human interaction was always restricted by the normative liability of conventional rules based on a tacit consensus about universal validity-claims.

By universal validity-claims I understand, along with Jürgen Habermas,[25] the following claims that are involved in human speech:

1. The meaning-claim or understandability-claim connected with speech-acts as illocutionary acts;

2. The claim of truthfulness or veracity connected with the expressive function of speech;

3. The truth-claim connected with the representation-function of propositions but possibly made explicit by performatives such as "I hereby assert...";

4. The claim of normative rightness or practical liability connected with speech-acts of social communication (and thus with the appeal-function of speech).[26]

23. Cf. Apel, *Die Idee der Sprache in der Tradition des Humanismus*.

24. Cf. Apel, "Transcendental Semiotics and the Paradigms of First Philosophy," *Philosophic Exchange* 2, no. 4 (1978), pp. 3-22.

25. Cf. Habermas, "Towards a Theory of Communicative Competence," *Inquiry* 13 (1970), pp. 205-18; also, Habermas, *Communication and the Evolution of Society* (Boston: Beacon Press, forthcoming).

26. This amounts to a critical reconstruction of Karl Bühler's famous "Sprachtheorie" (Jena, 1934) with respect to its three functions of speech. Cf. Apel, "Zwei paradigmatische Antworten auf die Frage nach der Logos-Auszeichnung der menschlichen Sprache," in *Kulturwissenschaften*, ed. H. Lützeler (Bonn: Bouvier, 1980), pp. 13-68.

Human communication as social interaction is characterized by the fact that in conflicts of interest even the four universal validity-claims may be called into question. It is a historical fact that in the so-called ages of enlightenment these questions could not be anwered by recourse to conventional rules of legitimation, including religious rituals and mythical explanations of the world. In such a situation a reflective separation of strategical and discursive or consensual rationality of social interaction must come about. It does not suffice in this situation to reestablish agreement between the social partners by means of negotiation or rhetoric (not to speak of open fighting); in order to take up and respond to the challenge of questioning validity-claims, the social partners methodically must suspend the strategical rationality of interaction and the underlying subjective interests of self-maintenance. They must suspend all this in favour of the transsubjective interest of a consensual redeeming universal validity-claims, which may be called the interest of reason that underlies communication by language.

This is what happened, for example, when Socrates established the philosophical *logos* as the principle of argumentative discourse.[27] From that time, theoretical philosophy (including a methodology for the developing sciences) and practical philosophy (including jurisprudence) have fulfilled the function of mobilizing and displaying the nonstrategical rationality of argumentative discourse in the interest of critique and redemption of truth-claims and normative rightsness- or liability-claims. (I maintain this, although since the time of Weber strong doubts regarding the rationality of philosophy and its social function, especially in the realm of norms and values, have been expressed.)

Furthermore, in connection with the so-called *critique of ideology* (from the Sophists through Bacon, Nietzsche, and Karl Marx) and with psychoanalysis, a systematic critique and redemption of the claim of truthfulness or veracity of human speech and its products was attempted. This attempt was based, I suggest, on mobilizing, within the context of communicative understanding, argumentative strategies of self-unmasking against the unconscious strategical rationality of self-deception. Finally, in connection with the recent linguistic "turn" in philosophy, even the attempt at a systematic questioning and redemption of the meaning- or understandability-claim of human speech was made. (I am thinking in this context of Wittgenstein's or Carnap's suspicion of "nonsensicality" (or, respectively, "meaninglessness") of philosophical or metaphysical speech. I think this attempt has at least led to the insight that truth-claims cannot be redeemed independently

27. Cf. Dietrich Böhler, "Entwicklungsprobleme und Entwicklungsschwellen der praktischen Vernunft," in *Reader zu Funkkolleg: Praktische Philosophie/Ethik 1*, ed. Karl-Otto Apel et al. (Frankfurt: Fischer, 1980).

of an examination of the specific meaning-claims of language systems or language games.)

Let me now try, in the last part of my paper, to draw some conclusions from my description of the nonstrategical rationality of consensual communication with regard to ethics.

IV

In the preceding I have tried to show two things:

1. We must presuppose a type of consensual-communicative rationality of social interaction in contradistinction to the strategical rationality of interaction, since without this presupposition we have no chance to come to a rationally grounded consensus about this question, that is, about the meaning of rationality with respect to social interaction.

2. The nonstrategical rationality of consensual communication has its own dimension of progressive development on the level of argumentative discourse. On this level the universal validity-claims of human speech can and must be redeemed by a critical reflection and consensus-formation that has separated itself a priori from strategical means-ends rationality.

We have thus uncovered a dimension of rationality and of possible rationalization of social interaction that was obviously overlooked in Weber's conception of the "occidental rationalization process." The significance of this fact should be the following: It seems clear that, in contrast to the Weberian concept of means-ends rationality, the consensual-communicative rationality of redeeming the four universal validity-claims is not *value-neutral*. For not only the definite redemption of the four claims but also the presupposed critical reconstruction and judgment of the respective intentions of the actors must have the character of a valuative understanding. According to the validity-claims in question (namely, understandability, veracity, truth, and rightness or practical liability), the respective valuations must proceed in the light of presupposed normative measures or standards.

At least one of these standards was recognized, at least implicitly, by Max Weber as a legitimate normative standard, namely that of *truth*. For it is obviously a presupposition of his postulate of "value-neutrality" of science that only on this condition "objectivity" and thus far the possibility of an approximation of truth may be conceived of. Hence, striving for truth is a presupposition for Weber's principle of "value-neutrality." However, Weber, strangely enough, did not recognize that striving for objectivity (or, respectively truth) is the paradigm-case of a human activity that cannot be understood without valuing. (Thus a historical inquiry that lays claim to an "internal" reconstruction of scientific progress toward the truth must imply valuative judgments of the facts of history as is demonstrated today, somewhat surprisingly for many social scientists, by the new discipline of the history of science.) For Weber, however, the point of his postulate of value-neutrality lay in his conviction that precisely a progressive discovery of truth by science is bound up with a renunciation of valuation in general because valuation, in contrast to stating the truth about facts, cannot be valid intersubjectively. From this conviction it becomes understandable that Weber did not reflect on the non-value-neutral character of the history of science (that is, of stating the truth about strivings for truth) but rather combined his postulate of value-neutrality with the historical thesis that the occidental "process of rationalization" must be connected with a corresponding process of "disenchantment" with regard to binding value-orientations in general.

Compared with this Weberian assessment, the perspective of the progressive development of the discourse-sciences, which from the Greek enlightenment have been in charge of a reflective critique and redemption of the four interconnected validity-claims of human speech, suggests a completely different conclusion.

It is true that, even from this perspective, one may state that the process of enlightenment and rationalization of human culture has been necessarily connected with a process of disenchantment. But, contrary to Weber and the Western complementarity-system of scienticism-instrumentalism and, on the other hand, irrationalistic existentialism (see page 15), one must not interpret the process of disenchantment as necessarily a process of losing all universal value-orientations in favor of a privatization of morals in the sense of ultimate, subjective, and irrational value-decisions. Rather, one may interpret the process of disenchantment that goes along with enlightenment and discursive reflection as that of a dissolution of the indisputable validity of traditional (mythical-religious) world-views and pertinent conventional moral norms. At the same time, however, one can expect that the progressive mobilization of discourse-rationality may amount to a historical compensation for the process of disenchantment by a methodical redemption of all universal validity-claims of human speech by way of the discursive rationality of consensual communication.

The process of disenchantment, no doubt, undermines and even dissolves the non-universal validity of moral norms that are relative to cultural traditions and conventions. But at the same time it permits the acknowledgment, on the level of argumentative discourse, of a new universal metanorm of a post-traditional and post-conventional foundation of moral norms (and of a critical legitimation of legal norms), namely, the demand for a discursive consensus of all affected people (or at least of their representatives) about their interests and thus about acceptable norms.

This concept of a rational compensation of the process of disenchantment implies, among other things, a new assessment of the relationship between the theoretical rationality of science and that of practical reason. Since the four universal validity-claims of human speech are inseparable from each other in the last resort, it should be possible to conceive of the methodical redemption of the truth-claim of speech, as it is carried through in science (or in a philosophical theory of science) as an enterprise that presupposes the redemption of the other three universal validity-claims of speech. That is to say, it should be possible to overcome the scienticist isolation of theoretical rationality that conceives of it only in terms of a capacity of domination and control that may be employed in technology, that is, as a basis of value-neutral instrumental and strategical rationality.[28]

I think that the Weberian postulate of value-neutrality (of science) is justified in the last resort, not by the alleged fact that valuations may not be intersubjectively valid but by the technologically mediated cognitive interest of natural science (and of quasi-naturalistic social science, that is, predictive behavioral science in the service of social technology).[29] For insofar as we are interested in controlling facts we want to instrumentalize in the service of our purposes, we must dispense with valuating them because *natura non nisi parendo vincitur*, as Sir Francis Bacon said. Thus, in predictive behavioral science or in social technology even the motives of human beings (for example, of consumers or voters) are not interesting as good or bad reasons but only as causes or antecedent conditions to be taken into account in a quasi-nomological scheme of explanation and prediction of events. But this is quite different in the context, for example, of a history of science, where we are interested primarily in understanding and valuating the good or bad reasons of former scientists as members of that indefinite community that is in charge of redeeming truth-claims by argumentative discourse.

Thus it is clear that the postulate of value-neutrality of (natural and quasi-natural) science with regard to its objects which is justified by our technological interest, and hence by instrumental rationality, is not justified for a science that reflects on science as an enterprise of consensual communication about universal truth-claims by discursive rationality. This point may even be extrapolated with regard to ethical

28. See my papers cited in note 1.

29. Cf. Apel, "Types of Social Science in the Light of Human Interests of Knowledge," *Social Research* 44, no. 3 (1977), pp. 425-70; reprinted in *Philosophical Disputes in the Social Sciences*, ed. S. Brown (Brighton: Harvester Press, 1979). Cf. also, Apel, "The 'Erklären/Verstehen' – Controversy in the Philosphy of the Human and Natural Sciences," in *Contemporary Philosophy. A New Survey*, vol. 2, ed. G. Fløistad (The Hague: Martinus Nijhoff, 1982), pp. 19-49.

valuation, I suggest, for the scientific pursuit of truth presupposes an ethics of nonstrategical social interaction within the scientific community. Furthermore, since the ethics of the scientific community is primarily an ethics of argumentative discourse, it is not restricted a priori to the enterprise of science but may be extrapolated once more by the insight that by each argument we have implicitly acknowledged an ethics of consensual-communication about all kinds of claims that may be represented by arguments. By this last step of reflection on the presuppositions of science as a social enterprise, we have obviously caught up with our previous reflection on the rationality of our own activity of asking and answering questions on the rationality of social interaction.

It should be acknowledged, I think, that the crucial obstacle to realizing that an ethically relevant rationality of consensual discourse is presupposed by science and technology is provided by the traditional prejudice of methodical solipsism. This is the deeply rooted conviction of modern epistemology, from Descartes through Husserl, that valid cognition and hence science may, in principle, be an achievement of one subject of intuition and of inference. For Husserl, even the intersubjectively valid meanings of language were in the last resort to be a constitutive achievement of (the intentional acts of) a single, although transcendental, consciousness.[30] If one starts from this presupposition in philosophy, then it may appear as if intersubjective validity of knowledge could be conceived of, in principle, without the presupposition of social interaction, that is, of consensual communication about truth-claims and, prior to this, about linguistic meaning-claims.

(Truth, then, could be conceived in an abstract sense by a metaphysical ontology, or by a logical semantics, to be a matter of correspondence between facts and propositions, which is criteriologically meaningsless, or to be a matter of private evidence about the correspondence of my propositional intentions with the self-given phenomena. The latter concept – that of classical phenomenology – is indeed neither dispensable nor criteriologically irrelevant, but it obviously does not consider the fact that my evidence about self-given phenomena is

30. Cf., for example, Edmund Husserl, *Cartesian Meditations*, sections 11, 13, 42 ff., 62. Husserl's methodical solipsism in these places consists in the fact that the meaning of other egos, as any other meaning, is considered to be a constitutive achievement of the intentional acts of the "primordial ego," which is considered the only residual of the "epoche." Contrary to this, within a *transcendental semiotics*, the meaning of the primordial *ego* would already presuppose for its own constitution the existence and function of a language and a communication-community and hence would be equally original as the meanings of the others (that is, of *you, he, she,* and the like), although this transcendental-reflexive insight must be evident for every consciousness of an ego.

always dependent on the linguistic interpretation of the phenomena and thus on the regulative idea of an ultimate consensus upon all manner of truth-criteria – evidence of correspondence, theoretical coherence, pragmatic fruitfulness, or so on – in an indefinite communication-community.)[31]

If these presuppositions of valid cognition are overlooked, then ignored too is the fact that subjects of knowledge must also form a community in an ethically relevant sense, that is, they must presuppose a possible consensus not only about the meaning and truth of propositions but also about the moral norms that are implied in communicative acts as acts of social interaction. These norms as pragmatic rules of the game of argumentative discourse may be made problematical and justified only by argumentative discourse.

In short, the nonvalue-neutral presuppositions of science (and hence of instrumental technology) are overlooked because, from the perspective of methodical solipsism, the subject-cosubject-relation of communication is ignored as a precondition of valid science. Hence, the scientistic monopolization of the value-neutral rationality of the "objectivity" (that is, of the subject-object-relation of science and technology) comes about.

The normative-ethical orientation of persons is also understood on the basis of methodical solipsism, for example, as a matter of an ultimate choice of value-axioms on the basis of private, irrational decisions of conscience. Thus, from Weber to the present the existentialist-subjectivist supplementation of scienticism within the framework of the Western ideological complementarity-system has been the last word on ethics.

At this point the internal connection between methodical solipsism and decisionism becomes visible. For, on the level of theoretical reason, valid knowledge is supposed to be possible without presupposing a rationality of consensual communication. The same supposition has been made on the level of practical reason.

Kant and Fichte considered it possible that the autonomy of my free will should not only be a necessary but a sufficient reason for grounding the moral law. Still, Kant and Fichte believed in the intersubjective validity of the moral law and thus at least integrated the idea of a generalized reciprocity of a communication-community of rational beings, which is a transcendental precondition of morals, into the concept of the moral law that was to originate in the legislative autonomy of my free will.

31. Cf. Apel, "C.S. Peirce and the Post-Tarskian Problem of an Adequate Explication of the Meaning of Truth," Part 1, in *The Monist* 63, no. 3 (1980), pp. 386-407; Part 2 in *Transactions of the Charles S. Peirce Society* 18, no. 1 (1982), pp. 3-17 ff.

This belief in the intersubjective validity of a moral law, however, has been dropped in modern irrationalistic existentialism (or, for that matter, decisionism) together with the belief in the possibility of a rational grounding of moral law. Instead, it is considered possible that the individual might replace the rational grounding of moral norms by his or her decision of conscience, which would ground a moral norm that is valid only for the subject of the decision. An extreme but representative version of this modern belief has been formulated by Karl Popper. On the one hand, Popper, along with Charles Peirce, realized that science as a community enterprise must presuppose an ethics. On the other hand, Popper, along with Weber and the Western complementarity-system, supposes that in the last resort everybody must decide by a "prerational" and hence "irrational" "act of faith" whether science, with the "criticist frame" of discourse and its moral implications, ought to be.[32]

This response, as far as I can see, meets with widespread approval in present-day philosophy for two reasons that may be characterized as fundamental errors of decisionism and of methodical solipsism.

1. The pertinent error of *decisionism*, in my opinion, consists in a confusion of the problems that goes back to the voluntaristic tradition of Duns Scotus and William of Ockham. On the one hand, it is correct that following ethical norms must ultimately be dependent on a decision of free will if such a thing as ethics is to make sense at all. This decision cannot be enforced by arguments and thus far is not justifiable rationally. On the other hand, voluntarism does not see that this fact of an ultimate decision of conscience is compatible with the fact that the fundamental norm or law of morals can and must be grounded as being capable of intersubjective consensus by argumentative discourse. This problem of grounding and hence of discursive rationality is simply confused with the problem of practical decision; hence a decisionistic substitution of an ultimate choice in the place of ultimate grounding occurs.

2. Even deeper rooted, I think, is the error of *methodical solipsism* that is connected with that of decisionism. Here, it is supposed to be possible to conceive meaningfully of a decision in favour of reason from a standpoint outside reason (that is, from a standpoint of a radical solitariness and arbitrariness). Against this it can be claimed that the very concept of a decision that could be understood as such by other people presupposes the subject's belonging to a community of rule-following and possible discourse. (This may be considered, I suggest, as a transcendental-pragmatic interpretation of Wittgenstein's insight that

32. See Karl Raimund Popper, *The Open Society and Its Enemies*, vol. 2 (London: G. Routledge & Sons, 1945), pp. 231 ff.

it is not possible to follow a rule privately.[33] If this argument against the possibility of an ultimate decision in favor of reason from outside reason is correct (that is, if the rationality of consensual communication is a transcendental condition of the possibility of a meaningful decision), then our argument regarding the rationality of ethics being a presupposition of all other forms of rationality may be deepened in a crucial way by the following arguments.

1. Since ethical rationality of consensus-formation with regard to all possible conflicts about norms is a condition of the possibility of serious arguing and hence of valid thinking, and since arguing or, respectively, thinking cannot be transcended or circumvented by itself, therefore our account of the rationality of consensual communication has opened a possibility of an ultimate foundation of ethics, a foundation not by deduction, but by transcendental-pragmatic reflection[34] on the conditions of the possibility of arguing or, of valid thinking.

2. Moreover, the following point should become clear. The ethical rationality of consensual communication which is presupposed by a discursive redemption of truth-claims cannot be understood simply as a minimal ethics just of argumentative discourse. For by the will to argue we have necessarily acknowledged the fundamental norm or law of morals that we ought to strive to settle all conceivable conflicts of interest among human beings by discursive consensus-formation. Thus we have acknowledged, not a special ethics of a particular language-game, but a *metanorm for the rational foundation or legitimation of concrete norms*. The latter, of course, must be related to situations and hence dependent on historical boundary-conditions. In short, the fundamental norm or law of consensual discourse may be considered as a (normative) deciphering of Kant's formula of the "fact of reason," a deciphering that shows that it is not an empirical fact from which to derive norms – such would amount to a "naturalistic fallacy."[35]

33. Cf. Ludwig Wittgenstein, *Philosophische Untersuchungen*, vol. 1, sections 199, 202, 206, 243, 257, 293. Cf. also Apel, *Towards a Transformation of Philosophy* (see note 13).

34. Cf. my paper cited in note 14.

35. Cf. my argument with and against the metaethical criticism of Kant's grounding ethics by the "fact of reason" in *Towards a Transformation of Philosophy* (see note 13), pp. 271-72.

TIME-CONSCIOUSNESS AND HISTORICAL CONSCIOUSNESS

DAVID CARR (Ottawa)

If we wish to reflect philosophically on history, one of the things we need to do is consider the nature of our awareness of the past. Husserl's 1905 lectures, *The Phenomenology of Internal Time-Consciousness,*[1] are one of the most brilliant examples of phenomenological analysis, and he deals with just that topic. It is true that Husserl is concerned there with our consciousness of our individual pasts in memory, and that the historical past is usually thought of as that past which lies beyond our individual experience, the past of others. Nevertheless, I think our best clue to a phenomenological clarification of historical experience is to be found in those lectures – a better one, actually, than what Husserl says explicitly about history in his later works, and a better one, in my opinion, than what most phenomenologists have said about it. But what Husserl offers us is no more than a clue – or a series of clues – and in order to appreciate them we have to attend to certain aspects of what he says and be prepared to extend and revise his theory in important ways. One of those, of course, must be concerned with getting beyond our individual pasts to the past of others. But that is only the last step.

What I propose in the following is first of all a reading of Husserl's central time-consciousness theory – a very personalized and non-scholarly reading, I admit – which will bring out those features of the theory most useful for our topic; then I shall proceed to the criticisms, extensions, and revisions I think necessary; and I shall conclude with some suggestions as to how a revised time-consciousness theory can contribute to a phenomenological clarification of history as a phenomenon.

1. Edmund Husserl, *Zur Phänomenologie des inneren Zeitbewusstseins*, Husserliana 10 (The Hague: Martinus Nijhoff, 1966); transl. J.S. Churchill as *The Phenomenology of Internal Time-Consciousness* (Bloomington, Ind.: Indiana University Press, 1964).

Cho, K.K. (ed.) Philosophy and Science in Phenomenological Perspective.

ISBN 978-94-009-6115-9

I. HUSSERL'S THEORY

The first thing that must be noted about Husserl's theory is that it is not an account of time itself but of how we experience time. And how we experience time is to be distinguished from how we may try to represent or conceptualize time. So far phenomenology's approach to time parallels its approach to space. And just as we have no experience of space except by experiencing things in space – things that take up or inhabit space, so we experience time by experiencing things in time, that is, things that take time, things that happen, events. The central core of Husserl's theory is its account of our experience of something *happening*, something that *takes place*.

This being so, the core of Husserl's theory is an account not principally of our consciouness of the past, but of our consciousness of the present. But of course, consciousness of the present involves consciousness of the past. So much had already been seen by Brentano and other predecessors. But they thought the simple distinction between consciousness of the past, called memory, and consciousness of the present was enough to account for our experience of an event. Husserl's great and most original contribution is to have recognized two distinct forms of consciousness of the past, which he calls retention and recollection, or primary and secondary memory. It is the former of these that figures in our consciousness of the present, while the latter is what we usually think of when we speak of memory or recollection.

It is easy to misunderstand this distinction, to take it for something like the cognitive psychologists' distinction between short-term and long-term memory. Even Husserl seems to have though of it this way in some of his earliest reflections on time – he speaks in early manuscripts of "fresh" versus "more distant" memory[2] – and aspects of his terminology in the 1905 lectures contribute to this misunderstanding, as when he speaks of retention as consciousness of the "just past."[3] The 1905 lectures are hobbled by the fact that the one notion which is in my opinion the key to the concept of retention, that of horizon-consciousness, had not been worked out by Husserl and was not fully at his disposal.

There is no doubt, however, that this is the key to the distinction. Retention is the consciousness of the past as the horizon or background against which the present stands out. The parallel to the experience of spatial objects is helpful. I cannot see an object in space except against a spatial background. Likewise, I cannot experience an event except against a temporal background. To experience an event is to be con-

2. See, for example, p. 165 of Husserliana 10.
3. Ibid., section 12.

scious of something *taking place*, that is, its *taking the place* of something else. What is replaced or deplaced recedes into the background but is not lost from view; I am still conscious of it but in a different way.

The whole configuration, impressional and retentional consciousness, foreground and background consciousness, make up what it is to *experience* an event in the sense of *Erleben*, to live through it. To *recollect* the event, by contrast, is to *re*live in memory an event that I am not living through. I *re*produce it in memory, according to Husserl, including all its original temporal aspects, i.e., the original configuration of foreground and background. Thus, to recollect an event is to be conscious of a recollected now and a recollected horizon of retention.

Retention can be looked at as a horizon-consciousness, then, that belongs necessarily to the makeup of our consciousness of the present, and indeed, in a certain sense, of any consciousness whatever; whereas recollection is a particular mode of consciousness whose focal object is a past event. We *need* not recollect, as far as I can see, in order to be conscious of the present, in the sense that we must have retention; whether a full-fledged conscious subject must have recollections as well as retention is a question which, as far as I know, Husserl does not take up.

Once the distinction is put this way, it becomes clear that it is utterly different from the long-term short-term distinction. Whether I am conscious of some event in retentional or recollective consciousness is not a question of how far removed it is from the present; it is rather a question of whether it figures for me in the background of the present I am living through or whether I am attending to it in its own right by reliving it as a segment of the past.

This point can be clarified by returning for a moment to the comparison with spatial perception. My desktop is the immediate background for the paper on which I write these words; the walls and bookcases of my study are further away, but they are likewise part of the background. Every perceived object must indeed have its immediate background, but that has a further background, etc. In time, whatever happens does so against the background of the "just past;" but that has its own just past, etc., etc. As Husserl says, every retention is retention of retention.[4]

Retentional consciousness differs from recollection somewhat as my marginal awareness of my bookshelves differs from my imagining the Canadian Parliament Buildings a half-mile from my study. But it is not a question of distance; I can turn to the window so that the Parliament Buildings enter the margin of my vision while I conjure up an image of

4. Ibid., section 11.

the bookshelves behind my back, or indeed the back of my own head or of the paper on which I'm writing. Likewise, I can recollect and vividly relive something that occurred just an instant ago; whereas something that happened quite a while ago may form the retentional background of my present experience.

Though he does not devote to it the analysis it deserves, Husserl recognizes that the *future* constitutes a similar horizon or "background" for present experience. Whether the future "in itself" is or is not completely undetermined, and whether or not it turns out other I expect it to, I am conscious of it. But again one must distinguish between explicitly attending to the future – thinking about it, imagining it, worrying about it – on the one hand, and the immediate horizon-consciousness of the future, which Husserl calls protention, on the other. As with recollection, we need not be attending to the future in order to be conscious, but we always have some protention of it, however vague. The point to be stressed about this whole analysis is that experienced time, like experienced space, is a complex structure; one can no more experience the present in isolation from its past and future than one can see an object apart from its spatial surroundings. What I am doing, seeing, feeling *now* is part of a temporal pattern that makes it what it is for me, gives it its meaning. In Husserl's terms, time-consciousness is what *constitutes* the present as present.

II. CRITICISMS, EXTENSIONS, AND REVISIONS

Having laid out the core of the theory, we proceed now to some extensions and revisions. We have relied up to now rather heavily, perhaps even more than Husserl himself, upon the comparison between time and space-experience. But one must always remember Bergson's warning against thinking of time in terms of space; and indeed in many respects this comparison is misleading.

Husserl himself was misled, I believe, into conceiving of retention as constituting a *field* comparable to the visual field. One aspect of this comparison is helpful: as we shift our visual focus from one thing to another particular things can shift from a position of more or less vivid copresence in the background toward the vague margins and finally pass entirely out of view without ever crossing any distinct boundary.[5] So the retained, metaphorically speaking, recedes from view until it passes into forgetfulness, no longer figures in the background. But we tend to think of the visual field as if it had a more or less fixed "size" even though it has no sharp edges. Though this size might differ from one person to the next, and be severely contracted in some case of visual

5. Ibid., section 8.

impairment, it could be measured in objective terms – indeed, that's the only way it could be measured – and the question of whether a given object was inside or outside it could be determined by measuring its objective distance from the center of focus, or perhaps the incidence of an angle formed by focus, eyes, and margin.

Actually, I'm inclined to suspect, without having ever tried to verify it empirically, that the objective "size" of the visual field varies considerably depending on the nature of the focal object – whether it is near or far, large or small, etc. In any case I am convinced that the "scope," as we might call it, of the *temporal* field varies considerably and expands and contracts depending on the nature of the temporal focus. Engrossed in a piece of music, to use Husserl's example, at any moment it is the entire piece, from its first note to that moment, which forms the vivid background of what I am hearing; the music is all around me, so to speak; what happened before it began has sunk without a trace. But depending on the length of the piece, this vivid horizon can be four minutes or 40 minutes long, objectively speaking.

Comparing the visual to the temporal field in another respect, Husserl commits a double error, to my mind. He speaks of a temporal perspective, comparable to spatial perspective, whereby objects "contract" as a function of their "distance" from the present.[6] What he has in mind is perhaps a row of telephone poles, which, according to laws of perspective, supposedly seem not only smaller but closer together the farther away they are. But of course they seem nothing of the sort; what I see is a row of equally tall telephone poles equally far apart; and the laws of perspective are just rules to follow for creating the illusion of this appearance on a flat plane. What Husserl could have meant by applying this notion to time is hard to imagine; surely he didn't mean that the first few notes of a Sousa march seem in retention closer together in time than the more recent and the present ones. In fact, what I retain is the unfolding of a steady rhythm, not a march which began *molto vivace* and has gradually slowed down to a stately *maestoso*.

The example of a row of telephone poles calls to mind another instructive comparison which needs to be introduced by way of extending and revising Husserl's account. Consider an example of the well-known Gestalt-shift phenomenon in perception of space. Entering the cloister of a medieval monastery I gain a view of the lovely garden in the center, its fountain and floral arrangements illuminated by sunlight. But I view it through a row of arches, so that the spectacle is divided into a series of framed segments separated by black spaces. By shifting my focus and shading my eyes, these black spaces are recognized as

6. Ibid., section 9.

intricately carved sets of columns, themselves now separed by gaps of empty space. When we shift our focus now to time, events similarly exhibit temporal gaps as we experience them, I think. I arrive at the theater, engaged with my companion in a heated discussion of an important matter. We take our seats for the performance of *Hamlet*. At intermission we continue our discussion, then return to the theater for the rest of the performance. Now when we resume our conversation at intermission, the genuine horizon of retention into which it fits is part of the conversation that preceded the play. We "take up" the conversation, as we say, where we left off, not explicitly recalling its details but just continuing it. The intervening first part of the play is not obliterated, but it acquires the status of a gap, an interruption in the flow of our talk. But once we return to the theater and the performance continues, it is our conversation which now acquires that status. The horizon of retention, then, not only spans quite different objective lengths but also assumes varying phenomenal features, depending on the event which is the focus of my conscious attention.

There is another aspect of the comparison with the visual field that needs to be treated with care. In describing the experience of space, Husserl himself, in some familiar passages in the *Ideas*, distinguishes, in effect, between visual field and horizon of space.[7] An object visually perceived in space is indeed surrounded by a visual field. But that field is itself experienced as a segment of space indefinitely extending in all directions. And it must be emphasized that this space is experienced, not just conceived or thought. True, we are speaking of what is not sensibly presented; but Husserl has taught that much is experienced that is not presented. Just as the objects I see have their hidden sides, so the visual field as a whole has its hidden "depths," as we might say. What's more, some aspects can be quite determinate, especially in familiar surroundings, as when the other rooms of my house loom behind the walls of my study as provenance and potential destinations for my own movements. And they "loom" in this way, in all their determinateness, without at all being the objects of explicit consciousness; they *figure* in the overall space I inhabit as the extended horizon of that part of space which presents itself directly to my senses. If there is an apt comparison, then, which will help us understand the temporal horizon, it is not merely with the visual field but with the horizon of space as a whole. This reinforces our critique of the tendency to consider the horizon of retention as short-term memory. For those determinate spatial landmarks that loom behind and around our visual field can be quite distant, extending, for example, beyond the house which surrounds me to the streets of the city in which I live and encompassing

7. See *Ideas* I, section 27.

those points which figure in my ordinary routines; whereas objects close by, even objects *known* to us, may not figure in any way in our perception of space. Likewise, I would argue that the temporal horizon can consists of "landmarks," metaphorically speaking now, quite distant from the present, which still form the background for the present without being the objects of an explicit recollective consciousness.

A final criticism of the comparison between spatial and temporal experience is much more far-reaching. It concerns the very notion of focus and horizon, or foreground and background. We maintained that this is the key to our understanding of Husserl's notion of retention, and so it is. But like Husserl we have located the temporal "focus" or "foreground" in the *present* and considered the past as its background. The future was then added on as a second kind of background from which the present stands out.

Now while this model is helpful in overcoming some misconceptions of temporal experience, it lends itself to others. It is too closely tailored to the kind of experience that serves as Husserl's prime example, the hearing of a melody, i.e., a relatively passive experience. But remember that we are trying to understand what it is to live through events; and many of the events we live through are our own actions. I would suggest that if there is a focus or a foreground for consciousness in performing actions, it lies in the *future* and not in the present. If that is so, and if the foreground-background image is to be retained, then we arrive at the old consequence that the present figures in the *background* of our temporal experience, as does the past.

But I don't think we should find this odd. I believe Husserl may have been misled not only by the comparison with space, but by some ontological and epistemological prejudices as well. He correctly saw that time-experience must unite a consciousness of what *is* with that of what *is not*. A remnant of the view that actuality is prior to potentiality in the order of being may have led him to suppose that same priority for consciousness. Husserl's use of the Humean term "impression" suggests another source of his view. Something like the distinction between vivacity and weakness may be at work in his theory. As we know, the Husserlian view that I am questioning becomes even more important in his later years. The *Quellpunkt* or bubbling fountain metaphor for the present, in the 1905 lectures, becomes the *lebendige Gegenwart* of the C Manuscripts later on.[8]

Against all this I would claim that for consciousness, the protentional future is in some respects more vivid, more central, in our living through ongoing events than the present, and I find no difficulty in con-

8. Ibid., section 36.

ceiving of the present as *its* background. But we should go even further. What should be retained from the comparison with spatial perception is not so much the focus-background scheme itself, as the idea that the various elements in the scheme make up a *Gestalt*, a whole which is prior to these elements, and determines their sense as they determine each other reciprocally. The foreground-background analogy helps us to get beyond the naive linear model of time and the simple perception-plus-memory notion of time-experience. But a more sophisticated use of the analogy would recognize that future and present as well as past, can be considered the background against which the other dimensions stand out, just as each of the dimensions can be considered as the focus.

There is a further reason for reconsidering the foreground-background scheme, and this goes for experienced space as well as time. It should not be thought that all experienced space displays the foreground-background structure. If I start indulging in some mathematical reasoning, or if I begin to daydream about a sun-drenched beach in the Carribbean, and my eyes assume the well-known "far-away look," what happens to the space I am actually inhabiting? The best way to characterize it is to say that this real space as a whole recedes into the background and that, if there is a foreground, it is not perceptual at all, not a part of the real space about me, but just those irreal or absent objects on which my mind dwells. The real space I inhabit by no means disappears; I continue to dwell in it bodily and to experience it. But in a certain sense I do not perceive it; I don't look at or even see anything in particular, nothing presents itself to my view.

Something similar happens, it seems to me, when we indulge in recollection, or what Husserl calls secondary memory. I still inhabit present time, I continue to live through it, but no part of it figures as the focus of my interest; present time as a whole sinks into the background while I dwell on the past. Yet all the dimensions of present time are functioning: though I focus on a past now, with its own past retentions and protentions, I am, after all, doing all this now, i.e., in the real now, and my present experience is continuous, with its own protentions and retentions. A past time can be the foreground, then, and present time its background. So much to demonstrate just how confused the foreground-background analogy can become, useful as it may be.

This affords us the opportunity to sum up now the various criticisms and revisions of Husserl's theory that we have been proposing. In general they have been designed to overcome the tendency to construe the horizon of retention as short-term memory, and to combat some of the implications of this misconstruction. One implication, strongly reinforced by some of the things Husserl himself says, is to think of *recollection* as a mental process in which I retrieve something that lies *beyond* the horizon of retention, out there in the dark as it were, bringing it back into the light. But if we think of the horizon of retention as extending indefinitely, with its vague and sharp contours, its landmarks and obscure recesses, then we are more inclined to think of recollection as a process in which I pick out something *within* this horizon, something from the vast background of my present experience, and focus m my attention upon it.

To make this point, the analogy with space can be useful one more time. When I exercise my imagination and daydream about that sunny Carribean beach, I am not only conscious of the bleak northern reality against which it so tantalizingly stands out; I am also vaguely aware, perhaps with some melancholy, of the vast distances I would have to cross in order to reach it. Note well: if I were daydreaming of Shangri-La or revelling in the delights of Plato's forms or Gödel's numbers, no such relation would exist. But here I am imagining a location in real space. What I am calling to mind lies within the ultimate horizon of my present space. Looked at the other way around, the imagined horizons of the imagined object extend to join the real horizon of the real present.

In time, similarly, when I recollect something, say my trip to Boston last year, the object of my present recollective experience is equally an element in the retentional horizon of my present experience. Or, again to reverse it, the past event I recollect has within its future horizon the very present act in which I recollect It. Husserl spoke of this in section 25 of the 1905 lectures. This is, of course, what makes it a case of recollection, and distinguishes it from my imagining some event in a past which is not my own, an event I never lived through. To genuinely recollect something I have to have experienced it in the first place. But this means precisely, in our interpretation of Husserl's theory, that it lies inside, not outside the horizon of retention.

III. TIME-CONSCIOUSNESS AND HISTORY

How can all this contribute to our understanding of the historical past, or rather, our understanding of the nature of our awareness of the historical past?

This topic is often approached, especially in the context of the critical or analytic philosophy of history, in the following way: We assume the existence of a full-fledged historian, equipped with all the aims, interests, and skills of his profession, but of course firmly rooted in the present. We note further that within the scope of his present experience are some documents and ruins, and then we ask: How, on the basis of this meager evidence, can our historian reconstruct the events and persons of a past he can never experience? How does he move from ignorance of the past to knowledge of the past?

Against this approach, and in keeping with our treatment of Husserl's time-consciousness theory, I want to suggest that we have two distinct modes of being aware of the *historical* past, and that they differ somewhat as retention differs from recollection. The first of these, which amounts to a sort of background- or horizon-consciousness, is something we all have, whether historians or not. If I am right about this, we shall be forced to revise our conception of the historian's approach to the past, which is more akin to recollection.

But in what sense do we have a consciousness of the historical past that is comparable to Husserl's notion of *retention*? Once again we must avoid giving too much importance to the distance from the present. By "historical" we do not usually mean only what happened before one's birth or a long time ago. Historical events are going on today. By historical events we mean not just human as opposed to animal or physical events, but those events that involve or affect society as a whole, either now or later. They may be earthquakes or diseases, actions of individual politicians or scientists, riots or elections or price increases – and so on. Excluded would be events that affect nobody's lives, but also events that are quite significant for an individual or even a small group, but have no effect beyond that.

Given this understanding of historical events, how does the individual experience them? There is a kind of spectrum: I can read or hear about them, I can see them on television or hear them on the radio, I can be an eyewitness or a participant, or finally I can be one who single-handedly carries out a historical action. As for participation, it is to be noted that I can participate in an historical event – in the sense of contributing to it – without realizing that I am doing so, as when I run up a large debt and thus contribute to inflation without seeing my action as anything but an individual choice. I can also be an eyewitness to an historical event without recognizing it *as* one, such as a secret meeting of the emissaries of two countries at war. But in these cases I would not be experiencing the historical event *as* such. And our question here concerns experience: Husserl asked how it is that we experience events, and we are asking in particular how we experience *historical* events.

Let us now apply to such experience some of the things we said about the temporality of unfolding events. If I am hearing an important speech by a political leader, or participating in a demonstration or casting my vote in an election, each of these has its own internal or "short-term" temporality in which each phase is experienced in the context of the unfolding event or action as a whole. But this event or action "as a whole" is experienced against *its* background, which is not just a sequence of the various things that have happened to *me* leading up to it, but rather its own proper temporal context. The election is the conclusion of an electoral campaign; the demonstration is the collective response to a perceived situation, and the result of some planning; the speech is the prime minster's pronouncement on an increasingly aggravating economic situation, and so on. Note that each of these temporal "contexts" or "backgrounds" constitutes an *interrupted* sequence, like the play and the conversation of our earlier example. To experience a historical event is to experience it against not just any temporal background, but against the historical background to which it properly belongs. Or to put it another way, to be able to recognize and event *as* historical is to have at one's disposal the historical context which gives it its sense.

I want to claim that we all have such a context at our disposal, though its extent and details differ considerably from one person to the next. Our experience of events places them in different temporal contexts, as the example of the play and the interrupted conversation shows. There, we shift from the social and aesthetic event of the performance to the interpersonal event *à deux* of the conversation. Likewise, we have the ability to shift from these varying social and personal contexts to that of the larger-scale social events that make up historical reality. The various events we experience are not simply in sequence, then, but take place on different levels, each with its own temporality.

If we grant this much, we can discern something like a retentional consciousness of the historical past. It may be thought that such awareness is extremely short-term and would consequently not encompass what we usually think of as the historical past. But here again I think we should take the spatial metaphor of "background" seriously, in the sense that the immediate horizon has its own further horizons, and so on indefinitely. The social and political world in which we live and act, and in which things *happen*, is part of a continuum extending indefinitely into the past. And an awareness of this extended background is built into our experience, however vague its contours, however much it is riddled with obscurities, gaps, empty spaces.

Still, much as we want to insist on the potential vastness and indefinite extention of this historical background for our awareness, at the same time we must remember that it is precisely a horizon and a horizon-consciousness we are speaking of here. In other words, however extensive it is, it is inseparably linked to the present, and its status for us is precisely that of being the context for the present. What we are claiming is that independently of its becoming an object of explicit concern in its own right, whether in the discipline of history or in other ways, the historical past figures in our awareness in the manner of a horizon. Husserl showed that to experience the present we must be horizonally aware of the past. I want to say that to experience the historical present, we must be horizonally aware of the historical past.

But here a serious objection may be raised to the comparison we are proposing. Retention is a horizon-consciousness, but it is one in which we retain what we have originally lived through, directly experienced, as present. The examples we used of historical events – the speech, the demonstration, the act of voting – are perhaps events that we may live through, directly experience. But what we called the proper temporal context of these events, what leads up to them, may not have been directly experienced at all. Such a background or context may consist of an amalgam of things heard about, read about, i.e. acquired second- and third-hand. Are we not running together here two things that must be phenomenologically distinguished, namely that which is, as Husserl would say, only "emptily intended," i.e., that which we may merely think or know or believe, on the one hand, and that which is directly given, on the other?

It is true we are running together things that can be thus distinguished, but we need to do this because they are in fact run together in our experience itself, especially at the level of social reality. In his time-consciousness lectures, Husserl made things easy for himself by restricting his examples to sounds or notes in a melody and considering them as pure hyletic data. But he realized that the flux of consciousness he was describing consists of complex intentional experiences with objects, horizons, and contexts at many different levels. As we pointed out earlier, it was Husserl himself who taught us, by contrast to the simplistic sense-data theories of his predecessors, that perception is much broader, deeper, and richer that what is presented to the senses. At the level of social experience especially, it seems to me, we must recognize a complex interaction of the given with the merely meant. It is one thing to hear a person talking, another to hear the prime minister giving an economic speech; one thing to see a lot of people running, another to witness or participate in a demonstration; one thing to pull a lever in a booth, another to cast a vote. Or rather, these are not different things: I experience the one *as* the other, and I do this by virtue of including in the horizon of this particular event many things I have not directly experienced.

It is because experience at the social level is such an amalgam that the horizon of the historical past can extend so far, indeed into the distant past before one's birth, etc. Once we acknowledge that hearsay, acquired opinions, and beliefs belong to the context within which we experience events, our notion of what belongs to the horizon of retention need not be limited to those events one actually has lived through. At the same time we must emphasize once again that it is a horizon-consciousness we are speaking of. In other words, it is not a question of explicitly thinking about the past; nor is it a matter of all those things I may *know* about the past – the dates and stories I remember from my history classes – and may be able to recite if asked. Rather, it is knowledge of the sort that Husserl called *sedimentation*. His well-known geological metaphor suggests that which has sunk below the surface but continues to support what is on the surface. Husserl availed himself of this metaphor in his later work precisely in order to elucidate what has the status of knowledge or belief rather than perception, but which recedes into a position comparable to a spatial horizon. It is that which *figures* in my awareness of the present, frames or sets it off without my having to think about it explicitly.

We have already attributed various features to this historical horizon which accord with our revised version of Husserl's time-consciousness theory: its status as background for the present, its character of extending indefinitely into the temporal "distance," its comprising gaps. interruptions, vague areas, and sharp contours or landmarks. Let us add to this the fact that it seems to expand and contract, or to change its salient features, depending on the focus of the present. To give two examples of historical events lived through by Americans in the recent past: Demonstrations against the Vietnam War took place in the relatively short-term historical context of the war itself and the growing opposition to it; civil-rights struggles belong properly to a context that encompasses the whole history of racial oppression including slavery, abolition, and the Civil War. A further feature to be noted: to the extent that we are not passive observers but active participants in the historical scene, its proper focus is for us the future rather than the present. In any case its various dimensions – past, present, and future – are experienced as a temporal Gestalt in which each determines the nature of the others.

What all this amounts to is an attempt to cast light on the obvious truth that we live the historical past as part of the continuing present before we ever turn our attention explicitly to the past. We have seen how the horizon of the historical past may be compounded of bits and pieces of hearsay, things learned in school, etc. It is also more directly encountered in the streets and buildings of our cities which comprise a social context for the most part older than we are. When we do turn our attention to the past, as in historical inquiry, we are not venturing out into an unknown domain to reconstruct something of which we are totally ignorant, on the basis of a few scraps of evidence; rather, we are picking out something from within a pregiven and familiar horizon of more or less clear shapes and contours. What we pick out may itself be some familiar landmark, like a recent war or famous political event; or it may be something hidden in the recesses amongst the familiar landmarks, something that puzzles us precisely because it is a gap in the terrain.

In these respects, our explicit attention to the historical past is like what Husserl called *recollection*. It is to relive or reproduce events I am not now living through. Of course, unlike recollection proper, the events in question may not have been lived through by *me*. But as belonging to the real past they are nonetheless continuous with the time I am living through, and they belonged before I explicitly turned to them, to the horizon of my present.

It may be pointed out that the purpose of historical inquiry is not merely to call to mind and bring into clear focus things we had only a vague awareness of; it is often designed to revise or even fully overturn our naive views of the past. Of course this is true; and historical inquiry, after it has carried out this task, can actually change even our background awareness of the past, once the knowledge it brings us has become sedimented. But to see all history as revisionist history merely confirms my point that such inquiry always begins with a conception of the past, and not in a vacuum. Also, while historical inquiry may set out to overturn our view of particular parts of the past, it nevertheless situates those parts within a larger historical context it does not question. Thus the retention-like horizon of the historical past encompasses and surrounds what we know or think we know explicitly about the past.

In this way we can gain a new conception of our relationship to the historical past, a relation that exists as a horizon-consciousness before becoming explicit in the form of historical inquiry. But the term "historical consciousness" that appears in our title usually means something much broader than either just consciousness of the past or historical inquiry. It indicates a preoccupation with the past, a fixation on it almost, that has run parallel with the growth of knowledge and is made possible by it even as it spurs it on. In all its forms – from veneration of the old, antiquarianism, preoccupation with restoartion of the authentic, historical nostalgia with its concomitant devaluation of the present – in all these there is a note of desperation, as if we were trying to hold on to a past we have almost lost, one which is no longer continuous with the present as the background which gives the present its sense. Perhaps the present analysis can, among other things, help us to understand these phenomena. It seems we are living in an age in which the continuity with the past seems not to take care of itself and needs to be restored by voluntary action.

THE AESTHETIC OBJECT AS "DIE SACHE SELBST"

MIKEL DUFRENNE (Nanterre)

I have always thought that aesthetics was a privileged path for philosophy – at least for a philosophy that goes "toward the concrete," as Jean Wahl said, and cares more for describing than for systematizing. Such a philosophy starts from examining the first relation of the being in the world with the world, i.e., perception; but this phenomenology of perception does not prevent going further, up to metaphysics or ontology. I would like to show that the phenomenology of the aesthetic object can achieve this step.

I am immediately confronted with a preliminary objection. Fink asserts that for such a move of thought we cannot invoke Husserl. Husserl, he says, does not open a path for speculative thinking. He is interested in science; he elaborates a method which must leave history and the ontological work that goes on in history in order to look for a radical beginning. Then man becomes the measure of all things. The real is what appears to man, a phenomenon. But the phenomenality of the phenomenon is not interrogated by Husserl. The being is reduced to the statuts of an object, object for a subject, and "the relation object-subject as a whole, with all its noetico-noematic structures henceforth becomes the proper theme of phenomenology."

We know how patiently Husserl has undertaken the analysis of intentionality. But this study of the intentional life may open the way to speculative thinking, although perhaps not the Heideggerian kind of speculation which Fink recommends. For Heidegger pretends to be immediately solicited by the meditation of Being, even when he does not go beyond the analytics of *Dasein*. He is on his way – *unterwegs zu* – on *Holzwegen*, but is already arrived: every road leads to Rome, that is, to the haunting question of Being. Whereas a thought which follows the path opened by Husserl reaches the stage of speculation only after a long way, since it has recourse to method – *Weg*, not *Holzweg* – rather than inspiration.

So I will make mine Husserl's proceedings, not as a historian, but by

Cho, K.K. (ed.) Philosophy and Science in Phenomenological Perspective.

ISBN 978-94-009-6115-9

focusing on the aesthetic object. As a matter of fact, I still keep close to Heidegger, for Heidegger summons the work of art in order to throw light on his ontology. But it is not the work of art I want to call for, it is the aesthetic object, that is, an object essentially offered to *aisthesis*, that is, revealed – should we say constituted? – within aesthetic experience. This difference has to be stressed: the aesthetic object is indeed the work of art, but as perceived, and by a perception that does it justice. It is the Greek temple, but also the parade of Panathenees ascending to the Acropolis.

The contemporary practice of art – including the contestation of art by nonart or antiart – invites us to enlarge the field of the works well beyond the samples Heidegger gives, to include in it the carnival or other events such as performances or happenings which can be experienced as aesthetic objects. For Heidegger, the truth of the peasant's boots as usual objects needs Van Gogh's mediation to be manifested; today the boots can be directly proposed to an aestheticizing act. In environments like Kienholz's or Brent's, any object may be commuted into an aesthetic object; so it is as far as it is present to a lively experience and associated with a certain pleasure (which can itself be loaded with anxiety). Significantly, the word "pleasure" does not figure in Heidegger's essay; we are tempted to say his reflection upon the work's truth keeps being linked with the philosophy of representation, for not showing how the work accomplishes itself in presence.

Now, in Husserlian perspective, the aesthetic object is well in agreement with the motto prescribed to phenomenology: back to things themselves. The aesthetic object is the thing itself – even if it does not reveal the thingness of the thing or its thing-structure, as some works such as Greek temples do, or even if it has the unsubstantial and ephemeral character of a fireworks display. The German language avoids any equivocation: the thing as thing itself is not *Ding*, but *Sache*. The *Sache* is what gives itself to a consciousness aiming at it, may it be an essence, ideal object, a relation, formal object, a predicable quality, or a thing properly speaking, and of course the perceived thing.

Grasping the thing itself to make it an object of reflection implies the phenomenological reduction, the act by which the thought, going from living to philosophizing, neutralizes any position of existence, any, I believe, practical interest, and limits itself to examining this thing and the modes according to which it gives itself to consciousness.

The point is that it gives itself, and that implies it is at first aimed at: any consciousness is consciousness of. Intentionality defines consciousness as the power of aiming at, and this aiming determines the way the object gives itself: as conceived, perceived, imagined, remembered. But what is aimed at must also be attained; the intention has to be fulfilled. This fulfillment requires the intuition, intuition of essences or perception of things in the world. The second one, the sensible intuition, is the intuition par excellence; it gives its object *leibhaftig und in schlichter Weise*. It may entail an indefinite multiplicity of potential acts, but this succession is "like one single act which lingers on," says Levinas, and aims at the same given object.

This idea of intuition as *Fülle* and the priority bestowed on percepception free Husserl from the objection raised by Sartre: Husserl is not doomed to idealism, *esse* is not reduced for him to *percipi*. What Husserl calls unreal is only the *esse* of the *noema*, and he carefully distinguishes *noema* and object; *noema* is the correlative of *noesis*. It stays in the immanent of the lived, but "it relates to the object," as in Frege the *Sinn* relates to the *Bedeutung*, the signification to the referents.

This object is no longer the still-immanent *object-pôle*; it is a real and transcendent object. Its meaning may well be constituted by a sense-giving consciousness; its being is not so: it is the being of a being. Consciousness may well posit a thesis of existence when it seizes at the same time the *quid* of the *noema* and the *quomodo*, but the existence imposes itself on it.

In the *Logical Investigations* Husserl says: "the difference between the significative apprehension and the intuitive apprehension is a phenomenologically irreducible difference." We know why: because the "intentional character of perception is, as opposed to the simple representation of imagination, the present." So the transcendence of the perceiving consciousness is not illusory. If we give all its strength to this transcending, we might say with Sartre that consciousness is nothing because it breaks away; it "breaks itself towards" and that is how man is actually a being-in-the-world, present to things, instead of having things represented in his consciousness. What Sartre calls the ontological proof frees phenomenology from the equivocal idea of constitution, whose meaning, says Fink, "oscillates in Husserl between sense-giving and creating." Sartre tells us: "to be conscious of something is to be in front of a concrete and full presence which is not consciousness." Presence of the world.

This decisive theme of being-in-the-world is used by Fink against Husserl: "More originally than any being, than every object, than every subject, there is the world. Thought is, according to its proper essence, the operation of opening man to the world.... Being itself is the space-time of the world which embraces any thing which is."

But is it fair to oppose this idea of the world to Husserl? After all, Husserl has spoken at length about the *Lebenswelt*. Commenting upon him, Levinas may say in terms which anticipate Sartre: "the subject is a being who, as far as he exists, stays already in presence of the world, and that constitutes his very being." Fink himself admits that Husserl finally "conceived a universal process in which the opposition of subject and object is included within the concrete totality of the intentional life."

Such, I think, is the germ metaphysics may develop. But if totality is thought over, should we still confer a privilege to consciousness? Levinas seems to think so when he says: "The decisive steps achieved by the *Ideen* consists in thinking up to its radical consequences the idea of intentionality and in realizing that the opposition of consciousness and object is meaningless, and that it is in consciousness, in intentionality that we find the truly first and concrete phenomenon, the source of the very opposition of object and subject."

Yes, but the question is: Should we now identify intentionality and consciousness, or at least locate intentionality in consciousness? Should we not rather make intentionality the source of a reciprocity and locate consciousness in intentionality? Then intentionality would be given a properly ontological meaning, which might lead, as we will see, to a philosophy of nature.

The reflection on the aesthetic object may orient us in that direction. If for Husserl the perceived thing is par excellence the thing itself, we can add that the aesthetic object is par excellence the perceived thing. At first, this object requires a kind of reduction in order to be seized: not the decision of suspending any thesis of existence but the decision of playing a certain game, the game of aestheticization, and so suspending the attitudes called for by knowledge or practice. When we go to the movies, we intend to see a film; our whole being is concentrated in the act of looking, and we will come back to our problem when we leave. We might be willing to conclude from that that the work of art is unreal – an imaginary, as Sartre says. I prefer invoking Kant and his idea of aesthetic experience as disinterested. For this disinterestedness qualifies not only the pleasure but the free play of the faculties and their accordance. The aesthetic object unfolds itself in a free space, a play space where the daily world is put into brackets, and the perceiver has only to welcome and savor it: on these conditions the aestheticizable object accomplishes itself as aesthetic object.

I have here to open a bracket, because my analysis seems to privilege contemplation. Contemplation may have been required by an art withdrawn from life. But it happens that the aesthetic experience of nature, or even of works of art in cultures where art is not institutionalized or refuses its institutionalization, requires a more active involvement of the receptor; so it is for the mountain climber or for the spectator who is at the same time actor. The harpoon is better achieved as an aesthetic object when it is used by the Eskimo fisherman than when it is exhibited on the wall of an anthropological museum. When used, the object is no less perceived; the aesthetic experience is not aware of itself, but is lived in the action that it metamorphoses. When art is not cut from life, the activity itself, instead of being reduced to a purely utilitarian practice, becomes aestheticizing and aims less at a specific object such as the harpoon than at the world where this object plays a function. But we should pursue that analysis of a spontaneous aesthetic experience lived within life itself, which makes life a game.

Anyway, aesthetic perception is a modality of perceptive intention, intentionality brought up to its higher intensity, "culminating into a kind of alienation of the receptor similar to the alienation of the creator who sacrifices himself to creation." The intention is now fulfilled: the aesthetic object gives itself to the seeing or listening which aim at it. And we could say the generosity of the gift is in proportion with the intensity of the aiming. For we know that every perception is in essence inadequate: the perceived thing only offers itself through *Abschattungen* that always indicate other aspects for an indefinite series of possible perceptions; and we are all the more aware of this limitation than our perception is inspired by a cognitive interest. But the apprehension of the aesthetic object seems to be less inadequate. First, because the intentional act does not care for knowledge. Then, because when the thing summoning its epiphany in perception is a work of art, it manifests in its structure a character of totality that makes up for its inexhaustibility. One must walk along a monument, indoors and outdoors; the monument proposes itineraries to the walker, as the painting does for the eye that grazes it; but it can also offer some privileged perspectives, some points for the view to embrace what may be called the essential of its being, because the more significant elements of the visible are brought together and articulated here. So classical architecture emphasizes the facade, that is in relation with the monument what the face is in relation with the body, so that the building is to be looked at as a spectacle, from a specified point of view, just as classical painting requests it from the motionless spectator. Later on art will give back this spectator his freedom, at the same time it takes into account the sphericity of his eye and mingles the focal zone with the peripheral area of the visual field. But this deconstruction does not imply the dislocation of the specific object, or rather the possibility of grasping it "in person" and "with one stroke."

Another parenthesis, please, to observe that this analysis should be extended to the arts Lessing called temporal. If we may need time to explore a monument or a painting, we necessarily need it to listen to music, read a poem, or see a movie. But the temporality of the work does not summon us in the same way as a logical argument which must be followed or an idea which must be thought over; the time we live is not the time requested by the search of an evidence slipping away from us, it is the time of a presence which does not get away, given in a perception that lasts. The object still gives itself in one stroke, but it is a lasting stroke because the object is a becoming whole.

Now, another reason for the privilege of the aesthetic object is that its proper being resides in its appearing. That does not at all mean it is unreal, or its consistency is only that of a representation in a consciousness. It claims, on the contrary, the full reality the work is entrusted with, a work laboriously produced and sometimes bearing the marks of this labor. But, let us say it again, the aesthetic object is this work as perceived, and if we had to choose for it an ontological region, we would place it in the sensuous, the *aistheton*. It is in the field of the sensuous that the qualities unfold, and precisely in order to bear witness to the materiality of the work, what Heidegger calls its "thingness," its part of earth affronting the world. It is for the sensuous, without naming it, that Heidegger calls in order to show how matter reveals itself "in the openness of the work's world. The rock sustains the temple and rests in itself; the metals come to their resplending and their twinkling, the colors to their shining, the sounds to their resounding, the speech to the saying." In this field the analysis may distinguish several registers: visible, sonorous, tactile, olfactive; anatomy warrants these differentiations, and art reckons at least with the distinction between sonorous and visible. But let us not forget that many artists have dreamed about a *Gesamtkunstwerk* and that, within or outside of art, synesthesia can produce multiple correspondences between these registers. Merleau-Ponty stressed that, defending a certain imperialism of vision. We could extend what we are saying about the aesthetic object to any perceived thing, but only the spontaneous reduction achieved by aesthetic experience displays and enjoys the sensuous as such. So we may again say aesthetic perception is more adequate: it is truly perception.

Do not believe that when the sensuous is emphasized the identity of the object is endangered. For the sensuous carries in itself a sense which is a powerful principle of unification for the object and of recognition for us. An immanent sense, that perhaps is not conceptualizable, but is experienced without ambiguity and may be said in the vocabulary of affect, as when Heidegger speaks of the solemnity or the sacrality of the temple. Such is the phenomenon of expressivity, which I have stressed at length. The aesthetic object illimitates itself and opens a singular world, that, conversely, feeling opens us to. So this object is both totalized and totalizing: totalized by the sense it expresses, totalizing because this sense unfolds into a world. Hence we can say this object is a quasi-subject. Its sense is immanent, but by this sense it transcends itself, it "breaks up" itself toward the world it gives access to. Here we may be Heideggerian: the work is true insofar as it manifests this power of *Offenheit*, which also implies a power of withdrawal and dissimulation, that is, insofar as it opens a world and belongs to earth. But rather than of "work" I speak of "aesthetic object," for the work is powerless as long as it is not perceived and promoted to the sensuous.

This drives us back to Husserl. For it seems that the emphasis put on the sensuous may throw some light on the Husserlian notion of constitution. It is evident that the aesthetic object only reveals itself to a consciousness aiming at it. But must we conclude from that that consciousness constitutes this object, or gives it its sense? No, if indeed the sense dwells in the object which expresses it, instead of being added to the object by a subjective free interpretation. What is required from the subject is only his being available and open for the sense to be recollected within him; and the work is real enough to impose this requirement. It must be promoted to the sensuous for the sensuous in its turn to deliver its sense and this sense to resound in us. We have to aestheticize ourselves; Valéry used to say poetry produces in the reader a poetic state. But it is also necessary, in order to grasp the sense, that we be in a preliminary accordance with it, thanks to what I have called an affective *a priori*. And the object must also lend itself to this agreement, being animated by a sense that is in it a constitutive a priori. Such are the conditions of possibility for being-in-the-world.

But can we not go further in the vicinity of the speculative thinking Fink wishes? Let us remember the Aristotelian sentence: Sensation is the common act of the sensing and the sensed. The sensuous is the product of this common act. We have just said what the partners are involved in by this act: in an amorous intimacy, where pleasure may somehow have the character of orgasm; it is not, to speak as Heidegger, the struggle of earth with world, but the *corps à corps* of the work and his guardian. I said the partners are in this game alienating and losing themselves; the subject abolishes himself, being fascinated by the sensuous, as lovers for a while fall into the *petite mort*. But could we not now say the opposite – that object and subject do not pre-exist to their intimacy, and instead of losing themselves discover themselves in it? In other words, the sensuous seems to be the product of their cooperation only because it is the place of their common birth; therefore the *petite mort* mimicked by their intimacy is as well the prelude to a little birth, a renascence. Of course, in ordinary perception we refer the sensuous to the thing it qualifies: the color is the color of a determined object, like the red of a face which means fever or shame. The sound is produced by a given source at a given distance; the sensuous is dealt with as an instrument for thinking or acting; it is subordinated to knowledge and explained by what is known.

But aesthetic experience renders the sensuous to its enigmatic being without denying its expressivity. The sonorous overflows me, wraps me up, dancing within me as I am dancing within it and through it; the visible is seeing me as I am seeing it; the tactile touches me and moves me. Such is the beginning that neither object nor subject may claim priority or initiative; and precisely this experience of the sensuous brings us back to beginning. Says Merleau-Ponty: "The sensuous world is older than the universe of thought." It may be called a world only because it is all: not as a totality but as an element. Merleau-Ponty names this element "flesh." Ultimate notion, says he, last because first; flesh is the name of the originary. But is it truly ultimate? Merleau-Ponty has been driven to this notion because his reflection had started from the body, and he had to look for what is playing in the body and makes it play, makes it consubstantial with things and makes things "secret fold of my flesh." But because flesh is the place for a double dehiscency, of seeing into visible and of visible into seeing, should we refuse it any substantiality and make it an element? Flesh then would be thought of as "a going between." But if this *entre-deux* deserves consideration, if it is not merely a relation instituted by the thought of an outsider, then it must give birth to both, to the beings that shall be and assert themselves for their own account. And if we bestow on it this power, should we not call it nature? That the originary breaks up means man and world surge from nature as belonging to the same race. But the originary keeps being there and bearing them: they are not born once and for all, they never break the umbilical cord, for, says Merleau-Ponty, "there is only one breaking up of Being that is forever." Every flesh is *flesh-of*, multiplied flesh of an indefinite plurality, and *the* flesh is flesh of nature, is nature as flesh. The sensuous is the figure of this flesh when, through the movement of reversibility which happens in it, it has access to appearing. The aesthetic object is precisely this object which surges into the appearing: the thing itself.

This development still may claim Husserl with caution. It may proceed from and stay in accordance with his notion of intentionality. Intentionality, says Levinas, "makes the very subjectivity of the subject"; it is the apparently sovereign act of a consciousness, especially when the aiming is empty, as in significative acts; for it is consciousness that can introduce in the presence this emptiness, the distance specific of representation. But Merleau-Ponty comes to speak of consciousness as "an intentionality without act," and then to deescribe "the subject as field." When intention is perceptive, when it achieves plenitude because the object gives itself as present as the aesthetic object does, we may wonder if this intuition that Husserl calls originary because it founds the other ones does not bring us back near the originary such as Merleau-Ponty understands it. The intentional relation phenomenology describes between the sensing and the sensed might be the unrelative both proceed from. Then the transcendent description ascribed to consciousness may be attributed to the originary as breaking up toward man and world. And if consciousness keeps being also transcendent – if the *Da-* of *Dasein* is still this glade where light can spread out – is it not as called for by and similar to a nature for which it is all the same to transcend itself and to naturate? Here thinking attempts to the ground.

But it cannot sejourn there; man only approaches it when, in aesthetic experience, he lets the sensuous be up to letting himself be fascinated. The aesthetic object is the sensuous being – this piece of flesh – which does not belong to the world nor to him, but which manifests the naturing power of nature; it opens a world, it invites a consciousness which is itself a sensuous flesh to enter it. It opens the realm of truth. And so we can again say: it is the thing itself. But not as an already natured thing, already determined, already assigned a place in space and time, which we would have only to detect among other things; not the thing I aim at, but the thing that aims at me, an in-itself that is for me as far as I am for it, not a being, neither object nor subject, but an a priori, appearing as a radiance out of which subject and object appear.

Certainly this object is only delivered to us in an experienced limit. We could say about the aesthetic act what Kant says about the moral act: it has never been accomplished. How could man radically relive his own birth? He is always already born, and he can only approach the originary. Merleau-Ponty says in other words: "The immediate is at the horizon," or more explicitly, "When my perception is on the verge of becoming pure perception, thing, being, it extinguishes itself; when it lights up I am already no longer the thing."

THE IMPLICATIONS OF MERLEAU-PONTY'S THOUGHT FOR THE PRACTICE OF PSYCHOTHERAPY

MARTIN DILLON (Binghamton)

I

In his monumental work on Freud, Ricœur argues that Freud's archaeology needs to be supplemented/counterbalanced/integrated with its own incipient teleology, and he turns to Hegel to find what psychoanalysis has left undeveloped.[1] I am convinced by Ricœur's critique, but not by his prescription: I agree that Freud's preoccupation with the past needs to be contextualized within a more comprehensive and integrated understanding of human temporality, but I propose to look in Merleau-Ponty's thought, rather than Hegel's, for that context. Both Merleau-Ponty and Hegel understand freedom and reason to be the goals which define human teleology, but Hegel's absolute reason is incompatible with Merleau-Ponty's conception of reason as essentially finite. Without pausing to argue the case, here I shall simply opt for finitude and proceed to examine the implications that Merleau-Ponty's teleology of freedom and reason has for the practice of psychotherapy.

Although Merleau-Ponty writes frequently on psychological themes, his concerns are largely cognitive/developmental. Merleau-Ponty did not articulate a theoretical viewpoint with regard to psychotherapy, although some fragments of his writings do bear directly upon that subject.[2] Consequently, although the thoughts I am about to present are,

1. Paul Ricœur, *Freud and Philosophy: An Essay on Interpretation*, transl. Denis Savage (New Haven, Conn.: Yale University Press, 1970), Book 3, chap. 3. Ricœur purports to discover "in Freudianism a certain dialectic of archaeology and teleology that is clearly evident in Hegel" (p. 461).

2. Maurice Merleau-Ponty, *Phénoménologie de la perception* (Paris: Editions Gallimard, 1945), pp. 180-202. *See* Martin Dillon, "Merleau-Ponty on Existential Sexuality: A Critique," *Journal of Phenomenological Psychology* 11, no. 1 (Spring 1980); also, Merleau-Ponty, "Le Problème de la passivité: le sommeil, l'inconscient, la mémoire," *Annuaire du College de France* (Paris: Imprimerie Nationale, 1955), pp. 161-64; "Preface" to A. Hesnard, *L'Oeuvre de Freud et son importance pour le monde moderne* (Paris: Payot, 1960), pp. 5-10.

Cho, K.K. (ed.) Philosophy and Science in Phenomenological Perspective.

ISBN 978-94-009-6115-9

in part, extrapolations, I will do what I can to keep my inferences from merging with his implications.

II

There are many areas in which contemporary theories of psychotherapy[3] are faltering, as is made evident by the conspicuous lack of consensus on fundamental issues; but the most serious failure, in my judgment, is the failure to articulate the values which necessarily underlie the practice of any form of therapy. Therapy aims at change, change from worse to better; thus it is intrinsically teleological and intrinsically bound to the values implicit in its goals. By and large, however, theoreticians have been reluctant to state and defend the values informing what must be normative theorizing. Mental health remains undefined.

Perhaps this is a legacy of the early positivism of the human sciences. In seeking to be scientific in the manner of their more respected cousins, the hard or physical sciences, the soft sciences attempted to confine themselves to description, to facts, to observables. The dogma that science – knowing – must ground itself on fact, to the exclusion of value, is predicated on the belief that values do not admit of cognitive grounding. As ordinary mortals we may have to make value-informed decisions, but once one has chosen to be a scientist, one refrains, qua scientist, from making value judgments.[4] When, however, the scientist undertakes to practice psychotherapy, he confronts a dilemma which betrays the contradiction embedded in his posture of value neutrality. On the one hand, he must acknowledge that there is something wrong with his patient; there is something bad in the way the patient is living his life, something that needs to be improved, made better. On the other hand, the therapist believes that he must refrain from imposing his values on the patient; as scientist he "knows" that his own values have no greater claim to objective validity than the values of the patient, and he "knows" this on the basis of the above-mentioned dogma. There can be no resolution to this conflict – because there is no way to mediate a simple contradiction – but the characteristic way in

3. "Contemporary theories of psychotherapy": the phrase names everyone, hence none. It is intended to allow the shoe I am constructing to be worn by as many feet as it will fit. The dilemma of value-neutrality instantiates itself in every major school of psychotherapy being practiced today that I know of. The exceptions, of course, are the "cult" schools: they are not at all value-neutral, but they encounter other, perhaps more serious, conceptual problems.

4. See Barton, *Three Worlds of Therapy* (Palo Alto, Calif.: Mayfield Publishing Co., 1974). "A theory that hopes to sustain and foster life-values should not select one set of values over another..." (p. 429).

which it works itself out is for the therapist to enforce his values nonverbally without having to defend them thematically. The therapist makes no assertions, he continually refers the patient back to himself as ultimate judge of his own value positions; and yet the therapist unabashedly offers positive reinforcement to the patient who learns to make "healthy" judgments. Thus can the therapist claim to have cured the survivors while disavowing responsibility for the casualties.

The situation is different, but not much better, in the case of the existential psychotherapy that has grown out of the early writings of Jean-Paul Sartre. As is well known. Sartre never wrote the ethics he promised at the end of *Being and Nothingness.*[5] It is also generally conceded that that work was itself a disguised ethics predicated on the value of freedom. Regarded as an ethical treatise, *Being and Nothingness* is doubly a failure. In the first place, by refusing to acknowledge and defend the prescriptive implications of such key terms as "bad faith," Sartre evades responsibility for his own moralizing. Secondly, and more importantly, the thesis of radical freedom set forth in that work cannot bear the weight of its own covert ethics. Hence, the therapist who relies on Sartre also confronts a dilemma and a contradiction. The prescription to confront/actualize one's freedom collides with the thesis that one is condemned to be free, that every act is equally an upsurge of freedom grounded in nothingness. As Merleau-Ponty demonstrates in his *Phenomenology of Perception*, Sartre founders on his own polarization. Either one is absolutely free or one is absolutely determined; for Sartre, there can be no in-between. But, if one is absolutely free, every act, including a futile act of self-deception or bad faith, is as groundless and free as every other.[6] As conceived by Sartre, the value of freedom cannot function in the assessment of behavior; the therapist cannot consistently affirm one set of actions as freedom-enhancing and criticize another as evading freedom – the distinction having been forsaken in the initial polarization.

Here, again, no resolution is conceptually possible, but one finds a praxis of elevating self-consciousness. The measure of the validity of an action becomes the degree of self-awareness accompanying it. One cannot choose an action freely unless one is aware of choosing it. If one responds automatically, one is a machine, an automation in service

5. Jean-Paul Sartre, *L'être et le néant* (Paris: Editions Gallimard, 1943), p. 722.

6. "If, indeed, freedom is equal in all our actions ..., if the slave attests to as much freedom in living in fear as by breaking his irons, one cannot say that there is any *free action* at all; freedom underlies all actions, and in no case would one be able to say 'Here freedom is manifest' since, in order to discern it as such, a free action must detach itself from a background of life which is not free or not as free [qui ne le fût pas ou qui le fût moins]." Merleau-Ponty, *Phénoménologie*, p. 499.

to a role (or essence) into which one has fallen (or been pushed by the look of the undifferentiated Other). The reflective/prereflective distinction thus serves to resurrect the free/determined distinction – thereby contradicting the thesis of radical freedom – and provides a basis for covert moral assessment. Bad faith is now lack of awareness, unconsciousness, a kind of lapse into the reifying swoon of a Leibnizian monad.

This is a point of convergence between Sartre and Freud. On the surface, there is the controversy over repression, where Sartre argues that Freud's topography cannot adequately account for the function of censorship. Sartre claims that isolating superego from ego does not eliminate the problem of contradictory awareness; at some level or other, he argues, there will have to be both awareness and unawareness of the repressed contents because recognition of the contents as inadmissable is required in order to identify them as to be repressed.[7] But this capacity to deny what one knows is precisely what Sartre labels bad faith. So, beneath the controversy, there is agreement on the fact of a self-dissembling denial – i.e., repression – as a fundamental structure of the psyche. Their disagreement concerns only the (il-)logic of this denial, and the extent to which it is conscious/volitional. Further beneath the controversy, one may discern another concordance which takes us a step closer to our central theme.

"Where there was id, there let ego be."[8] Freud's prescription coincides with the Sartrean elevation of self-consciousness. In both cases, there is an inchoate ethic founded on a teleology whose proximal goal is self-awareness, which is, itself, in service to freedom or deliberate choice. And, in both cases, this teleology is conceived through its essential agonist/correlate: the archaeology that binds the psyche (or For-itself) to its past (or situation). The *requirement* for a teleology is thus deeply embedded in the thought of Freud and Sartre, but the theoretical *possibility* of that teleology is problematic in both cases. In the case of Freud, as Ricœur shows,[9] the economics of desire grounds all

7. "It does not suffice that [the censor=superego] discern the condemned tendencies, beyond that it is necessary that it grasp them as *to be repressed*, which implies at the very least a representation in the censor of its own activity. In a word, how could the censor discern the repressed impulses without having consciousness of discerning them? Can one conceive a knowledge which would be ignorant of itself?" Sartre, *L'être et le néant*, p. 91.

8. Freud, *New Introductory Lectures on Psychoanalysis* (New York: W.W. Norton & Co., 1933), p. 80. "*Wo Es war, soll Ich werden.*"

9. *Freud and Philosophy*, III, 3, p. 492: "Ultimately, the task of becoming I, of becoming the ego, a task set within the economics of desire, is in principle irreducible to the economics." Hence, the *theory* of psychoanalysis grounds all explanation in repression. But, as I have noted earlier, the *practice* of psychotherapy presupposes a progression, hence a goal. As Ricœur puts it: "in a direction

motivation ultimately in the archaisms of instinct with the result that human behavior must always be understood as flowing from its past and never as drawn toward an elected destiny. And, in the case of Sartre, as Merleau-Ponty has shown, the teleology is undermined by the impossibility within Sartre's theory of distinguishing degrees of freedom, i.e., by the theoretical impossibility of recognizing a *progression* toward liberation.

The positive result of this critique of Freud and Sartre is the recognition of an inner link between the practice of psychotherapy, the attainment of higher levels of self-awareness, and freedom as a progressively realized value or goal. The negative moment was necessary to open the underlying problematic – that is, the nexus of problems that emerge when freedom is posited as a value. The core of that nexus lies in the fact that freedom cannot function as the final term of a teleology (although Freud implicitly and Sartre explicitly assign it that function). To anticipate conclusions yet to be substantiated: freedom cannot function as the final term of a teleology, because the formal structure of a teleology requires positing an answer to the question of the "for-the-sake-of" which freedom cannot answer. Freedom from the archaic (itself a problematic notion, as we shall see), raises the question of freedom for –? and that cannot be answered satisfactorily by a further appeal to freedom.[10] However, to ground this assertion and understand its bearing upon the practice of psychotherapy, it is necessary to raise the question of freedom in the context of its correlate, reason.

III

It is the deficiency of reason that defines the patient as such, and the degree of that deficiency is the measure of his illness. But the reason I speak of here goes beyond mere verbal lucidity, which can be highly developed even in severe cases of psychic disorder: it is an *operant*

---

contrary to the regressive movement psychoanalysis sets forth in theory, there must be supposed an aptitude for progression, which analytic practice puts in operation, but which the theory does not thematize" [ibid.].

10. It should be noted at this point that the problematic of positing freedom as a value is identical with that of positing authenticity as a value. Authenticity, as that term is understood within the existential-phenomenological tradition, is defined in terms of freedom, reflection, and resolution. To be authentic is to act with resolute awareness of oneself as free. If one accepts the conception of degrees of freedom, it follows that there are also degrees of authenticity. Thus, the teleology of becoming increasingly authentic shares with the teleology of increasing realization of freedom the problem of articulating the final term: authenticity for the sake of (*what*)?

reason, an ability to *act* as well as think and talk cogently. A patient in analysis may be able to deliver a competent theoretical analysis of his neurotic symptoms but still not be able to free himself from them. Indeed, verbal theorizing may be identified by his therapist as a technique employed by a patient to evade more direct and emotional confrontation with the archaism that has him in its thrall. For example, to recognize the Oedipus complex as underlying psychical impotence is not, *ipso facto*, to restore sexual vigor; something more than calling it by name is needed to cast out the demon. There has to be an emotional component to the intellectual enlightenment before the symptoms begin to abate.

Here, where archaeology collides with teleology, we arrive at the matrix of freedom and reason. The patient behaves irrationally to the extent that he cannot free himself from the past – from the personal past of his infancy as well as the impersonal past of his culture and species. Operant rationality, i.e., behavior commensurate with a thematically posited ideality, is thus conditioned by the degree of freedom the individual has wrested for himself from the determining influence of his past.

At this point we must distinguish two sets of problems which, albeit interrelated, must be approached sequentially. The first set of problems has to do with understanding what it is to win freedom from the past and achieve a style of behavior that is rational in the sense of being commensurate with one's goals. The second problematic concerns the positing of the goals themselves. Rationality in this context consists in grounded goal selection, i.e., in understanding what our freedom is freedom *for*. The intermingling of the two becomes apparent when one reflects on the fact that the choice of goals, the commitment to one teleology rather than another, is not made *in vacuo*, from the standpoint of weightlessness, but is rather a situated decision and stands thereby in relation to one's history. As we shall see, the overall problematic is one of finding an integrated mode of temporality, one in which the present moment of decision can be reconciled with one's historical situation and the ideality posited as the end of one's projects.

A. *Archaeology and freedom from.*

> It is by what phenomenology implies or unveils as its limits – by its *latent* content or its unconscious – that it is in consonance with psychoanalysis.[11]

11. Merleau-Ponty, Preface to Hesnard's *L'Oeuvre de Freud*, transl. Fisher, in *The Essential Writings of Merleau-Ponty*, ed. Fisher (New York: Harcourt, Brace & World, 1969), p. 86.

In welcoming the unconscious into the domain of phenomenology – if only as a limit which must constantly be tested and pressed back – Merleau-Ponty has clearly broken with those of his predecessors, notably Husserl and Sartre, who remain circumscribed within the immanence and false lucidity of the Cartesian cogito. To venture beyond the thematic contents of an ongoing intentional act is to forsake apodicticity in the interest of laying tenuous hold on truth. The truths to be sought in the domain of the unconscious concern those "relations which a consciousness cannot [by itself] sustain: man's relations to his origins and his relations to his models."[12] Here Merleau-Ponty associates the unconscious not only with "our archaeology" but also with the sphere of intersubjectivity and the significant others dwelling therein. This may shed some light on the meaning of "the unconscious" or, at least, Merleau-Ponty's intent in using this least felicitous term of Freudian jargon.

In Sartre's polarized thinking, there are phenomena which are immanent and those which are transcendent, but none which are both. For Merleau-Ponty, all phenomena are both immanent (i.e., manifest in some manner) and transcendent (i.e., opaque to some degree), but no phenomenon is entirely one or the other.[13] One might conceive the phenomena of conscious life as a continuum ranging from those of greater lucidity, transparency, and particularity to those which are more opaque, general, and anonymous. Toward one end of the spectrum, the one approaching greater immanence, we would find the Cartesian cogito; at the other, the Freudian unconscious.

One immediate consequence of conceiving the unconscious this way is to render it in some degree available for phenomenological description and analysis. This, in turn, has the effect of keeping the unconscious from being the inaccessible repository of occult forces/drives/instincts which purport to explain while themselves remaining inexplicable. A phenomenology of the unconscious has, indeed, been undertaken by Merleau-Ponty, although not under this rubric; the domain

12. "Preface," pp. 86-7.

13. This is an area of inconsistency in Sartre's thinking. In the "Introduction" to *Being and Nothingness* he asserts that all phenomena must be regarded as both immanent and transcendent: "... immanence can only be defined as the grasp of a transcendent" (*L'être et le néant*, p. 29).

But, when he analyzes specific phenomena, he typically insists upon regarding them as sheerly immanent or utterly transcendent, and refuses to grant the possibility of a phenomenon being indistinguishably immanent and transcendent. This is especially apparent in his treatment of the body. My essay, "Sartre on the Phenomenal Body and Merleau-Ponty's Critique," addresses the differences between Sartre and Merleau-Ponty on the issue of immanence and transcendence as it bears on their treatments of the lived or phenomenal body. [*Journal of the British Society for Phenomenology*, Vol. 5, No. 2 (May 1964)].

Freud labels unconscious Merleau-Ponty investigates under the heading of the prereflective. There are important differences, to be sure, as there are between Freud, Jung, Adler, and other psychologists who theorize about this aspect of the psyche, but the salient fact is that Merleau-Ponty uses the same concepts to characterize the unconscious that he uses in describing the prereflective, and assigns to the prereflective many of the theoretical functions classical psychoanalysis assigns to the unconscious.[14]

The zone of the prereflective has already been described as a domain of latency, opacity, generality, anonymity. It encompasses the lived body's sense of its own orientation in the world, hence encompasses as well an unthematized sense of the world as its situation, as background (or *fond*) of its being and doing. In this regard, there is an intimate link between the prereflective and the perceptual.

> All consciousness is, in some degree, perceptual consciousness. In what I call my reason or my ideas at each moment – if one could explicate all that is presupposed in them – one would always find experiences which have not been made explicit, massive sediments [*des apports massif*] from past and present, an entire "sedimented history" [*une "histoire sédimentée"*] which concerns not only the genesis of my thought, but which also determines its sense or meaning [*sens*].[15]

Merleau-Ponty's intent here is not to identify thinking with perceiving, but rather to point out that thinking and other thematic "mental" activities take place against a background of nonthematized experience which is fundamentally perceptual – but perceptual in a maximally broad sense which includes the personal and cultural significance sedimented in the perceived world and makes that acquisition somehow visible. The domain of the prereflective is thus coextensive with the latent sense of world or being, which is the orienting and meaning-endowing context of all thematic activities.

How does this shift from the unconscious to the prereflective bear upon the problem of operant rationality, or freedom from the archaic?

Note first that if the forces or contents of the Freudian unconscious are truly "intemporal" and "indestructible,"[16] then there can be no question of freeing oneself from them; the best one could achieve would be resignation before ineluctable necessity or Ananke.[17] But the

14. See Merleau-Ponty's critique of the notion of the unconscious in his *Phénoménologie*, pp. 187-202 and 433-452.

15. *Phénoménologie*, p. 453. In his reference to "une 'histoire sedimentée'" Merleau-Ponty refers to Husserl, *Formale und transzendentale Logik, Gesammelte Werke*, Bd. 16, ed. Van Breda (The Hague: Nijhoff, 1950), p. 220.

16. "Preface," p. 86.

17. "The very expression 'resignation' or 'submission' to Ananke points to a

practice of psychoanalysis offers more promise than this; one speaks, after all, of the "talking *cure*." So, if there must be change in the latent contents for there to be a cure or, in our terms, a freeing, the question arises as to how this is possible.

> Psychoanalytic treatment does not effect its cure by provoking a conscious grasp of the past, but first of all by binding the patient to his doctor by new existential connections [*rapports d'existence*]. It is not a matter of giving scientific assent to the psychoanalytic interpretation and discovering a notional sense/meaning [*sens*] of the past; it is rather a matter of reliving the past as significant in this way or that, and the patient attains to this only through *seeing* his past in the perspective of his coexistence with the doctor.[18]

The function of transference, as described here by Merleau-Ponty, is to restructure the past, to bring about an actual change in the way it is perceived. It is not merely to rethink the field of latency, the context of the prereflective; it is rather to relive it. Abreaction is no longer a magical healing process which works by virtue of some ill-defined economics of catharsis; it is rather a taking up of a new perspective on things, an authentic (as opposed to merely notional) binding of oneself to a new and better/healthier way of perceiving the world, achieved in some measure through the power of the doctor as the vehicle of truth.

> The complex is not dissoved by a non-instrumental freedom [*une liberté sans instruments*], but rather is displaced by a new temporal pulse [*pulsation du temps*] which has its own supports and motives. The same thing occurs in all conscious coming to grips [*prises de conscience*]: they are effective only if they are supported by a new commitment. And this commitment in turn is made in the domain of the implicit.[19]

As Merleau-Ponty continues here to unfold his thought, it becomes clear that the Freudian dialectic of determinism has given way to a dialectic of freedom and commitment. In classical psychoanalysis, the patient trades the values of his father for those of his surrogate-father, the analyst. The phenomenon of transference binds the patient to the analyst as to his father and thereby endows the former with the archaic power of the latter. The patient's values, the complex of ideality and

---

total wisdom that is more than the mere reality principle, psychologically considered as the perceptual testing of reality. Is it not the case that it is only when reality is accepted with resignation that it becomes Ananke?
Ananke ... is a symbol of a world view, and not simply the symbol of a principle of mental functioning; in it is summed up a wisdom that dares to face the harshness of life." *Freud and Philosophy*, II, III, 3, p. 328.

18. *Phénoménologie*, p. 519 (emphasis mine).
19. *Phénoménologie*, p. 519.

guilt constituting his superego, are, as it were, ladled from one mold to another – certainly with the complicity of the patient, but without very much in the way of rational, critical evaluation on his part. Indeed, it is difficult to conceive how this evaluation might take place. Evaluation presupposes critical comparison of one set of values against another, the one serving as foundation for the assessment of the other – yet the patient's ground values are precisely those which are being displaced.

By contrast, in Merleau-Ponty's existential model, the encounter with the analyst takes place against the backdrop of the world. Granting that this encounter involves the patient as a rational-emotional totality – granting, that is, that it engages the patient's being as a mere discursive confrontation could not – still, there is the perceived world to serve as the measure of validity. One might object that it is precisely the patient's perception of the world that is at stake. That is true. And it is also true that the patient's understanding of this world is the result of a kind of negotiation between the patient, his analyst, his history, his culture, and the significant others populating his proximal sphere of intersubjectivity. But – as post-Freudian theorists (notably Jung and Rogers) have come to see – the dialectic of determinism in Freudian thought is incompatible with the freedom intrinsic to any self-consistent conception of rationality or mental health. And, as I hope to show shortly, the function of the therapist in the patient's project of orienting himself within the world is conceived in existential theory as that of restoring the patient's freedom and responsibility rather than force-feeding an established doctrine regarding reality perception and evaluation. The operative distinction here is the one Heidegger draws between "leaping in" (*einspringen*) for another and taking over a freedom/responsibility that is properly his, and "leaping ahead" (*vorausspringen*) of him in the attempt to return his care to him in an authentic way.[20]

Yet another step is required to arrive at an understanding of psychotherapy which conceives its practice in a manner that is consistent with the freedom and rationality of the patient. The problem we confront here is that of treating a latency that is, by definition, subrational in a manner that develops and enhances (rather than thwarts and undermines) the patient's autonomy. Stated in other terms, the problem is that of assisting a patient in gaining freedom from his thraldom to archaic structures without violating that freedom in the process. The existential critique of behaviorism chastises that praxis for use of manipulative techniques as it chastises Freudian praxis for inducing

20. *Being and Time*, transl. Macquarrie and Robinson (Harper and Row: New York, 1962), I, 4, sect. 26, pp. 158-159.

dependency (albeit only temporarily); the question is how a consistently existential approach could produce results without opening itself to the same kind of criticism.

It is clear from the outset that no such praxis is conceivable within the context of Sartre's thesis of radical freedom. Indeed, such a praxis would not be necessary, since for Sartre consciousness is absolute and can contain no latency, no opacity. Since, further, the situation is only what consciousness makes of it, there is no medium through which the archaic can persist in influencing the For-itself's constitution of the world. As Merleau-Ponty characterizes the Sartrean position: "there is only intention immediately followed by effect, an idea very close to the Kantian idea of an intuition which is as good as an act."[21] Since the world does not resist, there is no resistance to be overcome – hence nothing for freedom to exert itself against, nothing for it to do, and "the very idea of choice disappears."[22]

As Merleau-Ponty construes it, however, freedom is intrinsically circumscribed and continually brought up against the world it inhabits. It is the world, prereflectively taken for granted, that constitutes the zone of latency containing the archaisms in contention with which freedom must be won. Hence, it is the world that must be changed. It is as simple and as difficult as that. The therapist has to help the patient change his or her world, either literally (as in a case reported by Merleau-Ponty of anorexia and aphonia brought on by the refusal of one patient's mother to allow her access to her lover)[23] or ontologically, when sedimented guilts and other life-defeating structures are perceived as constituting reality. Indeed, in the context of Merleau-Ponty's ontology, it must be both – for "... in the exchange between the situation and the one who assumes it, it is impossible to distinguish what 'comes from the situation' from what 'comes from freedom.'"[24]

The question becomes one of how the therapist can guide his patient to a new – and truer – description of reality, and, beyond that, get the patient to commit himself to that understanding. This is a problem familiar to any teacher – in this view therapy is, ultimately, a kind of teaching – and, as we all know, admits of no specific or technical solution. On the other hand, a general answer can be given: the function and task of the therapist is to let the truth be *seen* as the truth, to let the patient *perceive* the world in a way that is better – truer – than the diseased – false – modalities grounded in the archaisms sedimented

21. *Phénoménologie*, p. 499.
22. *Phénoménologie*, p. 499.
23. *Phénoménologie*, pp. 187-188.
24. "*... Il est impossible de délimiter la 'part de la situation' et la 'part de la liberté.'*" *Phénoménologie*, p. 517.

in his world in the early, precritical days of its creation. I stress the verbs "to see" and "to perceive" because they involve the individual's body – indeed, his total being. Merleau-Ponty speaks of a "perceptual faith" and that is exactly what is at stake here. It is not a merely discursive understanding – the entertaining of a representation or consideration of a possibility – that is intended; it is, rather, the kind of *Verstehen* Heidegger describes as an *Existentiale*, or "existential structure" of *Dasein.*[25]

As one who banishes specters and lets the truth be seen, the therapist has the world as his accomplice. How does one convince the totality of an individual that what he discursively "knows" is true really is true, hence a worthy basis for commitment? At most, one can point; the world must do the rest. At most, one can show; the world must do the convincing. The faith of perceptual faith is not produced by an act or leap of faith; it is a consequence of the nature of the real to dispel our illusions, satisfy our doubts, and command our belief.

The truth is not easy to see, which is why there is need for teachers and therapists, but must rather be won. The listening attunement of *Gelassenheit* is necessary, but far from sufficient. It is possible that, in listening, one hears only the voices of the dead; that is a malaise we all contract at birth, a kind of original sin that must be expiated. The dead must be buried, returned to the earth, put out of sight and hearing; that is a universal task at which some need help. The intellectual task is the never-ending one of thematizing and critically examining one's presuppositions. The existential task, equally endless, is that of summoning and confronting one's ghosts, the all-too-unwitting architects of our emotional space.

Ultimately, it is the issue of truth that separates the existential from the otherwise-kindred theories of psychotherapy. The value of truth, under the banner of authenticity, permits no temporizing, no mind-easing fiction, no palliating metaphysical comfortizing. The ghosts must be confronted, and so must the specter of death that awaits us all. The uncomfortable fact is that, although all are called to the confrontation, not all are equal to the challenge. And, for them – that is, for most of us most of the time – there is only the uneasy solace of everyday dwelling in a prereflective world whose darker corners are too ominous to be approached. Or there is madness – when that darkness begins to encroach.

I conclude this section on archaeology and freedom from, at this point, because we have reached a point of closure and because another issue must be resolved within the rapidly diminishing space allotted. Before going on to that issue, however, I want to mention some themes

25. *Being and Time*, I, 5, sect. 31, p. 182.

which bear on the matter of freedom from the archaic. First, there is the sphere of intersubjectivity which is coextensive with that of the perceived world as prereflectively lived. The point here is that the truth which I have argued is the main touchstone and value of therapy is, at the same time, the main touchstone and value in the negotiation of reality with the others who cohabit our world. Thus, the Other, both in particular and as undifferentiated presence, calls me to truth insofar as he contests my perspective, and leads me from it insofar as he conspires with my ghosts. Secondly, there is the matter of my own body (*le corps propre*), which, as Sartre points out, lends weight/gravity/seriousness to my emotions[26] by vibrrating with them, but which, as Merleau-Ponty points out, also draws me out of my illusions through its *Wahrnehmung*, the truth-taking that is intrinsic to its perceptual activities at the prereflective level. Finally, there is the underlying issue of hermeneutics, which has been circling impatiently at the periphery of this discourse and begging for notice. Here I can afford only to say that the transcendence of the perceptual world offers a ground for cognitive optimism as well as emotional stability that separates my viewpoint from the neo-skepticism currently in vogue; the perceptual world does not provide equal accommodation for any and all interpretations of it, and in that rich recalcitrance offers release from the circle – and from madness.

B. *Teleology and freedom for.*

Operant rationality has been defined as behavior commensurate with a thematically posited ideality or set of goals located some distance into the future as the end of a telic process or project. Thus conceived, rationality is inseparable from teleology. The question we approach now is that of the extent to which the ends posited are – or can be – freely chosen. This question is actually two: (1) Do *I* choose my ends, or are they preordained by my history? (2) Can I make a nonarbitrary choice of goals, or are all values equally groundless and my free choice thus no more than the empty freedom of whimsy? Both questions call into question the rationality of goal selection; they are questions about the foundations of value decisions. The first asks if those foundations are determined by the elements constituting my situation (including the

26. "In order for us truly to grasp the horrible, it is not only necessary to mimic it; we must be spell-bound, flooded by our own emotion; the formal frame of the behavior must be filled with something opaque and heavy which serves as matter. We understand in this situation the purely physiological phenomena: they represent the *seriousness* of the emotion; they are phenomena of belief." Sartre, *The Emotions: Outline of a Theory*, transl. Frechtman (New York: Philosophical Library, 1948), pp. 73-74.

archaisms discussed above), and the second asks whether there can be any valid foundations at all.

Merleau-Ponty's responses to these questions might best be illumined by considring his critique of the answers put forward by Sartre. Sartre denies that my choice of ends is dictated by my situation on the grounds that the meaning of my situation is determined by my act of constitution. The mountain has the significance of obstacle only in the context of my project to climb it. Since I have chosen the project which confers meaning on the mountain, it is I who am responsible for assigning the meaning to the mountain. This is the classical example; let me take up another that is more germane to the issue of psychotherapy.

Consider the girl who has been forbidden by her mother to have further contact with the young man she loves. Her response to this situation is to lose her appetite and her power of speech. In the Sartrean analysis, the girl has chosen her anorexia and aphonia. It is she who constitutes the young man as her beloved and endows him with the significance that makes contact with him vital to herself. Likewise, it is she who has constituted her mother as a legitimate authority, someone who cannot be disobeyed. When these two value systems collide, it is up to the girl to choose between them. But neither possibility – forsake the lover/forsake the mother – is acceptable. Hence the girl opts for a "magical" resolution;[27] she withdraws from the world in which the impossible decision is oppressing her. It is through her mouth that she eats and maintains her vital ties to the world; and it is also through her mouth that she communicates and maintains the world as the context of being with others. Faced with what she cannot do – choose between impossible alternatives – she does what she can do; she magically transports herself out of the oppressive world by distancing herself from her mouth, the organ that sustains the world for her.

What is wrong with this account? Here I shall have to construct the reply Merleau-Ponty would have given,[28] for he brings up the example in a critique of Freud and does not mention Sartre in this context. Let me note first what is missing from the account before us. Missing is the girl, herself, her mother, her lover, and the whole concrete situation.

27. "We can conceive of what an emotion is. It is a transformation of the world. When the paths traced out become too difficult, or when we see no path, we can no longer live in so urgent and difficult a world. All the ways are barred. However, we must act. So we try to change the world, that is, to live as if the connection between things and their potentialities were not ruled by deterministic processes, but by magic." *The Emotions*, pp. 58-9.

28. As I have constructed the Sartrean account. Sartre does not take up Binswanger's case study, but it is possible to put together a Sartrean analysis by bringing his general conceptual schemata to bear on it.

Merleau-Ponty gives us only the outline of the situation, its abstract schema.[29] Hence, we cannot tell if the girl is employing her illness in a power struggle with her mother, whether she genuinely loves her young man (and, if so, how) or is using him as an instrument of liberation or revenge, whether the mother's prohibition is grounded in genuine concern for her daughter and realistic assessment of the young man's probable effect on her life, and so on. I mention this absence of data to make an important point: the origin and measure of value lies in the world, and it is to the world that we must always return to formulate and assess our understanding of it.

Nevertheless, we do have enough to point out the flaws in Sartre's account. Let us start with the obvious. The girl did not choose to be born, to be born of this particular parent, or to encounter this young man as a possible love object. She did not choose her mouth or her mouth's functions anymore than she chose her kidneys and their functions. Nor did she choose the vital link between her mouth and the world of interpersonal relations. All these are given, as the mountain is given. Also given is the issue of parental authority. It is given as an issue. The girl can choose to obey or to disobey; she cannot choose, except in the magical mode of her illness, not to have obedience as an issue she must confront. The same can be said with regard to her erotic life; she can choose to confront the structures of eros in this manner or that, but she cannot choose not to confront them at all. Indeed, her manner of withdrawing from the confrontations in question is, precisely, a manner of contending with issues forced upon her, i.e., her own status as a daughter and as a sexual being.

The point here is that the transcendence of the world manifests itself in the fact that there are situations to be contended with. And it is in the nature of situations to limit the range of responses possible. That is the point of Merleau-Ponty's doctrine of circumscribed freedom.

The interesting aspect of this example is the ambiguity that surrounds the idea of choice. Can it be said that the girl has chosen her illness? Let us assume that her withdrawal from the world had the character of a recoil; she is thrust back from participating in a world which offers no viable resolution to a situation that, for her, simply cannot be borne. Her love for her mother is as necessary for her existence as her love for her young man; she cannot choose between them, because a world from which either love is absent is a world in which she cannot live. Is she then caused to be ill – and ill in just this way – by external forces impinging upon her? Clearly not, because she is complicit in her loves, assents to them, sustains them in her very flight from the world

29. Binswanger, *Über Psychotherapie* (Nervenarzt, 1935), pp. 113 ff., is cited by Merleau-Ponty as his source for this case study.

in which they have collided. Yet, on the other hand, she does not maintain her illness by choice, either. As Merleau-Ponty points out, her aphonia is not a deliberate or voluntary silence; while in thrall to her illness, she has literally lost her voice and does not have speech as a real possibility open for her to choose.[30] There is a fundamental ambiguity here.

On the one hand, the girl's aphonia "represents...a refusal of coexistence"[31] and as refusal elicits the categories of freedom. "Without doubt, aphonia is not a paralysis, and the proof of this lies in the fact that, treated by the medications of psychology [*des médications psychologiques*] and left free by her family to see the one she loves again, the girl regains her speech. [On the other hand], however, aphonia is not...a deliberate or willed silence." "To be aphonic is not to keep silence: one keeps silent [*se taiser*] only when one can speak."[32] The girl cannot speak, and that fact seems to demand that the categories of volition be replaced by those of causality. Yet, as should be apparent, neither set of categories can, by itself, do justice to the phenomenon before us.

Resolution may be found by restoring its temporal thickness to the situation and taking a diachronic view of it. In the diachronic analysis, the girl's complicity in constituting her world is more evident. Through a thousand inconsequential decisions she casts herself in the role of dutiful daughter, and the cumulative weight of these decisions amounts to something that is consequential. In refusing to participate in the world that demanded a choice between duty and love, she once again made a series of small decisions that gathered themselves into something of magnitude. One can imagine the early phases of her refusal – I cannot reply to this verbal demand, or that, or the next to follow – accumulating and endowing the moment of refusal with its own autonomy. Thus is constructed an island of solitude, a place of refuge from impossible demands, which finally becomes a prison. Thus help is needed from the outside to engineer an escape.[33]

In this case, the cure involved changing the girl's world. It was changed into a world in which duty and love were compossible. Who/what brought about the change? Details are not available, but it is safe to assume that her mother rescinded her prohibition at the urging of the doctor called in to treat the aphonia and anorexia. Under one de-

30. *Phénoménologie*, pp. 188-189.
31. *Phénoménologie*, p. 187.
32. *Phénoménologie*, p. 188.
33. "At each moment that passes, freedom degrades itself and becomes less probable. ... It is necessary ... to admit at least that sulking or aphonia, to the extent that they endure, become consistent like things, that they make structures of themselves...." *Phénoménologie*, p. 190.

scription, then, the girl's world was changed from the outside, by her family and doctor. Under another, it was the girl herself who, in refusing the impossible world, demanded that changes be made and enforced her demands with her refusal to live on the conditions imposed by others. A third description, which I tend to favor, would understand the change as occasioned by a resignation of freedom and responsibility on the part of the girl. She swoons into passivity, placing her life and destiny in the hands of others. Understood in this way, her refusal is a refusal of freedom as much as a refusal of existence and rejection of the world. What we do not know – and might not be able to ascertain even at first hand – is the degree of deliberation and calculation involved in the various decisions that precipitated the illness. But it is clear that, at some point along the way, the girl ceased to be a rational agent. It is this that needs to be understood.

Regardless of the degree of deliberation/calculation that may or may not have obtained prior to her loss of speech, there is a point at which she ceases to be an agent of her own destiny. To say that she is then no longer a rational agent is tantamount to saying that she is no longer a teleological agent: she is not behaving purposefully. And from this we may conclude that teleology, the structure of purposiveness, is a necessary aspect of understanding the girl and her situation. Conceive her as an automaton and there is no longer conceptual space for illness; there is only a thing recoiling from this set of external circumstances or that. Furthermore, to place the mechanism of recoil/response "inside" her psyche – to conceive her responses as codetermined by present external forces and the psychic programming imprinted by external forces in the past – is not to improve the conceptual poverty of the causal explanation. Whether it be this cause or that, the present circumstances or the past, there is no way to distinguish between a sick response and a sane one. The structure that makes sense of psychotherapy is that of rationality, interpreted here as purposiveness, and that presupposes freedom and its correlate, teleology.

I do not purport here to have "proven" freedom or rationality. Indeed, I acknowledge that they have been presupposed all along. My intent has been simply to show that (1) no sense can be made of psychotherapy without presupposing these concepts; (2) they are implicitly presupposed in psychological theories which explicitly repudiate them; and (3) the concept of freedom that is required is one which conceives freedom as circumscribed by a situation – because, unlike the concept of radical freedom, the concept of situated freedom is commensurate with choice and rationality.

To bring this to conclusion, I return to the issue of teleology raised at the beginning of the paper in the context of the question concerning it posed at the beginning of this section.

At the beginning of the paper I argued, with Ricœur, that the archaeology of psychoanalysis (or any other theory underpinning a therapeutic praxis) must be understood in correlation with a teleology. I argued further that, although teleology presupposes the value of freedom, that value cannot serve as its final term. Finally, at the beginning of this section, I posed the question whether there can be a free choice of finalities, whether it is possible to make a nonarbitrary choice among values. Let me attempt now to tie all these strains together into the unity of a single thought.

The classical term that stands at the end of the "for-the-sake-of" in a teleological progression is happiness. I shall adopt this term, but, at the same time, acknowledge the difficulty associated with it: "happiness" names the place of an intrinsic good, but – and this is the problem – does not name the content or adequately describe the nature of that good. When happiness is given a specific denotation, as has been attempted in utilitarianism, one faces the difficulties of defining and defending that denotation: e.g., what is pleasure and why is it good? The latter challenge can lead to what might be called the "why regress" – for any value X posited as an ultimate term in the "for-the-sake-of" progression, that value itself must be defended. That demand for defense is implicitly a begging for answers to the question "What is X good *for*?" Hence, to the extent that one replies by listing the benefits following from X, one has undercut one's own claim for the ultimacy of X. In the attempt to avoid this regress, I shall employ a different sort of defense. The goodness of the X I shall posit as contributing to the definition of happiness is substantiated by arguing that its absence is palpably bad.

Although theories of psychotherapy have been loathe to acknowlledge the positive values implicit in them, there is one negative value that all seem to acknowledge. It is described in different ways in the context of different theories, but underlying them all is the basic Freudian metaphor of *splitting*, which names an opposition or conflict within the psyche that sets it at odds with itself. The idea is that each element in the opposition has its own teleology and the various teleologies are incompatible: to fulfill the aim of one element is to frustrate or violate the aims of another. Thus are id and superego at odds in Freud's later topography. The absence of splitting would be integration, and that is the term I propose as constituting in part the ideal of happiness.[34]

34. "Sexuality is not ... an autonomous cycle. It has inner ties to the total cognitive and active being. ... We reunite here the most durable acquisitions of psychoanalysis. Whatever the theoretical declarations of Freud might have been, psychoanalytic research in fact leads, not to explaining man by a sexual infrastructure, but to retrieving in sexuality relations and attitudes which have hitherto passed as relations and attitudes *of consciousness*; and the significance of psycho-

IV

This is hardly the place to articulate and defend a theory of value, but there is a series of points that should be made by way of bringing these thoughts to closure. For the sake of brevity, I will simply enumerate them.

1. The value of integration is never defended by Merleau-Ponty as such, but it appears throughout the corpus as the final term of rational teleology. It is one of the fundamental ideas of Gestalt theory which inform the entirety of his work.[35]

2. I have argued above that freedom cannot function as the final term of a teleology because it begs the question of freedom for–? Yet there is an inner relation between freedom and integration that links them as values: splitting, as the opposition of incompatible teleologies, is a threat to freedom because it denies the possibility of realizing all of one's goals. One who is divided against himself is not free authentically to be himself.

3. Conceived in this way, the value of integration marks the point of intersection between freedom from and freedom for, that is, the intersection between archaeology and teleology. To be freed from the conflict between opposed values located in the world structured by one's past is to be freed for the pursuit of becoming one with oneself. It opens the possibility, for example, of fulfilling one's sexual destiny without being oppressed in that very project by the archaic guilt attaching to sexuality through the structures of both one's personal past (castration fears) and one's impersonal past (cultural taboos) as well.

4. I acknowledge, in deference to Ricœur, that Hegel's absolute names the ideal of rational integration. It is true that the movement from the contradictions of consciousness dispersed and at war with itself at lower levels to that of integration at higher levels is one that is clearly predelineated by Hegel – as by Parmenides, Plato, and others. Indeed, I share with Hegel the belief that this goal lies on the far side of human experience. But there is this crucial difference between us: as I construe it, the value of integration is an open-ended regulative ideal whose symbols are those of human love and are essentially tied to the lived body and the finite experience of time; whereas, for Hegel, both corporeality and temporality denote moments which the dialectical process of the return of Reason unto itself must overcome and leave

analysis is not so much rendering psychology biological as in discovering in the functions believed to be 'purely corporeal' a dialectical movement, and in *reintegrating sexuality into being human.*" *Phénoménologie*, p. 184 (emphasis mine).

35. See my essay "Gestalt Theory and Merleau-Ponty's Concept of Intentionality," *Man and World*, Vol. 4, No. 4 (Nov., 1971).

behind. The symbols of incarnate existence seeking integration with itself are the symbols of carnal love, and the symbols of the oneness of the divine are purely spiritual.

5. The implications of these thoughts for the practice of psychotherapy have been stated in the course of the paper. They center around the need to take thematic responsibility for the values of freedom, reason, and integration as these values inform the therapeutic praxis. Beyond that, however, is the culminating thought introduced a few sentences ago. Merleau-Ponty takes us up to this thought, but stops short of it. Hence, in articulating it I am stepping beyond the security of his authority. The symbols of finite integration are, I claimed, the symbols of carnal love. One can, I think, read Freud's corpus as the gradual surfacing of this thought. This thought raises basic questions about the role of the therapist, and specifically about his two main sources of power, i.e., transference and wisdom. To what extent does wisdom allow transference to manifest itself as eros? To answer such a question requires a phenomenology of love, which I have undertaken elsewhere in another context,[36] but which cannot be summarized here. Suffice it to say that wisdom is essential to counterbalance the dangers of power, and that there is no wisdom apart from love.

36. "Toward a Phenomenology of Love," *Soundings*, Vol. LXIII, No. 4 (Winter, 1980).

THE HIDDEN DIALECTIC IN EDMUND HUSSERL'S PHENOMENOLOGY

JAMES M. EDIE (Evanston)

As is well known, Husserl was throughout his life quite disdainful of Hegelian philosophy. It was only with great reluctance that he even mentioned Hegel a few times, even in those sections of his work in which he necessarily gave his own summary of the development of Western philosophy, namely in *Erste Philosophie* and in *Krisis*. And even when he was constrained to mention the philosophical contribution of Hegel, there was never any full discussion of dialectical logic. For a philosopher with such a deep concern for logic and the transcendental foundations of logic, this refusal to engage Hegel is puzzling, but certain. As my own early teachers of Husserl correctly insisted: If there is ever any doubt as to Husserl's logical position on any disputed question, one will never go wrong in interpreting him in an anti-Hegelian sense. In the very few places where he forced himself to say something positive about Hegel, the best he could come up with was that Hegel's thought provides us more with a *Weltanschauung* than with a strict philosophy.[1]

It is true that certain French commentators on Husserl, most notably Sartre and Merleau-Ponty, but also such rigorous logicians as Suzanne

1. Edmund Husserl, *Prolegomena zur reinen Logik, Logische Untersuchungen*, vol. 1 (Tübingen: 1913), p. 226; and "Philosophy as Rigorous Science," tr. Quentin Lauer, *Phenomenology and the Crisis of Philosophy* (New York: 1965), pp. 77 ff. At this point I would like to acknowledge a debt to my former colleague, Errol E. Harris, whose forthcoming book on formal, transcendental, and dialectical logic has taught me many lessons. His argument that formal logic presupposes transcendental foundations and that transcendental logic presupposes dialectical foundations is something to which I was totally impervious until a short time ago. I am, certainly, not yet ready to follow Harris all the way into dialectical logic, and am definitely not ready to surrender the great achievements of linguistic structuralism to dialectics, but I have been convinced that Husserl's dismissal of dialectical logic was premature and not based on thorough investigation. Though Harris does not deal at all with this aspect of Husserl's work, his own investigations caused me to do so in what is still a most preliminary essay.

Cho, K.K. (ed.) Philosophy and Science in Phenomenological Perspective.

ISBN 978-94-009-6115-9

Bachelard, have accustomed us to hearing Hegel's name linked with Husserl's method but there has never been any doubt, even in their own minds, that they were departing from the intentions of Husserl himself and, as Merleau-Ponty said, "forcing Husserl to go further than he wished to go."[2]

From the *Phenomenology of Perception* onward Merleau-Ponty gave a highly Hegelian cast to his expositions of Husserl. But even such a sober commentator as Suzanne Bachelard says that Husserl was "unconsciously oriented toward a dialectic."[3]

Bachelard finds this inner dialectic in the necessary opposition involved in the duality between transcendental subjectivity and the forms in which it necessarily manifests itself. Why there should be just these forms (perception, imagination, thinking, etc.) and not others is a question of ultimate, brute facticity and can in no way be *deduced* from an analysis of subjectivity itself. In short, subjectivity ultimately finds itself in a factical situation which it cannot explain but can only describe.[4]

In the *Phenomenology of Perception* Merleau-Ponty begins with a discussion of the central concepts of Husserl's phenomenology, such as the concept of the reduction to experience, the concept of the experience of other persons in "transcendental intersubjectivity," the concept of the notions of fact and essence, and the concept of the notion of intentionality. His style of exposition from the beginning of this work – unlike his earlier writings – is dialectical, not to say Hegelian. We shall return to this.

From the period 1949-1959 he began to abandon this dialectical mode of exposition in favor of linguistic structuralism, only then to return to it in his last work, *The Visible and the Invisible*. But here in *The Phenomenology of Perception* he is completely dialectical. The phenomenological reduction, he says, is both possible and impossible at one and the same time. There is a truth of solipsism and a truth of intersubjectivity, and both must be maintained in their opposed balance. Every fact is the instantiation of an essence and yet no fact can exhaust its essence. The world of experience can be known and at the same time not known; its evidence is eidetically certain and yet only "presumptive." Consciousness is a "project of the world," which transcends itself toward what it is not and will never be, and yet consciousness is, at one and the same time, the "pre-objective" possession

2. Maurice Merleau-Ponty, *The Primacy of Perception and Other Essays*, ed. James M. Edie (Northwestern University Press, 1964), p. 72.

3. Suzanne Bachelard, *A Study of Husserl's Formal and Transcendental Logic*, tr. Lester E. Embree (Northwestern University Press, 1968), pp. 222 ff.

4. Ibid.

of itself in immanence. Consciousness is that ambiguous paradoxical reality which is both transcendent and immanent at once.

After the opening discussion of these paradoxes of phenomenology the main dialectical resolution which runs through and unifies the rest of the *Phenomenology of Perception* is the dialectical opposition and unity of intellectualism (subjectivism, idealism) on the one hand and naturalism (realism, positivism) on the other. Because of the "ambiguity" of the human body, which is the locus and vehicle of the embodiment of consciousness, as we can experience it, both intellectualistic and naturalistic descriptions of human reality have their own truth and yet neither can be exclusively true. The truth lies in seeing that experience justifies both kinds of explanation at the same time. This is the sense that Merleau-Ponty gives to the ancient distinction between body and soul. There is, in reality, *no* distinction between body and soul, because human reality is completely body and completely soul. The bodily behaviors themselves are intentional and endow the experienced world with meaning and value, and yet this wholly embodied, meaning-bestowing activity goes far beyond the body as a "physical" or "natural" entity. The lived-body, as the source of the "visible and the invisible" (in all the many senses Merleau-Ponty gives to this term), is itself the subject of experience.

We have attempted elsewhere to sort out the number of structures of consciousness involved in this account of *omnium visibilium et invisibilium*, which originates from the lived body. A partial list is as follows:

1 The perception of objects which are not, strictly speaking, given to me in perceptual presentation but which I nevertheless perceive, such as "objects behind my back."
2 The experience of imagining absences, possibilities, potentialities, contingencies, counterfactual conditionals, the subjunctive, the optative, etc.
3 The perception of others insofar as the perception of the other presents a body (surface) in which there is a (nonspatial) mind, the body being "visible," the mind being "invisible" (in the sense of the Husserlian appresented object). The experience of my own mind in my own body which is "posterior" to the experience of embodiment.
4 The silence which surrounds language, as *la langue* "precedes" and surrounds *la parole*.
5 Consciousness and unconsciousness.
6 The Husserlian distinction between fact and essence.
7 The relationship between the present state of a science which is moving toward a more perfect stage of the same science, which will be recognizably the *same* science, though it does not yet exist.

Etc.[5]

Husserl would certainly not have liked this style of exposition. Nevertheless, if not exactly faithful to Husserl, we can see grounds in Husserl for Merleau-Ponty's method. In his own more hyperbolic leaps Husserl sometimes defines phenomenology as a "genuine realism" or even a "genuine positivism." A philosophy which can be called both "phenomenological positivism" (Merleau-Ponty's term) and "transcendental idealism" (Husserl's more favored and usual term) must somewhere have dialectical roots and possibilities. The view which I wish to present for your consideration at the present time is that there lie deeply hidden in Husserl's phenomenology at least three *principal* doctrines central to the whole of his thought, which require a dialectical logic to unravel (whether it be Hegelian or not), namely (1) the theory of perception, (2) the theory of science, and (3) the notion of intentional history developed in the *Krisis.*

I. THE THEORY OF PERCEPTION

From his first phenomenology of perception in the Second Part of *Ideen I*, Husserl develops the concept of the "infinity" of the perceptual object. Precisely because of the situated nature of consciousness, in its being inserted in the world, both through its embodiment and through perception, no perceptual object can be given all at once. Such an object can perhaps be dominated by thought and *conceived* in a perfectly eidetic manner, but it cannot be so *perceived*. In fact, in the idealistic interpretation of this thoery of perception, one would have to say that a perceptual object is nothing other than the system of all of its possible presentations. Perceptual objects are given *Abschattungsweise*, which means that they are never given completely. *More* is always appresented than can be grasped in any actual and present presentation. That is to say, in good English, a perceptual object is both given and not given in the same perceptual presentation. It is given as having many aspects that are not now presented but which *could* be. And, if other persons are present, a given perceptual object is even presented as being de facto perceived from other viewpoints which I *could* occupy in principle but do not now and may never occupy.

This law of the infinity of the perceptual object pertains not only to the *x* limit-point, transcendent to the perceiver, but is true of the perceiver himself. Whenever we take ourselves as objects we find, beneath

5. James M. Edie, "The Meaning and Development of Merleau-Ponty's Concept of Structuralism," *Research in Phenomenology* 10 (1980), pp. 50-1.

the level of acts of consciousness, states and dispositions of the ego such that the ego itself is "transphenomenal" and transcendent to all possible experience in that very experience itself. If, for instance, I experience in myself a strong dislike, even disgust, or, at the limit, hatred for one of my colleagues or acquaintances, it may very well appear to me after repeated experiences that this is a disposition or "habit" of my consciousness in such wise that everytime the thought, image, or presence of that person is brought before me I will feel the same movements of disgust, dislike, anger, etc. In other words my ego with its "habits" or "sedimentations" always transcends any particular experience I can have of it by reflectively now taking it and its acts as objects.

II. THE THEORY OF SCIENCE

Throughout the *Formal and Transcendental Logic* Husserl is concerned with the investigation of the transcendental foundations of formal logic and formal ontology (the theory of objectivity in general). In the most general sense, since transcendental-constituting consciousness is the source and condition of the possibility of all objectification (all "having of objects"), there are transcendental presuppositions to formal logic and formal ontology itself. The most important and most deeply underlying of all of the various presuppositions which he uncovers is that formal logic plus formal ontology, as the study of the rules of objectivity in general, presuppose an *intention*, namely the intention of coming to knowledge. At no one point in the study of formal logic as such, nor even in the study of the rules of objectivity in general, is it ever stated explicitly that their purpose is to enable us to acquire knowledge. This presupposition goes unspoken but can be uncovered by a genetic analysis of the innermost intentions of the *mathesis universalis* itself.

Knowledge or science is undergirded by the formal constraints of logic and formal ontology, which provide us with the necessary theory for any possible science whatsoever.

What does Husserl mean here by "science"? The short answer is that a science is essentially a text which has this specificity, namely, that it is a text which gives us knowledge. It is a text, first of all, which is most stringently governed by the laws of the three levels of formal logic. That is to say, first of all, that all of the sentences which compose its various paragraphs or parts must be meaningful, i.e., must observe the laws of the *reine Formenlehre der Bedeutungen*, that is, the laws of pure *a priori* grammar, the first level of formal logic. Further, though it is necessary to avoid nonsense in any text, this is by no means sufficient. The sentences, however meaningful in themselves and taken one by one, cannot follow one another in random order. Here the second level of formal logic comes into play. These are the laws which will guarantee not only that the sentences are not mutually contradictory and contain no internal incoherencies but, over and above that, are compatible with one another, belong to the same realm of discourse, and in some sense implicate, follow from, lead to, imply one another. Finally such a text must be capable of clarification on the third, or truth-level, of formal logic: namely the linguistic statements which constitute the scientific texts must in some way be testable as to their truth or falsity by relating them to primary life-world experience. *Urteil* arises from *Erfahrung* and must be able to be brought back to it. It is in his concern to found logical structures in actual perceptual experience that Husserl is to be most sharply distinguished from the logical positivists and logical empiricists, even Hume, with whom he otherwise has so many points of affinity. The logical positivists agree with Husserl that all linguistic expressions, to be found true, must be brought back to primary life-world experience (*Erfahrung*), and they accept all the laws of formal logic, but they treat them as something to be "added on," as if they had no foundation in perceptual experience at all. Like William James in Chapter 28 of the *Principles of Psychology*, Husserl is not content simply to accept sense-experience and the laws of logic as if they had nothing to do with one another. His question, like James', is: "Why does the world play into the hands of logic?" What are the experiential foundations of logic, and how is it that the least perceptual experience gives us the ideal of objective truth? The primary question, which empiricism and positivism totally ignore, is the question of how the higher-order structures of thinking are founded in primary perceptual experience. This is the relationship of *Fundierung*, which is fundamental to all of Husserl's logical studies.

It is evident that in saying this, we have not yet come very far, but we have gained clarity about one fundamental point. That point is that no particular or specialized science of itself must necessarily study or concentrate on the laws of formal logic and formal ontology. Only philosophers do that. Only philosophers study *ex professo* those things which are so fundamental that all the sciences always already take them for granted. But we do know now that every science must be elaborated *according to* these coercive constraints of logic and ontology. We can know *a priori* that any scientist who violates any such law is liable to contradiction, incoherence, and error. Therefore, every science presupposes something more fundamental than itself.

Husserl delights in going on to show that even these most fundamental presuppositions of science are not themselves presuppositionless but that formal logic and formal ontology contain hidden within their very project a number of transcendental presuppositions which it is the job of the transcendental phenomenologist to uncover. This Husserl does brilliantly in the *Formal and Transcendental Logic*.

If we turn now to the theory of science as it is developed in the *Krisis*, we see that it is essential to every factually existing historical science, whatever it may be, that it be developing toward a greater state of exactness and precision. Any given science at any particular time is in an actual state of realization and has its own explanatory power in that historical situation but is tending towards a more perfect realization. Husserl had as acute an awareness of this as Plato. Recall that in the *Timaeus* Plato explains very well that because the physical universe is not as strictly knowable as the ideas, and therefore cannot become the object of an eidetic science, physics will never be more than a "likely story" based on empirical generalizations and probabilities. Therefore, at any period in the development of a theory of the physical universe we know most insistently that this theory will have to be replaced by another more perfect and more adequate to its object later on and, further, that that theory will itself be replaced by others more adequate, and so on, ad infinitum.

This does not absolve us from the need to elaborate the science of physics. It only means that we must do the best we can – Plato thought the theory of the Pythagorean Timaeus was as close to the truth about such matters that one could come in his day. But we know that the science of physics, for instance, will never be definitively completed, and that each "likely story" will have to be replaced by another, and then another, and then another, into the indefinite future. Husserl calls this the "teleological" thrust of science. The dialectical paradox – though, of course, he does not use the word "dialectical" – is that we can recognize a certain science as being the *same* science through a series of essentially relative states of development. The present state of development is necessarily *intermediary* between a less and more perfect state of development of the *same* science. In short, any given science at the present time both is and is not the *same* science that it was some generations ago or that it will be some generations ahead.

In short, the future in some sense lives in the present. There is a *telos* in the present, an end or *terminus ad quem*, toward which any given science is developing. There is, therefore, the same relationship between the future state of a science and its present state as there is between its present state and its past.[6]

6. This is the main thesis of André de Muralt's admirable book, *L'Idée de la phénoménologie* (Paris, 1958). Cf. pp. 17-20 ff. In this book de Muralt argues that phenomenology is not, strictly speaking, a descriptive science of the real, existing world, but a "logic" of significations. It has a "descriptive" dimension to be sure, but this is identical with its "transcendental dimension." He bases himself on Husserl's "exemplarism." The concrete, existing object is a "factual example" of its idea; the idea is the "ideal exemplar" of its object. The factual object enables us to define the idea; but only the idea enables us to comprehend the factual object. Suppose a given science in its actual, imperfect, historical state. Its "essential

Moreover we do not have, and know that we do not have, a completed science of anything whatsoever, not even of the eidetic sciences like geometry, or the new sciences like structural linguistics, which use non-Galilean methods of explanation. There is a diachronic development of science through time toward an absolute and completely definitive perfection. The *idea* of a perfect explanation of something aimed at by science is contained immanently within the science but is not yet realized and de facto will never be realized, though it can, like a perceptual object given through its profiles, be approached asymtotically, enabling us to progress and to realize this idea ever more perfectly.

That there should be such a perfect state of a given science present in our operating scientific activity at the present time is a postulate of reason. It has as its analogue in the phenomenology of perception the presumption that all experiences and all viewpoints on the world will, when all of experience shall have taken place, be found to be consistent with one another, all of one piece, all constituting the total englobing horizon which we call the *Lebenswelt*. But the *Lebenswelt* is never *selbst da*, never given in an indubitable presentation. It always transcends any number of particular experiences and therefore is the object of fundamental belief, the *Urdoxa*, rather than strictly demonstrated knowledge. We have a *presumptive certitiude* rather than an absolute certitude.

---

character," says de Muralt, involves a continual tendency toward greater and greater precision and exactitude. In its actual state of realization, any given science is essentially relative to a state of greater perfection; it is an intermediate state of development between a less perfect and a more perfect state. The completely realized and perfected state of a science is an ideal goal (*telos* or idea); as such it is an "open" or "indefinite" idea. By the same token the "ideal science" and the "real science" (the science in its actual state of development) are involved in a reciprocal exemplarity. The real or factual state of development of a science gives its meaning to the "idea" of science, but at the same time the "idea" alone makes it possible to understand the "real" as an intermediate stage in the realization of the idea. "The one is absolute, the other relative. The one is ideal, eidetic, the other is real, factual, *weltlich*." The ideal science (the idea of the "authentic" science) is the *exemplary idea* of the real science, while the real or factual state of the science *illustrates* the ideal. But this implies that the exemplary idea "structures" or "pre-scribes" the factual example, and this, says de Muralt, "is the constant teaching in the whole of Husserl's phenomenology." It is the universal principle of the mutual exemplarity of the real and the ideal.

In the realm of aesthetics one could apply this same distinction and interrelationship to the performance of a text which is not scientific but literary. Husserl's theory implies but does not work out a whole theory of literary criticism which, strangely enough, the phenomenologists (like Ingarden, for instance) who have dealt with literature have not touched.

III. INTENTIONAL THEORY OF HISTORY

Husserl's attitude towards history reminds me of nothing so much as that of the old Moslem philosopher Alfarabi, and certain other medieval philosophers, in their use of the history of philosophy in their writings. Husserl himself sometimes refers to the historical sections in the *Krisis* as "my novels," *meine Romane*. When Alfarabi wrote his book, *The Intentions of Aristotle's Metaphysics*, it was clear that he knew he was going beyond the letter of the text to give the inner sense. Husserl has the same attitude. His historical investigations are not *explications de texte*, or minute philological investigations into just exactly what a given author said. They are rather investigations into the sense of what a given author *meant*, or should have meant in any case. In his most theoretical vein Husserl writes:

> Only in the positing of a final foundation is this intention [of an historical philosophy] revealed: for only in starting out from it can one uncover the single direction of all philosophies and all philosophers; in starting out from it one can come upon the light in which one understands the thinkers of the past as they would never have been able to understand themselves.[7]

This is "intentional analysis." It discovers in a given philosophy or scientific endeavor a *Zweckidee*, a sense, that gradually comes to awareness in a given historical development. To grasp this idea, to isolate it in its ideal purity, will enable us to clarify the "inner meaning," the "true meaning," the "deeper meaning," of a given historical attempt. This will enable us to deal not just with the text of Descartes but with the intentions of Descartes, not just with the text of Galileo but with the intentions of Galileo, and so on.

Husserl likes to speak of the "true" problem, of the "hidden" problem of Descartes, Hume, Galileo, etc. The philospher is "the man of infinite tasks." Now it is evident that no particular science, and no philosophical theory, no discovery, no progress is ever definitive or absolute. Each discovery, each advance enables us to put what was previously known in a new perspective, to reorganize the same body of knowledge in such wise that each new state of a science appears as *more true* than the last. This truth is the rule in terms of which we judge the past. Merleau-Ponty likes to call this the retroactive effect of the true. If it turns out that Freud clearly discovered some of the laws that govern the operations of the unconscious in human beings, it immediately appears to those who understand these laws in a scientific manner

7. Edmund Husserl, *Die Krisis der europäischen Wissenschaften*, Husserliana 6, ed. W. Biemel (The Hague: Martinus Nijhoff, 1954), p. 74.

that they have been true all along, even prior to their discovery, and that Artistotle and Thomas Aquinas were governed by the laws of the unconscious as much as Freud, Adler, and Jung – only that they could not have *known* it. Or if the science of linguistics suddenly shows that men have been speaking natural languages according to strict laws of phonology without even knowing what these laws were until forty or fifty years ago, these laws nevertheless appear now as having held in some form throughout. Even in the ethical realm, if it turns out that such and such a person – for instance, Marshal Pétain or Michael Bukharin – was wrong, even guilty of treason in a certain act, we interpret his previous acts as leading up to that conclusion.

This is the problem of the relation between fact and essence, the *ideal* and the *real* in history, and its invariant structures. It is the problem of diachrony and synchrony. Thus, whether we are dealing with a historical text or a scientific text, or *any* text, the nature of the problem is the same. In this age of concern over the "textuality" of the text, Husserl's underlying theory is just now coming into its own. The *ideal*, the essential, which is immanent in history is, paradoxically, itself a product of history. This perpetual movement towards a truth which is *more true*, towards an absolute which is more absolute, expresses the eternal dynamism of scientific knowledge and defines its very sense, namely, the *idea* of an authentic science. It expresses the historical and constructed aspect of science constituted by generations of scientists. Science is thus both actual and potential at one and the same time. Its truth in the present is related to its present historical realization in a manner analogous to the way the *significant* (meaning) is related to the *signe* (sign) in language. If we had the time it would be worthwhile to relate, in this context, *la parole* (speech acts) to *la langue* (language as a formal system), performance and interpretation to the text-as-such, what Nelson Goodman calls the allographic to the autographic in works of art, all of which relationships seem to exhibit the same dialectical characteristics we have uncovered here.

No one can fail to see in these relationships affinities with dialectic, even the dialectic of Hegel. It seems to me, in conclusion, that if Husserl had taken up the project of Hegel in its broadest sense, namely, as an attempt to bring to the level of full reflection and to discover the concepts necessary to *think* our experience, he would have seen that his own project was not so different in its *ultimate intention*. The inescapable conclusion is that there is a *hidden dialectic* in Edmund Husserl's phenomenology.

TIME STRUCTURE IN SOCIAL COMMUNALITY

MANFRED FRINGS (Chicago)

The following is an attempt to show that the social forms of togetherness in which human beings find themselves possess a contiguous relation to the structure of time as experienced with others in such social forms.

We will refer to two forms of social togetherness only, but these two are the main forms first distinguished in the sociology of Tönnies and later elaborated by Max Scheler in his work, *Problems of a Sociology of Knowledge* (London: Routledge, Kegan Paul, 1979). These forms are: "society" and "life-community."

By "society" we understand a group which is artificially held together by man-made laws, constitutions, norms of behavior, or any other organized devices, and by a particular kind of thinking guided by "criteria" for truth such as, for example, "workable" or "not workable" (pragmatism). A group of people living in a society is largely characterized by "objective" thinking, i.e., they tend to perceive, handle, manipulate, work with, and negotiate things and states of affairs mainly in terms of "objects." In capitalism as a present worldwide mode of society such objects and things are commercialized, i.e., all things are subject to their being sold or stocked, including such things as a human voice, a mental product, or even religious objects. If capitalism is a mode of mind (rather than an economical system), all forms of socialism fall also under this mode of the mind perceiving the sellability and commercialization of things as one of their primary aspects. Furthermore, human beings living in a society live at a "distance" from each other. There is no mutual trust that would bind them or determine initially their social togetherness. Relations among them are, as it were, pre-established through all sorts of artificial conventions and contracts.

By contrast, members of a life-community are bound together by mutual trust. Forms of a life-community are "family," "clan," "home community," "tribe," and "people" (in nonpolitical senses of the term).

Cho, K.K. (ed.) Philosophy and Science in Phenomenological Perspective.

ISBN 978-94-009-6115-9

The life-community is the sociological base of what we call in general terms our "lived world." It is a "natural thinking," rather than reflective and objective thinking, that characterizes the human beings living in this social form. It is a "lived expression" of things rather than their objectivity that falls into the perceptive fields of these people. Truth is "plain" and not always evidential and sometimes contradictory to logical consistency and construction. In a life-community truth comes close to sheer presencing of what is, in the absence of criteria. A case in point is, sociologically, "truth" as *aletheia* among pre-Socratic thinkers like Heraclitus, Parmenides, and Anaximander, who lived in colonial Greek settlements and isolated villages far from the city, which is a political instrument of society. Let it be added that life-communities are held together by blood relations, traditions, and strong tendencies toward preserving the whole of the group.

We cannot go into the details of many other sociological aspects of such groups as they were elaborated by Scheler. It would go far beyond the aim of this paper, for example, to show that the structure of a group bears on the experience of intersubjective time, or better, that there exists a *contiguity* between time experience and social experience among the two groups mentioned.

As far as society is concerned, we can briefly point out that the experience of time found here is the well-known "objective" time that is and can be "calculated." Societal man is accustomed to "shift" his plans and objects around in a vacuum of empty time. We fill, for instance, the empty squares of our calendar with appointments and the like. We can "date" them and re-date them. What is at the bottom of this time experience is the "filling out" of empty time frames with whatever contents. It does not matter which matrix is used in this practice. Time itself appears here as a thing to be handled and conquered for man's practical use. Societal man "clocks" his existence.

In marked contrast to this practice, the time in life-communal existence is already *filled* with contents. This is to say that contents and time phases *coincide*, whereas in a society the contents and phases of time are separated. The coincidence of time phases and contents is hard to grasp because any explanation of it puts the mode of our time consciousness into a reflective one and, therefore, modifies the subject under discussion and perhaps beyond recognition. Let us furnish, therefore, some examples to help us overcome this difficulty.

First of all, while listening to the paper being read we experience this coincidence of contents followed and time elapsing in such a fashion that we are not "aware" of something like time. The contents and phases of time coincide, or time elapsing is filled with them. Likewise, in all experiences of "welling up" or "coming up" there is this peculiar coincidence. A feeling of hunger, for instance, "wells up" in me before my consciousness takes an active turn to it. This welling up is subconscious, i.e., prior to any objectifying mode. Once such a mode does "turn" to this welling hunger-drive, it can and does "place" the feeling of hunger, e.g., one can wait to eat, choose to fast, or quickly satisfy one's hunger. Clearly the content "hunger" and time are separated in this way. This state of affairs of welling-up pertains to all our drives. What is important for us is the fact that within the welling-up *itself* content and phases are "one." The same holds true in all occurrences of our "insights." It may happen, for example, that we are looking for a solution of a problem for many days without success and that all of a sudden the insight comes to us in one flash without our having thought about it at all. This coming up, i.e., prior to the insight before us, cannot allow of any separation between the contents involved and the time phases belonging to them. The insight "becomes" in its "own" timing. Both are conjoined. The same state of affairs holds in our own lives. We experience all our actions on the background of a "*duration*" of existence, the span of our lifetime, which cannot be clocked (unless we apply calendar time to it). The duration of an individual is filled with its own personal feelings of the world to which would belong a continuous moral tenor, a particular character of the individual, and particular directions of intentions. This duration of an individual's existence is analogous to the duration of a group whose generations come and go. Social time in this sense is tantamount to historicality making recorded history only possible as a typical societal occupation. It is no wonder, therefore, that life-communities of the more pure type, such as tribes, have little interest in recorded history. If they do, their historical accounts tend to be cyclic and not linear, as is the case with societal conceptions. Mythology would be the best example to prove the point. Recurrences of the same, reincarnation, etc. reveal a cyclic time experience in which the member persons try to objectify their lives. But in such cases the contents and time phases are still *made* to conjoin with each other. The Maya Indians, for example, have the world restart every 54 years in their calendar. This social time is, however, one of "duration" and not of "sequence" whenever there is a *more or less complete absence* of objectivation. True, also, a life-communal person meets his fellow men in sequences and their bodies in space. But the communality with others *itself* is neither objective nor sequential. For it is always the same type of human beings that meet and that represent the whole of the group-soul. Group feelings have no past, present, and future; rather, they are characterized by a durational, historical "present," which is "one" in content. In a societal attitude this belongingness to the group is covered up and pushed into the background of daily acts and actions. The concern for the "thing" and its manipulability turns societal time experience into a predominantly "objective" one. The thing is "in" time.

It is the contention of this paper to show that the durational present is a chief characteristic of time experienced in a life-community and that the direction of time experience is in marked contrast to that of society in which time stretches from a now-point forward into the future and backward into the past.

Strictly speaking, past, present, and future are artificial constructs in society, helpful as they are. Their construction consists in the possibility to define them ad libitum in relation to their positions assumed or wanted. We can place historical events into various pasts. We can date them further back or forward depending on historical research. We can also place future events to our conveniences, such as conventions that are cancelled and rearranged for another date than the one previously agreed upon. Both objective history and science make use of this type of past, present, and future. In short, we can graph it in the following manner:

Past → Present → Future

By-contrast, nonsocietal time, i.e., life-communal time, possesses an *inverse* direction. The future is "lived" in anticipations belonging to a nonchanging world-view (cyclic time experience). The past is "tradition," i.e., it is experienced in the "*present*" and not "*as*" past. Ancestors, for example, continue to play a vital role in the "present" of a tribe. The past "moves" into the present without being given "as" past. The present "possesses" and encompasses the past. The future, likewise, is encompassed by the present. It is the same type of anticipation, the same type of future content that beset the present as lived. Present actions function here in the name of the naturally "expected." We can graph also this time experience in the following manner:

Past → Present → Future

It is well-known how life-communal groups living in isolated areas experience little or no "progress." Entering such a community or joining its members (e.g., nomads), we make the observation that "time stands still." It may well be the case that tribes like the Hopi Indians show no use of past and future tenses in their languages because of this inverse time structure. It may also well be the case that objective time for this reason is little or not at all thematized among the aforementioned pre-Socratic thinkers. It is the *present as lived in duration* that allows, from a sociological stand, the well-known conjunction of being and time, or time and being, in the sense of the Being of becoming (Heraclitus) or in the sense of being as "one" (Parmenides). I do not wish to elaborate on this any futher and, instead, wish to come to more phenomenological aspects of the state of affairs involved; i.e.: How can the inverse experience of time converging out of the lived past and future into the duration of the present be understood on an *egological* level?

We mentioned before that societal people experience each other predominately as objects within artificially set-up relations. The very absence of such relations among life-communal people (no matter whatever little artificial relationships *may* occur among them here and there) makes their intersubjective experience "organismic." The members are held together by what I call a "psychic glue," in which blood relations and vital values play predominant roles for the sustenance of the tribe, family, extended family, clan, etc. Indeed, this psychic glue runs through their ancestors and generations to come as well: a tribal-, family-, and community-drive toward preservation of the *whole* of the group differs sharply from societal *self*-responsibility and its construction. In a life-community there prevails the *solidarity* of "all for one and one for all." The whole of the group is one of its highest vital values encompassing past and future generations. Our phenomenological question concerning the status of the ego in a life-community is the following: How can the intersubjectivity pertinent to life-communal experience be understood in terms of the ego/alter-ego relations among its member-persons?

The answer to this question is dependent upon whether we take off from Husserl's *Fifth Cartesian Meditation* or from Scheler's third part (C) of his work, *The Nature of Sympathy*. What must first be said about these treatises is that neither of them makes explicit reference to the element of time in intersubjective experience. Also, from a sociological stand, Husserl's *Fifth Meditation* appears to be a typical *societal* analysis, in that concepts like "assimilation," "association" among egos and bodies function in the explanation of the givenness of the "thou," indicating that transfers between embodied egos can be made and that they are bridgeable, so to speak. The "other" is still opposite myself in Husserl's *Meditation*. He is for me, I for him. It is for this reason that phenomenologists for a long time have voiced criticism of this *Meditation*. While some remarks against it (e.g., Dorion Cairns called it a "methodological mess") are rather strong, it may also be justified, I still believe, that Husserl had much the same in mind and intention as Scheler did in 1913, when the manuscript of the aforementioned part of his book on sympathy was completed.

As far as the time structure of ego/alter-ego relationships are concerned, we must first mention two irreconcilable alternatives of interpretation of them that occur in the literature. Either my ego constitutes that of the other, or the other's ego makes my ego possible. In the latter case the other is "pre-given." In the former view the other is through me. If my ego is alter-ego-constituting, one communality is derivable from it. If the alter-ego is pre-given, communality is pre-given. But if the alter-ego is pre-given so that it can constitute my ego, then my ego must have a trace "in" the alter-ego already because it cannot constitute my ego out of nothing. In that case any ego would possess alter-ego-ness and the same irreconcilability would come up again: Is the alter-ego, *within* an ego, constituted *by* this ego, or is alter-ego-ness, *within* the ego, that which generates this ego out of alter-ego-ness: Much as it seems to be impossible that alter-ego-ness generates ego the case could be likened to the status of light. A source of light lights up only when its rays hit *something else*. In itself, without hitting other things, a light source remains nonlight, i.e., dark. A universe consisting of only one light source and nothing else would be dark.

These and other aporias concerning the givenness of the other ego-logically were clearly seen by both Husserl and Scheler. Historically, the difficulties go back to Fichte. Fichte saw that the ego was "split." On the one hand we experience our own ego as a unity but, on the other, in looking at and experiencing our ego we know that there is no such thing as another ego looking but that this looking, too, belongs to the *same* ego experience. The ego's unity can, therefore, not be compared to the "unity" in a traditional sense. Recently, Hartmut Tietjen has furnished us with an elaborate comparison between Husserl and Fichte (Hartmut Tietjen, *Husserl und Fichte. Letztbegründung, Subjektivität und praktische Vernunft im transzendentalen Idealismus* [Frankfurt: 1980], 309 pages); he maintains that the two can only be compared in their earlier philosophy. What becomes translucent in such comparisons between Husserl and Fichte, and Husserl and Scheler, appears to be the impossibility of understanding the unity of the human ego in a traditional sense. We cannot apply "part" and "whole" to an ego. The alter-ego is no "part" of the ego, nor vice versa. The relationship between ego and alter-ego, be it within the ego, or in a monadic sense such that ego and alter-ego would have to be "bridged," reminds one, rather, of a unity that has a *topology of its own*, reminiscent of wholes and parts holding among transfinite numbers (Cantor), among whom, for instance, 1 + 1 = 1 or 2 x 2 = 2, or all even numbers having the same unitary power as all even + odd numbers. This *appears* to be indicated, although not elaborated upon, by Scheler, and I wish to sketch briefly this state of affairs which will help us to get the time-flux in intersubjective life-communal experience into view.

Intersubjectivity is tantamount to a psychic stream permeating egos but in itself being indifferent to such egos. The *initial* state of an ego (at or around the time of birth) is *non*egological, i.e., its existence consists solely in the "immersion" into others and in extraverted attachments to things. One can call this state (which Scheler describes in different ways) as extraverted ecstasis or ecstatic extraversion *devoid* of selfhood. This initial state does not amount to being "one" ego but to only an egological *diffusion* within the intersubjective stream mentioned. This Schelerian assumption of an intersubjective egological "vortex" remains an assumption, but it helps greatly to avoid the aforementioned "bridging" among bodies and egos of *adults* (a presupposition made in Husserl's *Meditation*). We all too often make this presupposition of taking it for granted that fully grown *adults* of society should function as the ultimate measure from which to elucidate human intersubjectivity. While this *can* be done if the explication remains outspokenly restricted to societal ego-relations it *cannot* and should not be done with regard to any nonsocietal group. Ancestors and future generations alike play a vital role here and must be included in a manner *different* from the way we take them into account in a society. This inclusion must function as importantly as the present generation in constitutive phenomenological explication. For ancestry and future generation belong *in fact* to the "lived" intersubjectivity and time experience among members of life-communities.

The initial egological ecstasis, the dynamic *inception* (not "beginning" in clock-time) and *diffusion* in intersubjectivity is directed to *already* existing egos whose egological contents and experiences must function for this initial ego as "*already*" there with the quality of the *past*. In this sense the diffused inception of an ego must not be pictured as being directed into and toward its own future, nor in the sense that it grows into the group's future. Rather, the *dif*fused egological state is first nourished by the contents carried by *already existing egos* and must be *con*fused in those contents that accumulated in the already existing egos in the ocean of intersubjective streaming. Thus, it is nourished by genuine *tradition* and fed from "behind," as it were, up to the point when the initial ego reaches the state of being able to set itself *off* from existing egos in terms of whatever little amounts of self-willing, probably around the age of two. In a life-community this self-willing remains on low levels, whereas in society it reaches a maximum. In a society a person can be *against* its whole, and may take arms against it; in a life-community being against its whole is tantamount to treason and results in severe punishment. From a moral point of view the life-community is beset with *co*-responsibility, a society with *self*-responsibility.

Inasmuch as societal egos are at distance with each other the problem of the time-flux among them can hardly come up and it has rarely been thematized as a peculiar *inter*subjective time. For we tend to take the egos to be "simultaneous." In a lived nonsocietal experience, however, the initial ego is nourished from *past tradition* and from what is already given and there for it; it is infected and contaged, as it were, by large amounts of traditional contents. The time-flux involved is that of the past into the present, as we mentioned before, and into a durational, not-objectified present encompassing anticipations which also bear the traces and styles of tradition.

But the *already existing egos* into which and among which an ego is born in its diffused state must *themselves* have been nourished from the past of their own egological already existing environment at the point of *their* ecstatic inception. Thus, it would appear that intersubjectivity of life-communal groups is shot through with gaps and holes of diffused ego-inceptions devoid of selves. This would appear to be an intersubjectivity not only consisting of fully grown egos but *a fortiori* of also ecstatic diffusions bare of ego-centers, i.e., a psychic stream permeating all egos but in itself indifferent to such egos (p. 90 below). The genesis from egological inceptions to fully grown egos must possess a "time" in which *no* differentiation and separation between past and future, contents and phases is at hand. The ego must "time" itself in its becoming without there being any past and future "*as*" past and future. All we seem to be able to assign to initially diffused egos is a durational present of the thereness of others and of things. As long as the genesis of the life-communal ego does not reach self-willing and individualization, its time-flux must be inverted toward its durational present, or, at least, *tend* to such inversion. "Sleep" seems akin to such ego-diffusion.

It is my contention that this experience of time is rooted in social experience. The more a human being lives in a life-communal group, the more the present will stretch backward and forward, i.e., both past and future *blend* into *continuous duration*. Lived time and objective time are two manifestations of time relative to the social group (community or society). In a life-community the past and the future are not experienced so much "*as*" being past and future. This "as" is characteristic for society, and it is difficult for a societal individual to place himself into a communal time blending all three time dimensions into one duration. If it is the case that, sociologically, life-communities are the foundation for the possibility of societies (an order of foundation we find also established in both Scheler's and Husserl's distinction between "generative" *Gemeinschaft* and *Gesellschaft*), the inverted time structure described must also be conceived as *continuing forth* in society, albeit covered up by objective time. It must be stressed that in practical experience we never find a *pure* life-community, nor a *pure* society. Every society possesses life-communal forms, and every life-community possesses at least tendencies toward societization. One cannot draw a sharp line between them but only speak of their predominance. It is therefore to be assumed that both objective time and lived communal time, i.e., time stretching back into the past and forward into the future, and time merging *from* the past and the future *into* a durational present, *themselves* form a complex *interplay of durations and se-*

quences depending upon our predominant sociation at hand. It was the purpose of this sketch to stress the sociological factor in the analysis of intersubjective timing; i.e., I do not believe that *inter*subjective time can be elucidated solely in terms of a *pure* time-consciousness, nor of a pure ego, if such a thing should exist. The transcendental, i.e., constituting, ego does *not* suffice to come to grips with the flux of the inter-ego time. Ego and alter-ego, no matter in which sense of these terms, are egos of *sociation* rather than *as*sociation and assimilation.

Whether the *social* sciences can at all be bracketed in this area of our time experience with others is highly doubtful.

The problem of the *contiguity* between interhuman sociation and time experience involves many more points than the ones I have tried to make. For instance, the entire difference between the status of *protentions and retentions* and the stretched "now" (*das Jetzten*) in Husserl's lecture on Time-Consciousness, as well as Scheler's concept of the same in what he called "immediate remembering" and "immediate anticipating" as opposed to factual recollection of something in an objective past and factual expectation of something in an objectified future, belongs to intersubjective time also. It may be argued that life-communal human beings live more in protended and retended nows, whereas societal people live more in the objectified past and future. But to just argue that this could be the case is of little use unless a *socio-temporal contiguity* could be established, i.e., whether or not, or to what degree interhuman sociation bears on the experience of time and history.

HEGEL'S IMAGE OF PHENOMENOLOGY

H.S. HARRIS (Toronto)

At the beginning of his commentary on Hegel's *Phenomenology of Spirit*, Howard Kainz poses an interesting question: "What," he asks, "is the literary form of the 'Phenomenology'"? But, although his consideration of the question produces some interesting comparisons, and quite a few incidental insights, he is not able to give a direct answer that is informative. "We conclude tentatively ... that this work is completely unique in the annals of philosophy."[1]

This will not do, and Kainz knows it. The object of asking the question is to get some guideline for reading the work; to discover whether there are any other works we are already familiar with that it resembles in a structural way and that can help us see the relation between the parts; and to orient ourselves as we go through it. Even if there is no other philosophical work like it, there must surely be other kinds of books that it resembles in an instructive, orienting fashion. Thus, the book Spinoza called *Ethics* is quite unlike any other ethical treatise,[2] but Kainz rightly points out that its obvious similarity to a textbook on geometry has an orienting significance for the beginning reader that is quite helpful. (He does not add that ultimately it may be dangerously misleading if we cling too tightly to it, but that seems to me to be another important truth that we should do well to remember in the present context.)

In lieu of anything better, Kainz offers five hints that supposedly have a positive value in orienting ourselves for the task of reading the *Phenomenology*. First, he suggests it has an "inward form" that will give us clues to its purpose (or purposes). So far as there is any positive

1. Howard Kainz, ed., *Hegel's Phenomenology, Part I: Analysis and Commentary* (University, Ala.: University of Alabama Press, 1976), p. 6. Kainz' entire discussion occupies pp. 5-9.

2. Except for some other works of Spinoza, and possibly some conscious imitations of this primary model, of whose very existence I remain complacently ignorant.

Cho, K.K. (ed.) Philosophy and Science in Phenomenological Perspective.

ISBN 978-94-009-6115-9

guidance in this, it amounts to the suggestion that the *Phenomenology of Spirit* is like a great prose-poem. This may be true, but it certainly is not a novel suggestion.[3] Moreover, it is of little use as a primary orientation. To begin with, Hegel himself was conscious of the imperfection of the literary form of what he had produced; he spoke of this in a letter to Schelling at the time of publication.[4] Thus, attention to the "inner form" runs the risk of leading to wrong conclusions, because the balance and relationship of the parts as literary elements is not what the author himself thought they ought to be.

Second, this way of looking at the work is only posing the problem again in a context we are more familiar with. Occasionally the author of a long poem or a novel will tell us in a straightforward manner at the beginning what he intends to do (just as Milton does in *Paradise Lost*). But more often than not his deeper purpose or meaning is hidden, and we have to struggle to find it. There is undeniably an element of concealment in Hegel's method. For there are references we can catch but which he could have made clearer; then there are others we can only speculate about, because the text is deliberately enigmatic. I am not sure whether more poets have written in this riddling and allusive way since 1807 than before, but I am certain that comparing Hegel with them does not help. For instance, I believe that Blake's great prophetic work, *The Four Zoas*, is an allegorical "phenomenology" of human historical consciousness that is far closer to what Hegel attempted, both in conception and execution, than any of the German Romantic parallels that Kainz suggests in his fifth hint. But there is no way that this belief will help me to understand Hegel.

(It is altogether more likely that an understanding of Hegel will help me read Blake. It might also deepen my appreciation of Goethe's *Wilhelm Meister* and the *Heinrich von Ofterdingen* of Novalis, if the basic hypothesis – that those works are intended to incarnate not just a typical pattern of individual experience but also the historic experience of the human community – is justified. Whether that assumption is correct I need not inquire further in this paper, because any potential beam of enlightenment goes from the philosophical work to the poetic, not vice versa.)

This brings us to the deepest reason for being wary of the poetic analogy. Poetry can have the purpose of conceptual explanation and

3. Kainz found it in Helmut Rehder's essay "The Significance of Hegel's *Phenomenology* for Literary Criticism," in *A Hegel Symposium*, ed. Don Carlos Travis (Austin: University of Texas Press, 1962), p. 133. We may remember that Croce, speaking not just of the *Phenomenology* but of the system as a whole, called Hegel a "poet of philosophy" in *What Is Living and What Is Dead of the Philosophy of Hegel*, transl. Douglas Ainslie (London: Macmillan and Co., 1915).

4. *Briefe*, ed. Hoffmeister, I, 161.

scientific enlightenment (as in Lucretius), but not usually. Philosophy, on the other hand, typically (though not necessarily) has this explicit aim, and no one was ever more categorical in his commitment to it than Hegel. We must concede this, no matter what our estimate of his actual achievement may be. If Hegel is indeed a "poet among philosophers," he does not rank with Lucretius and Dante, nor even with Plato and Kierkegaard. Thus, although it may be legitimate to conclude with Croce that Hegel was a poet of sorts, in spite of himself, we ought first to give him the fairest hearing we can manage upon his own terms. We must not tell beginning readers to approach the *Phenomenology* as if it were poetry, precisely because (as Kainz acknowledges in his second suggestion) Hegel was "heir to the rationalist persuasion in philosophy" and his objective was to describe "the world precisely as an organized System of Reason."

We ought not to take this scientific aim as our guide either, however, since "the description of the world" (if that is a correct characterization of Hegel's philosophical aim, which I take leave to doubt) is accomplished in the system itself, for which the *Phenomenology* is only the "introduction." The function of the introduction, as an independent whole – and especially as the "first part of the System of Science" – must be something distinguishable from that overall aim, something more particularly specifiable.

This leaves us with the two hints which Kainz derives (through Hyppolite) from the works of Fichte and Schelling. Hyppolite sees in Fichte's "deduction of presentation"[5] "a first model of what Hegel's *Phenomenology* will be."[6] But I do not think Kainz can possibly have checked the reference, for I can well remember puzzling over it when I was first beginning, not to read the *Phenomenology*, but to teach it. If there is any relation between what Fichte does here and what Hegel does, it extends to the first three chapters of the *Phenomenology* only; and it illustrates why Hegel criticizes Fichte in the Preface more than it illuminates what Hegel does.

As for Schelling, there is no doubt that his ideal "history of self-consciousness in epochs" influenced Hegel (though not as much as it

5. Fichte, *Wissenschaftslehre* (1794), *Werke* I, 227-46, ed. and transl. Peter Heath and John Lachs (New York: Appleton-Century-Crofts, 1970), pp. 203-17. The phrase "pragmatic history of the human spirit," quoted by both Hyppolite and Kainz, is applied by Fichte to his *Wissenschaftslehre* at *Werke* I, 222 (Heath and Lachs, pp. 198-99).

6. Jean Hyppolite, *Genèse et Structure*, I, 14, transl. Samuel Cherniak and John Heckman (Evanston, Ill.: Northwestern University Press, 1974), p. 8. Hyppolite does not give a direct reference to Fichte, but refers us to Guéroult's *Evolution et structure de la doctrine de la science de Fichte*, I, 225. I suspect that Hyppolite did not look at the relevant section of Fichte himself.

influenced Hyppolite).[7] But Kainz sends us rather to an *obiter dictum* which Schelling himself (as far as I know) never followed up: "Now we do in fact also maintain that no individual consciousness could be posited, with all the determinations it is posited with, and which necessarily belong to it, unless the whole of history had gone before.... Historiography, which otherwise has no object save that of explaining the present state of the world, could thus equally set out from the current situation and infer to past history, and it would be no uninteresting endeavor to see how the whole of the past could be derived from this in a strictly necessary manner."[8]

This is easily the most suggestive anticipation of what Hegel does than Kainz (or Hyppolite) have found for us (though neither of them focused attention on the crucial passage). But it leaves the basic puzzle of Hegel's *Phenomenology* untouched, since Schelling does not say why the derivation of the "whole of the past" from the "present state of the world" "with strict necessity" would be interesting. Instead he explains that the *ganze Vergangenheit* that is "deducible" does not include a great mass of people and happenings that are not properly "historical." This discussion too is helpful because it clearly parallels the way in which Hegel thought that an individual self-consciousness could recall and appropriate the formative process of the *Weltgeist*. But the optimistic version of Kant's critical conception of history that Schelling goes on to outline (history is characterized for him by an "infinite *tendency to progress*") is far removed from the "reverence towards fate" which Hegel always preached upon historical texts; and it is even further removed from the culmination of Hegel's effort of historical remembrance in an "absolute knowledge" which leaves all "infinite tendencies" behind. It is this climax that we have to comprehend if we are going to thread our way through the labyrinth that Hegel constructed. So we should do well to examine what Hegel says about it, and see whether he himself offers us any structural analogies which help to orient the beginning reader.

In fact he tried very hard to do this; and although his analogies are not perfect, the *Phenomenology of Spirit* is far easier to interpret from inside than it is through external comparison with other literary projects either proposed or carried out by his contemporaries. This is not

7. Schelling, *System of Transcendental Idealism, Werke* III, 395-531, transl. Peter Heath, pp. 47-154. A simple comparison of this part of Schelling's table of contents with the table of contents in Hyppolite will suffice, I think, to establish the influence; cf. *Genèse et Structure*, I, 14, transl. Cherniak and Heckman, p. 9. It must remain to the reader who studies Hegel and Hyppolite together to decide whether the influence was on the whole beneficial rather than baneful.

8. Heath, p. 201; *Werke* III, 590; cf. Hyppolite, *Genèse et Structure* I, 44 (Cherniak and Heckman, p. 40).

to say, however, that we must seek to discover the "inward form" that is "unique" to the book. For Hegel's own suggestions direct our attention to a type of literary work which is more variegated, less rigorously structured, than the class of geometry textbooks, certainly, but nevertheless quite easy to identify and to categorize. He offers us three images that we have to combine in order to understand what is supposed to be happening: the image of a path or a way to be traveled (a way that has already been made and mapped, not one that we have to make or discover for ourselves); the image of a ladder to be climbed; and the image of a plant growing through the cycle of its seasons to the point where the fruit can be plucked. Since the fruit here is "absolute knowledge," perhaps we might hazard the conjecture that the fruit that is meant is an apple (Hegel later mentions an acorn and an oak, but at that point he wants to use the analogy in an opposite sense – the acorn is the *seed* at the beginning, not the fruit on the tree at the end).

This is the first analogy that the reader is actually offered, and it is not explicitly offered as a structural guide to the book but as a criticism of the ordinary view of the history of philosophy.[9] It is not clear that Hegel's book is about the history of philosophy generally, but it is clear enough that it deals with the organic development of his ideal of philosophy as *system*, so the connection is not really a difficult one to make. That we are supposed to identify the fruit as an apple is never suggested, however. If my suggestion is right – and Hegel's own development of the other analogies will show that it is – then his book begins by proclaiming its own sphinxlike character. It begins with a riddle.

The "ladder" simile is explicitly connected by Hegel with his own undertaking. For it is at the climax of his general discussion in the Preface, when he brings together his two main theses – that "truth is the whole, and its form is a scientific system" and that "the Absolute is Subject as well as Substance" – that Hegel remarks that "the individual has the right to demand that Science should at least provide him with the ladder to this standpoint."[10] In the very next paragraph he says that "this coming into being of science generally, or of *Wissen*, is what this *Phenomenology of Spirit* sets forth"; and he explains why the simple inversion of the standpoint of consciousness into the standpoint of philosophic science must be pictured as a ladder, by telling us that

9. Hegel, *Gesammelte Werke*, ed. Rheinisch-Westfälische Akademie der Wissenschaften (Hamburg: F. Meiner, 1968 ff.), cited hereafter as *NKA* (*Neue kritische Ausgabe*), IX, 10; Miller, section 2. The rigorous alternative of *Beistimmung oder Widerspruch* against which this analogy is set, is especially characteristic of Fichte. But it is Kant's characterization of precritical philosophy (in the "Dialectic of Pure Reason") that Hegel needs to overthrow.

10. *NKA*, IX, 23; Miller, section 26.

"in order to beget the element of science which is its pure concept" the "immediate spirit" of sensory consciousness (which is strictly "spiritless") must "work itself through a long road." The "ladder" image thus forms a bridge between the doctrine of a simple opposition of standpoints (with no possibility of a direct conversion from one to the other) and the developed conception of a *pathway* from one to the other. The bud-flower-fruit image has already suggested that the overarching cultural history in which the new "Science" forms the harvest phase, must be viewed as an organic sequence of reversals or conversion experiences. But at the same time the experience of conversion as an immediate transition, mediated by nothing more than the preaching of the word, or the proclamation of a new gospel, has been laughed to scorn. The "ladder" is offered as a religious image of that "seriousness, suffering, patience and labor of the negative,"[11] which is requisite in place of the edifying talk of Jacobi, Schleiermacher, and a host of others if we are to share in "the life of God and divine cognition"; and the laborious journey over the path traveled by the *Weltgeist* is a philosophic image of how the history of human culture has to be appropriated before the "sun-clear reports" and pistol-shot proclamations of Fichte can carry any conviction.[12]

That the "ladder" is a religious image is not stated, but its religious status is implicit in the fact that the ladder stretches between the earth of ordinary consciousness and the heavenly "aether" of philosophic science. Hegel underlines the fact that his concept of "Spirit" is much closer to Christian tradition and language than other contemporary formulations such as "the moral world-order"; and his careful explanation of why the name "God" is more of a hindrance than a help to the philosopher would make no sense if we did not see that his own aim is to define what that name refers to. His "ladder" is a religious image because it does imply the otherness of the world which it leads to. The "journey" image is a more ultimate one for Hegel – and hence it is developed much more fully – because the otherness of the destination (though it is real enough) still belongs to this world and this life. The "aether" of Spirit (or of science) is an element in which we must learn to breathe and to live here and now. The ladder we have to climb is therefore not a "thread of light" which we can follow (as Dante did) all the way to the presence of God in the other world and the other life. Indeed, the turning of the spiritual eye toward the other world (which

11. *NKA*, IX, 18; Miller, section 19.

12. *NKA*, IX, 24, 38; Miller, sections 27, 51. Hegel says we can find the religious form of conversion anywhere, and can "easily dream up something for ourselves and put on airs about it." (*NKA*, IX, 13-14; Miller, section 9). But he identifies the apostle of philosophical conversion unmistakably. This critique of Fichte is quite distinct from the attack upon those (Schelling's students certainly, and perhaps also Schelling himself) whose philosophic *science* is itself undeveloped because their *method* is only a "formal" (or mechanical) one.

Plato advocated, and the Church accomplished) has had to be slowly and painfully reversed again, Hegel's "science of experience" is the final consummation of this reversal. He wants to make "the lucidity, which only the things in the heavens used to have, work its way into the darkness and confusion in which the sense of this world's affairs lay."[13] So he is borrowing Jacob's ladder both to take us to Heaven and to bring us back to earth.

The ladder that Jacob saw (and Dante after him) was "set up on the earth, and the top of it reached to heaven; and behold, the angels of God," who prophesied for him not a heavenly but an earthly fate – that his seed would be spread abroad over all the earth, and that "in thee and in thy seed shall all the families of the earth be blessed."[14] That Hegel had this latter prophecy in mind I cannot definitely show; but only the two-way traffic on Jacob's ladder makes the ladder image appropriate to the connection between the earth of consciousness and the "aether" of science as Hegel conceived it.

But Jacob saw his ladder in a dream. Is not this typical of the rapturous enthusiasm of the religion of feeling to which Hegel was violently hostile? Can it be right to think that he has borrowed an image from one of the most famous stories of a religious dreamer, when he himself speaks so contemptuously of "God's own to whom he gives wisdom in sleep; what they in fact receive and bring to birth in their sleep are of course dreams"?[15]

This irony is far from conclusive against the interpretation I am proposing, because it is typical of the Preface as a whole; and we can quite properly take it as implying only a criticism of those who put Jacob's dream on the same level with that mighty wrestling all night with the angel, which left him lame for the rest of his days;[16] or, more immediately, it is a criticism of those who mistake images for science, or the orienting work of the Preface for the seriousness, suffering, patience and labor of the book itself. The Preface ends, we may note, by condemning those who think Plato's myths more important than the *Parmenides*, but this has not stopped Hegel from using the myth of the Cave himself, just as Plato did, for purposes of orientation – though, as we have already seen, he uses it for orientation in the opposite direction.[17] This sting in the tail of the Preface is certainly no accident, and we should take to heart its implications, both for the

13. *NKA*, IX, 13; Miller, section 8. (Whether Hegel is thinking of Dante we cannot be sure. But it is a plausible hypothesis. The reference to Plato's forcible liberation of his prisoners from the Cave is unmistakable.)
14. Genesis 28: 12-14.
15. *NKA*, IX, 14; Miller, section 10.
16. See Genesis 32: 24-32.
17. *NKA*, IX, 48; Miller, section 71.

interpretation of the Preface itself, and for the "scientific worthlessness" of this present discourse. But we must still try to follow the argument where it leads.

That it is right to look for the origin of Hegel's images in the Scriptures is finally confirmed by his treatment of the most experiential and this-worldly, hence the most philosophical and most fully developed, of them all: the journey. This is the last image to be presented in the Preface, but it was the first that Hegel thought of, for he had employed it already in his Introduction; and there can be no doubt that he means to compare his book not just to a typical life-journey, but to the climax of that quite singular and unique life-journey that provides the fundamental image of Christian experience: the Passion of Christ or the "way of the Cross."

In the order of exposition (which we should follow because we are maintaining that the book provides better orientation for its readers than we can find by going outside it, even when we go no further than our external knowledge of the order of its composition), this comparison is made gradually. First we are told only that the way is long and involves hard labor because we must attend to, and linger over, what goes unnoticed or is reduced to mere child's play in the natural course of our self-conscious *Bildung*. We need not, indeed we cannot, suffer what the World-Spirit has gone through in order that we may enjoy this heedless, or playful, process of self-formation; but the achievement of philosophical insight requires that we should appreciate all that suffering and patience. We cannot say yet that there is anything very Christlike about the much-emphasized "patience" of the World-Spirit, but we can recognize that what Hegel is asking of us depends upon the same imaginative capacity that made it possible for Christians to claim that God had taken "all the sins of the world" upon himself in the person of a single man.

Our task involves patience and labor but little suffering. What is familiar has to be made strange in order that we may take it seriously. The very first thing that we have to realize is that the form of conceptualization, which we so readily take for granted, is a state of death for all that is fixed in it: "Not the life that shrinks from death, and keeps itself pure of devastation, but that which endures it, and maintains itself in it is the life of the spirit."[18] This does seem reminiscent of Christ's death and resurrection, and the seemingly gratuitous comment that Hegel adds about "powerless beauty" ("beauty hates the understanding because it expects this of her which she cannot achieve") helps to confirm the reference to the miracle that the Apostles proclaimed. For Greece was the culture of the beauty which lacked the power to

18. *NKA*, IX, 27; Miller, section 32.

overcome the barbarians, and the mighty arm of the understanding that achieved universal Empire was Rome. Thus, when we study the transition from *polis* to Empire, and the ring of *Gestalten* round the manger at Bethlehem (as we find ourselves doing more than once in the course of the book), we are coming to terms with the most elementary transition in our everyday consciousness, the transition from sense to thought.

The "pathway" of Hegel's *Phenomenology* begins from this descent into the eternal living death of thought as "understanding." What we have to bring about (once we have comprehended what thought is) is resurrection of our thoughts as self-moving *Begriffe*, concepts that circle upon themselves infinitely in a self-consciousness that is not buried in the night of what is "familiar" because long-forgotten. The historical and mathematical modes of inquiry must both be rejected, because these approaches concentrate attention on "truth" in its understandable sense; and even the newest "formal" philosophies, though they claim to be philosophies of organic form, must be rejected because they ignore the transcended phases of truth's organic growth as being merely "error" that has been decisively superseded. All such views are just the presently existing forms of living death.[19] Truth must be comprehended in its development, and therefore the "science of experience" must be a prolonged wrestling match with the forms of "error" out of which it has emerged. (Hegel may speak of "lingering" with each *Gestalt* – *verweilen*, the word that Faust promises not to use imperatively – but the "magic power that turns the negative into being" is not the less strenuous because there is no blood and sweat in it.)[20]

The worst difficulty Hegel faces in describing the wrestling (*die Anstrengung des Begriffs*)[21] is created by the fact that the struggle and the victory go hand in hand. Thus he emphasizes what an effort is involved in speculative thinking, but at the same time he wants to say that speculation is a simple seeing, that we observe a pattern in the struggle because we are contemplating it from above. The quasi-historical character of his *Phenomenology* is determined by the need to create a distance between the struggling and the watching. But it is still our consciousness which reenacts the struggle of the *Weltgeist*, just as much as it is our self-consciousness that watches what happens. That the standpoints of earth (the struggle) and heaven (the contemplation) are thus dialectically united in our thought is what makes the book so diffi-

19. *NKA*, IX, 38; Miller, sections 51-2. This contemporary state is characterized as "flaying," an image that derives from Greek mythology; cf. Apollo and Marsyas. By implication, Hegel is accusing those he attacks of accepting the values and standards of the secular Enlightenment, and of not grasping the speculative significance of Christianity.

20. Cf. *NKA*, IX, 25 and 27; Miller, sections 29 and 32.

21. *NKA*, IX, 41; Miller, section 58.

cult to read. The most that Hegel can do about this in the Preface is to tell us what to expect, and to contrast his procedure with the simple "heavenly" mode of inspiration, and the simple "earthly" one of common sense. But his contemptuous remarks about the common-sense reader who relies on prefaces, and the inspired writer who can't be bothered to write a preface, are a warning to us that we must study the book itself if we want to understand this methodological part of *his* Preface properly. In this part of the discussion he gives us no image of his road, but only the contrasting images of a road that takes one nowhere out of one's armchair, and a road that is not there at all – and finally a rude comment about "scientifically worthless myths."

The goal which the Preface keeps continually before our eyes – whether in its true form or in its various illusory alternative guises – is the heavenly one of "participation in the divine life."[22] The Introduction, by contrast, is quite worldly. In the Preface there is a continual tension between the religious aims and language and the severely philosophical doctrine; the Introduction is more consistently philosophical in its language, as well as its thought. Yet the image of the "pathway," which is quite consistent with the most sober and common-sensical description of what is ahead of us, is rather surprisingly called a "way of despair" (*Verzweiflung*).[23] This is surprising because, although it is obviously necessary to emphasize that the dialectical difficulties and uncertainties of the *Weltgeist* are real (in contrast to the comfortable armchair doubt of Descartes, or of philosophers generally), despair is not a very noteworthy component in the organized "science of the experience of consciousness." The motto of the consciousness we shall observe is much more obviously the *nil desperandum* of the Trojan leader in Horace's famous ode. Consciousness is perpetually defeated, but it never despairs. The Spirit – and we who are its self-consciousness – learns and moves on after each defeat, while the *Gestalten* of consciousness itself are infinitely resourceful in their refusal to admit that they have been defeated.

It is essential to Hegel's conception of a "*Gestalt* of consciousness"

22. Cf. *NKA*, IX, 12-14, 17-19, 20-1, 22, 40, 46-48; Miller, sections 6-10, 16-20, 23, 25, 55, 68-70. We should not forget that the "Bacchanalian revel" (*NKA*, IX, 35; Miller, section 47) is the most primitive and immediate mode of participation in the divine life (cf. *NKA*, IX, 387; Miller, section 723). And the fact that the "shaking of the Subject" in the speculative proposition is applied first to Kantian self and then to "God" – and the use of the name "God" is then set aside for the sake of it – can hardly be accidental (*NKA*, IX, 42-5; Miller, sections 60-6; cf. IX, 20-1; Miller, section 23). When the whole pattern is considered, it seems to be impossible to resist the claim that a reference to the death and resurrection of the God-Man is intended at *NKA*, IX, 27 (Miller, section 32).

23. *NKA*, IX, 56; Miller, section 78.

that it can maintain itself, and in showing us why we must move on, Hegel is generally careful to show us also the shifts by which each *Gestalt* renders itself circular and so avoids moving. This is why the mood of our observant progress is so generally one of ironic amusement. To take the most crucial instance, even when consciousness comes to despair of itself and its life, officially and *ex professo* – in the "Unhappy Consciousness" – we are made to see how resolutely it organizes life on that basis, how tightly it clings to the "thread of light" that was mentioned in the Preface; and the way that it rounds itself out by finding forgiveness and justification even in this life provides us with the stepping-stone to the supremely self-confident consciousness of Reason.

Only once is "despair" really present and dominant in a *Gestalt* of consciousness. It is the necessary complement of the initial self-consciousness of the free ego; despair is the fate of its independence and self-will. Only a really genuine despair can mediate the transition from the life-and-death struggle to servitude. Hegel recognizes the possibility of a subjection that is merely expedient and "lives to fight another day" – or of a servitude in which independence and self-will have merely gone into hiding. But he tells us clearly that this is not the servitude in which the *Bildung* of self-consciousness properly begins. (This spirit of *Eigensinn* is rather the shift by which the *Gestalt* of the struggle preserves itself, and refuses to accept defeat.)[24] The *Bildung* of self-consciousness begins with the real "shaking of the subject" through the fear of death;[25] and Hegel probably wants to make us look for, and linger over, the significance of this "beginning of wisdom" when he calls the road to Absolute Knowledge a "way of despair."

All the same, his calling the whole path "a way of despair" (rather than "a way of defeat") is paradoxical, and the resulting puzzlement must immediately cause us to fasten on the description of the *Phenomenology* as the "way of the soul which traverses the series of its configurations as stations marked out for it by its nature" that Hegel has just given us at this point. "Stations of the soul" on a "way of despair" can only be the "stations of the Cross"; and this identification offered us at the beginning of our journey is confirmed in the last sentence of the book where "history comprehended" is called "the 'skull-place' (i.e. Golgotha) of the Absolute Spirit." If we go through the book with this analogy as our guide, then when we return to the Preface at the end – as we should – the language of death and resurrection that we find there becomes visibly the completion of the religious story with the resurrection into a new life.

But if Hegel's *Phenomenology* is thus modeled on the image of

24. See *NKA*, IX, 115-16; Miller, section 196 to the end.
25. *NKA*, IX, 114, 115; Miller, sections 194, 196.

Christ's Passion and Resurrection, then we can say what kind of book it is after all. Just as Spinoza's *Ethics* is philosophy modeled on a geometry book, so Hegel's *Phenomenology* is philosophy modeled on a manual of devotional discipline; and since several types of religious devotion are discussed and dismissed by Hegel himself, we can be more precise. It is not models of Christian life like the *Imitation of Christ* of Thomas a Kempis (which Hegel was certainly familiar with) or *Pilgrim's Progress* (which he probably never heard of) that the *Phenomenology* resembles. The closest parallel is a work like Bonaventure's *Itinerarium mentis in Deum*, but it is doubtful whether Hegel knew that little treatise existed. The work he did know was Dante's *Divine Comedy*. His *Phenomenology* should be read (so far as its literary form is concerned) as the "human comedy" in which the great religious symbols of the Passion and Resurrection receive a philosophical significance within the bounds of a logical comprehension of "experience." He does for the "age of knowledge" what Dante did for the "age of faith."

Apart from this great religious journey, which the poet remembers and interprets as he tells it, there is a contemporary work of philosophical "devotion," which Hegel undoubtedly had in mind as a stark contrast to his own book. This is the *Bestimmung des Menschen* of Fichte.[26] Dante goes from despair through vision to faith; Fichte moves from doubt through knowledge to faith (with the vision both of a better world and of a higher life). Hegel proceeds from doubt through faith (the "Unhappy Consciousness") to knowledge. His book is written in the declared belief that a new world is dawning, but there is no vision of the future in it. The crucial difference between Hegel and both predecessors I have identified is that for him there is no "beyond." The intellectual world, the aether of science, is "the daylight of the present." Hegel's ladder, like the rainbow, returns to earth. "The concept," as he taught his students at Jena at about the time he was first conceiving the *Phenomenology*, "is the mediator between itself and life."[27] It is true, to be sure, that since the *Phenomenology* leads us to the *Logic*, we can (if we want) think of the "System" itself as the Hegelian analogue of Dante's *Paradise* or of the noumenal Kingdom of Ends. But this parallel only illustrates a contrast, since the Hegelian System is a Platonic Heaven of Ideas, not a Christian Heaven of Souls.

A closer parallel to Christian salvation is offered by the "Concept's

26. Hegel may also be mindful of the newly published *Anweisung zum seligen Leben* (1806). The title is certainly suggestive, but he does not echo it in his Preface (which was the only part of the book written late enough to be affected by it). *Faith and Knowledge* is testimony enough of his critical study of *Die Bestimmung des Menschen*.

27. Rosenkranz, p. 182; Harris and Knox, p. 257.

mediation between itself and life." Because of this, we might say that – like Dante's earthly pilgrimage – Hegel's pilgrimage of Reason ends in the Earthly Paradise. This is what is suggested by two Greek allusions in the Preface that we have not yet considered. The famous comment, "Truth is the Bacchanalian revel,"[28] means not just that speculative truth is alive and dialectical but that it is a whole, embracing the life that is not speculative and self-consciously transparent, but natural, spontaneous, and unconscious or dark. On the other hand, Hegel also claims that "existence is Nous, as Anaxagoras first recognized its essence to be."[29] This takes us to the opposite extreme, but still in Greek terms. Just as the worship of Bacchus was an acknowledgment that we "live in God" in our sensory existence, so the doctrine of Anaxagoras was the first clear formulation of the view that the God in whom we live and move is Reason.

To unite these two extremes successfully would be to bring the beginning and the end of the *Phenomenology* together – the perfect mediation of the Concept between itself and life. To unite them in the way in which the Greeks did would be to regain the perfect form of "natural consciousness" – in other words, it would be "Paradise regained." I am not sure quite how Hegel envisaged this, except that it did not mean returning to the historic paradise of natural consciousness in the "religion of art." When Hegel realized that a new culture was not soon to be born and that the future was dark and enigmatic, he stopped talking about "the Concept mediating between itself and life." The *Phenomenology* itself was the only interpretation he ever gave for this mediation, and the *Phenomenology* is not a work of political prophecy. So it does not matter that Hegel's Earthly Paradise remains – like Dante's – empty.

It is not the parallel, but the contrast, that is important this time. The heavenly Paradise of Dante becomes for Hegel simply "our" philosophical standpoint of contemplative observation, as we watch the Divine Tragedy of the *Weltgeist* give place to the Human Comedy. Far more interesting than this displacement of Paradise, in which the difference is so radical that the comparison is hardly enlightening, is the transformation of the moments of *Hell* and *Purgatory*. Fichte's Hell is the horror of being swallowed up in the determinism of Nature as a

28. *NKA*, IX, 35; Miller, section 47. *NKA*, IX, 387 (Miller, section 723) shows that either this is only a very picturesque but very misleading metaphor, because it is valid only from the standpoint of ordinary consciousness; or else, as I say, it implies that "Truth is the whole" in a much more radical sense than its apparent cashing out as "scientific system" indicates. The doctrine that "the concept is the mediator between itself and life" seems to swing the balance firmly in favor of the second alternative.

29. *NKA*, IX; Miller, section 55.

whole. He is purged of this fear through the counsel of a "Spirit," which, like Dante's Beatrice (though a bit more Socratically), explains to him the significance of his natural knowledge.

For Hegel, the displacement of *Paradise* itself renders this dialogue function superfluous. His Hell has a much deeper affinity with that of Dante, in that for Hegel, too, the singular consciousness is damned, and only human communities can travel the way of salvation on the Mount of Purgatory. But his Hell is one of failure, not one of wrong choice; in this it resembles Dante's Limbo. For in the *Phenomenology* the singular self-consciousness finds only an empty tomb (the Holy Sepulcher).[30] When it loses that, it can finally be transformed into Reason. Singular Reason, however, finds first the skull that was supposedly never in that tomb,[31] and beyond that it finds only a Last Judgment that is mute (in "Reason giving and testing Laws"). Only the human community, having eaten of the apple of Greek philosophy and been expelled from the Eden of Greek poetic and political achievement, begins to find its way up the steep slope of social *Bildung*. But this time the road leads not to a skull but to the guillotine that turns the self into a skull (Hegel's mountain being, of course, the one on this side of the world that Dante was unable to climb, not the divinely organized world in which every sinner knows his sin and stands ready to aid his neighbor).

Whether the comparison with Dante will help a beginning reader I do not know. Certainly it can mislead him. Dante is, after all, more like John Bunyan than he is like Hegel (who has nothing at all in common with Bunyan, as his estimate of the supersensible moral world beyond the guillotine suffices to show). Hegel is interested in changing our conception of the world and of our place in it, not in order to change our behavior but rather in order to show us why we behave as we do (so far as he has a practical aim at all). Because his concern is exclusively with our self-knowledge, the *Phenomenology* has affinities with the work of a cloistered teacher like Bonaventure which it does not have with that of Dante. But in that it is a "science of experience" inspired by Christian canons, it is more like the *Commedia* than it is like anything else.

Finally, however, in terms of the problems of its own time, it is a definition of the "vocation of man." And it necessarily has affinities with works (like Fichte's) that it directly opposes, which it cannot have with the productions of an earlier age. But it derives its indubitable uniqueness from posing the problem of man's destiny in terms which its own age had forgotten how to use, not from posing the problem in a way in which it had never been posed before. That we must all travel the way of the Cross together is one of those doctrines we are so

30. *NKA*, IX, 126; Miller, section 217.
31. *NKA*, IX, 190; Miller, section 343.

familiar with that we have forgotten it. The finding of the right response to the Delphic injunction ("Know thyself!") in this doctrine was too paradoxical for the penny-plain individualism and utilitarian optimism of an enlightened century. But it would not have surprised Augustine.

PHENOMENOLOGY AND THE PHENOMENON OF TECHNOLOGY

DON IHDE (Stony Brook)

PREFACE

In the philosophy of technology there are a number of emergent questions which characterize the debates within this relatively new discipline. Without entering the specifics of those debates, I should like to take note of several of these.

First, in both European and North American contexts, the question of the relationship between science and technology has taken up a considerable amount of the debate. Coupled with this question is one of characterizing what shall count as technology vis-à-vis science. The dominant position is one which holds that science is primary and technology dependent – at least with respect to the modern era. Such a position necessarily must make a relatively strong distinction between traditional and scientific kinds of technologies, since, whether or not there has always been science, there has always been some kind of technology in historical and probably since human times.

In the face of this dominant position, that of Martin Heidegger stands in stark contrast. While he accepts a distinction between traditional and scientific technology, he nevertheless argues that Technology is ontologically prior to science. He then goes on to argue that the essence of Technology is, in effect, "Baconian" in that Technology is a mode of revealing which takes Nature, and ultimately even ourselves, as a kind of resource, "standing reserve (*Bestand*)."[1]

The position I have taken is that, while there may be some aspects of technology which are dependent upon science, there is also a counter-interaction, in that contemporary science is necessarily embodied in its investigatory aim by technology.[2] But in other respects, technology bears a relation with all our ontological relationships whether or not it is scientific or traditional.

1. Martin Heidegger, "The Question Concerning Technology," in *Basic Writings*, transl. David Krell (New York: Harper and Row, 1977).
2. See Don Ihde, *Technics and Praxis* (Reidel, 1979).

Cho, K.K. (ed.) Philosophy and Science in Phenomenological Perspective.

ISBN 978-94-009-6115-9

Whatever the outcome of these debates, there is a second area of disagreement which is equally acute with respect to the evaluative interpretation of the phenomenon of technology. The debate may be called, in its most extreme form, a debate between utopian and dystopian directions of interpretation. Here, whether or not there is a strong distinction between traditional and scientific technologies, it remains the case that the use of technology has been interpreted for many centuries now as either an ultimate fulfillment for humankind or an ultimate threat.

One extreme in this series of debates, the utopian, argues that technology, especially scientific technology, can be the means of freeing and fulfilling humankind's aims. Such claims, beginning (as Lynn White, Jr., has already shown us) with the Middle Ages, continue today with virtually every new advance and invention.[3] Contrarily, the dystopian doubt about technology has also continued to the present. The fear that technology – although invented by humans and originally designed for beneficent ends – could become a Frankensteinian monster, so powerful that it works on its own, is not new to the twentieth century but is already latently present in Christopher Marlowe's *Doctor Faustus*.

Again, while it is important to deal with both the evaluation of technology and the long-standing debates about its import, what is striking about both these sets of arguments is the rarity with which the proponents turn to the phenomenon of technology itself. That seems to be the needed task of a radical phenomenology, and is the task that I turn to in this essay.

THE PHENOMENON OF TECHNOLOGY

The radical and simple way of shifting perspective would be to boldly ask two question: What is the phenomenon of technology itself? And from this "thing itself," what is the truth of utopian and dystopian interpretations? In a sense this is the way in which the phenomenological philosopher Edmund Husserl would have approached the problem. And, equally boldly, it is the way in which his successor, Martin Heidegger, did address the problem, particularly in his essay "The Question Concerning Technology," where the question is: What is the *essence* of technology?

But to ask this question as boldly and directly as this simultaneously leads to the possible criticism that one believes he or she has found a

3. This is the argument of much of Lynn White's work; see especially his "Cultural Climates and Technological Advance in the Middle Ages," *Viator* 2 (1971), p. 171.

privileged perspective, perhaps even one exempt from interpretative prejudices, from which to gain a view of the "things themselves." Yet the shift to a kind of phenomenological empiricism does seem to me to be necessary if we are going to distance ourselves from an eternal dynamic of the standard debates. Thus, what I propose to do in this inquiry is to gradually approach the hopefully modest aim of asking: What is there in the phenomenon of actual human interactions with technology which gives rise to the current arguments? Then, from this set of observations I hope to show something about the *essential* possibilities of the human engagement in technology.

In undertaking this part of the inquiry, I shall employ most of the key methodological notions of a strictly governed phenomenological investigation, in particular the idea of a strict correlation between the concrete human experience of a world, i.e., intentionality, and a use of variational method, i.e., variations employed in such a way as to determine what is *invariant* (or structural or essential, as the case may be).

I begin with an imaginative exercise which, while an example of variational investigation, may be called the story of "From the Garden to the Earth." Could humans live without technology? And, if so, what would be the quality and situation of their life? Here I wish to begin with a very broad but concrete sense of what shall count as technology, a focused but open notion which preserves such features as the materiality of a technology, its creation or invention by humans, and its incorporation into a praxis. Thus a "technology" is some artifact or set of artifacts, incorporated into a praxis in such a way that some human activity is involved and expressed.

A simple example may be imagined – the archaic human who uses a stick to knock down an ordinarily unreachable bunch of bananas is employing a "technology." He is using a material artifact to "extend" his bodily reach to attain some desired end. In this primitive act he has already taken a technological step. But could he live otherwise in a pre- or non-technological way? Empirically we may already note that humans do not live this way, but we are not simply exploring an empirical generalization. We want, instead, to examine essential possibilities. So, we must construct an imaginative example, but within the limits of the concrete.

I think, as a limit-case, the answer is yes, but such an existence would be that of a "Garden." First, because the human is mostly hairless compared to most animals, human geography would be limited to some tropical place which reached neither extreme of hypo- or hyperthermia. Humans can populate the Earth only with clothing, which is *ipso facto* a "technology" (material artifact employed in a praxis which transforms a situation). Without clothes, only a Garden is possible. Second, with respect to food, the Garden would have to have an annual and plentiful supply of easily reachable, attainable, and digestible food: fruit, shellfish, berries, and an absence of large predators. Tools, weapons, fires, of course must be precluded if a non-technological existence is to be maintained. Again, human habitation would be that of a Garden, not the whole Earth.

One can very rapidly see where this example leads. Only those directly bodily and expressive activities would obtain. Existence in the Garden of pre-technology must be also preliterate (writing employs transformed artifacts), face-to-face and protected by a beneficent Nature. Any changes which might occur in this environment could only be threats to the very conditions of life. Contrarily, I hope you can see, that much of what we currently belive to be human need, even "necessity," implies "technology" in some sense. To have chosen to leave the Garden and inhabit the Earth – a mythical "choice" which was made in prehistoric times by every human society – is to have "chosen" a technologically mediated existence. Today, in fact, given world population and its impact upon raw nature, it would probably be impossible to return to this new concept of Eden.

In this imaginative construction I am suggesting that while it might be possible to live non-technologically, it would clearly be to live within limits probably no longer possible.

Here we must turn to an even closer look at the human interaction with technology: what happens to our experience of the environment, the *world*, when we take up the very technology which allows us to inhabit the earth? In this examination I shall be employing – but without a lot of technical terms – the central notions developed in phenomenology. I shall assume that human experience is focused, is directed first outward to an experienced environment, takes place within projects which involve us in wholistic fashion so that both our minds and bodies are committed, and that what results reflects back upon how we understand ourselves. All of this is implied in the complex idea of *intentionality* or what I may call the human-world interactive experience.

My first task, here, is then to distinguish between what at its limits would be a non-technological experience of the world and a technological experience of that same world. Again, variations between our story of a non-technological Garden and the inhabitants of an Earth may be instructive. I return to that simple example of the archaic human using a stick to extend bodily reach to some fruit.

Were we to look at that example closely – phenomenologically as a rigorous science of experience – we would note that there are subtle but marked differences between picking the fruit by hand and by stick. We may note this by concentrating upon the perceptual and bodily experience involved. I shall point to only a few features, which are nevertheless suggestive of a much wider set of essential characteristics implied in our taking up technology: The hand picker of fruit engages the fruit in a full, multi-sensory experience of the object (fruit). He sees it, feels its hardness or softness as bodily close, smells it and tastes it. In contrast, at least when limited to the instant of the picking, the technological picker of fruit experiences it both as mediated *through* the artifact or tool, and as limited with respect to its sensory dimensions. He may see the fruit, but in the moment of picking does not as fully experience the softness or hardness of the fruit, nor does he yet smell it or taste it – although the ultimate aim is to bring that fruit within reach of precisely those senses. He does, however, have a bodily or kinesthetic, though transformed experience of the fruit itself in the moment of picking. He feels the resistance of the stalk through the stick itself, and, contrarily, the stick as means, not the object of experience, is not primarily experienced except as incorporated into the picker's own bodily sense. I hope you can begin to see that our simplified example turns out to be both much more complex than the first thought, and yet filled richly with the very essential structures which mark at least one set of human-technology relations. Let us from the beginning link these to our interpretative background of utopian/dystopian directions.

A technologically optimistic fruit picker might well be the first human elated by the sense of power and attainment experienced in the extended reach which the stick gives. He is fascinated with this new ability to touch, to extend beyond his bodily limit. But simultaneously, he is not aware of, or overlooks what happens in that moment. The fruit itself, while technologically mediated, is not yet the full, multi-dimensioned object it will be when he then picks it up by hand and devours it.

Contrarily, the technological pessimist, seeking to remain in the Garden, pays primary attention precisely to that sensory nearness, to that basic immediate sense of the fruit. He is temporarily satisfied with just what is there or thought to be there. But he overlooks the other kind of richness which the tool user experiences, the reach into the previously unreachable. Thus at this simple and basic level, we can already see a potential for both utopian and dystopian interpretations of technology, but we can also see that both are reduced and focus upon different dimensions of the human technological experience.

Before moving to the next step, let us note that this simple example also contains precisely those experiential elements which pertain essentially or invariantly, not just to archiac tools but to even our most sophisticated contemporary technologies. The telephone, a technology much more complex than our stick, with its now world-wide connective system which includes everything from subterranean cables to satellites, when used displays the feature I have called an *amplification-reduction* structure. That is, the telephone extends our verbal reach, in this case far beyond the extended kinesthetic reach of the stick, throughout the world and we hear and are heard by another. But perceptually, as with the stick, this extension is also a reduction of our sensory experience of the other. Our experience is reduced to a mono-sensory dimension and even that is partially reduced to the still "tinny" or "phony" sound of the other's voice. Distance is diminished to a nearness, but that nearness remains the partially irreal nearness of machine mediation. Our gain is simultaneously a loss, or stated positively, we experience an essential ambiguity in our experience of what is the other through our technology.

If there is phenomenologically and essentially an ambiguous necessity involved with our experience of technology, then one could assert a thesis: careful, rigorous phenomenological analysis of the experience will show that *any and all technology is non-neutral*. And the word is chosen carefully so as not to prematurely decide that there is a dominantly bad trajectory implied in technology. But there is a *non-neutral* transformational effect to any and all technology.

Thus our mythical "choice" made in the new Eden is a choice fraught with significant and even dangerous consequences. To reach for the fruit technologically in order to inhabit the Earth is to step out in a way which is irreversible – at least historically and perhaps also ontologically. There is no return to the Garden, yet there is a residual sense in which every action refers back to the Garden.

By the reference back to primal experience, I mean that even in our most complex and high technologies, there is the need to bring results, effects, objects within the realm of human experience. "To know" still means, in some very basic sense, "to see," to be available from a perceptual position. I shall use a very recent example from physics: the atom, hypothesized by the Greeks and multiplied into a microworld of particles by the twentieth century, has always also been sought by our desire to *see*. By only after the development of highly complex microscopic techniques (it is a long way from the first lens systems of the eleventh century to the electron microscopes of the twentieth), tied to sophisticated photographic processes, did the first pictures of atoms become possible. Only two years ago some physicists at Stony Brook and Stanford claimed to have attained this first photographic representation of an atom (not a molecule, which had been photographed for some time). To see, to grasp, to eat, remains that primal base reference even in the midst of the virtual technological cocoons we utilize in the twentieth century.

Yet we are also now very far from the stick. What brought us here to the point in human history where the earth is interconnected by communications, where what were once tribal wars can now be global threats, where famine in one part of the earth may bring a response from its other side? I should now like to take a second step in this analysis of the phenomenon of technology. If the first step shows that all technology is essentially ambiguous, non-neutral, the second step shows that there is a latent trajectory to technologies such that technological directions occur which incline, though not determine human curiosity and desire.

The history of the development of lenses is illustrative. We do not know by whom or why the first lenses were invented, but already in eleventh-century Europe they were in use. Surely one very practical and basic use was for eyeglasses, one of the earliest applications. To be able to see clearly and distinctly when before one saw only a blur has its own obvious advantage. (But we must not forget that this gain is not unambiguous – the eyeglass wearer may overlook and almost forget that what he sees is accompanied by back glare, by the intrusion of the frame and by foreshortening of the depth of field even in the best of circumstances, but these "reductions" are more than compensated for by the correction of his bodily limitations.) From eyeglasses, it is not far to greater magnification, so before the scientific revolution of the Renaissance there were magnifying glasses and even compound lens systems which eventuated in the microscope and the telescope.

These latter developments, then complex technologies, allowed that same greater magnification (and often overlooked greater reduction) of the world than ever before. Unimagined wee beasties appeared in the drops of water seen through the microscope, and mountains and valleys upon the surface of the moon. It is not hard to imagine the fascination which accompanied such inventions – and with it the temptation to project wildly ever-greater extrapolations. Our engagement with our own artifacts can be one of fascination, a fascination which allows us a trajectory of development. If a little magnification yieldls the previously unknown, what can greater magnification give?

Here, however, I want to point up a possibly overlooked factor in our initial fascination with such technologies. Fascination can be accompanied by a forgetfulness, a forgetfulness which overlooks the essential non-neutrality which always also contains a reduction for every amplification or magnification of our experience through technology. To see the mountains of the moon through a telescope is to focus upon what might be called a micro-element of the whole. To see the moon through a telescope is, while it occurs, to lose it as a part of the heavens, to enclose it within a bounded frame. It is to reduce both its sense of distance and its relations to the surrounding stars and earth. And, as with all lenses, it is to decrease its focal plane to that of a certain kind of surface.

Naturally, we can be aware of that "trade off," as we now call it. But equally, we can become reductive utopians and forget that for every gain there is a simultaneous and necessary loss. In short, we are frequently *inclined* to follow that which fascinates and forget or at least allow to be recessive what is lost. If I may be so bold as to make a generalization, I think that at least one reason why today's most prestigious fields of scientific research are in the realm of the microworld is precisely this technological inclination. Particle physics (with its enormous atom-smashing tools), micro-biology with gene splicing and DNA-RNA research, and even psychology with its new time-lapse tools, are following the latent trajectory of high-technology instruments.

But technology does not have its own momentum. It is created and embodied only within a human community. But possible trajectories are suggested and some of these are frightening. Here the obvious example is weapons development. The first human who killed with a club amplified his bodily strength with a technology. Later even kinesthetic distance was overcome with spears and the bow, and later still but along the same trajectory the modern aircraft with the Exocet missile which sank Britain's finest advanced destroyer was in the same destiny of extension. To have power, greater power, and power at a distance is also a trajectory which, in the case of nuclear weapons, is a quantitative change which becomes a qualitative change.

Samson, however strong, might slay a thousand Philistines with the mere jawbone of an ass, but even his might is not universal in threat. With nuclear weaponry such threat of extinction is concretely universal in extent. The overkill power to extinguish 20 times rather than 10, while probably economically powerful enough to depress a worldwide economic development, does not raise the plateau of universality an iota. It is a trajectory taken to its total conclusion. I need to enter the tendency of the dystopian here, because in the face of such a trajectory, all of us may become dystopians. Yet I would remind you that the trajectory itself is latent from the beginning. It lies in the escalation of the amplifactory-reductive possibility of technology taken up. It is a burden we have "chosen."

I have now taken two steps in a phenomenology of technology. The first step points to the essential, non-neutral possibility of technology which structurally belongs to any and all technology. I have then pointed out that in our engagements with technologies, trajectories emerge, trajectories which refer back to our own imaginations and desires, but which by extending the amplificatory (and reductive) structure of technology, can actually result in qualitative changes with respect to human destiny. These are both positive and negative, and often they are two sides of the very same technology.

I should like to take only one more step before drawing a conclusion. It lies in a question hinted at before: given essential ambiguity and the possibility for projecting a trajectory, does technology incline nor determine our fate? It is here that we locate the very contemporary dilemma concerning technology, a dilemma which we can neither escape or dare to avoid. Once again I turn to a very simple example: variant technologies of writing.

Print, writing, or language "reduced" to writing is now at the center of much of the European philosophical interest. Speech, the language of the Garden, has become writing, the language of technologically inhabited Earth. For writing is technologically mediated. But my example focuses upon precisely that writing-technology interaction. It is an example which points to the question of inclination versus determination. My variants are three technologies of writing with respect to stylistic results.

I begin with a now-archaic example: writing with a dip pen or quill. In this case my experience of writing is one in which two elements emerge to suggest a trajectory for style. One is the relation between the speed of composition with respect to thought, and the other is the taking shape of the actual letters and sentences on the page. With respect to the speed of thought compared to the writing, I find that the writing is much slower than thought. I can revise a sentence, turn it over, edit mentally, if you will, while actually writing. By the time the sentence is complete, it will hopefully be well turned. Simultaneously, the sensuous form of the lettering can take on its own fascination. The curves and shapes can be well- or ill-formed; handwriting is craft or art in its own right. And perhaps these two elements even reinforce each other, for to write the visually beautiful script is to write even more slowly. And thus perhaps we discover a secret of the style of the belles lettres. The eighteenth century was a time when letter writing flourished (and before it the illuminated manuscript), enhanced in direction by the technology of quill or pen.

Now move to the fast electric typewriter. Here the author may now compose more rapidly, indeed, the accomplished composer can type at a speed which much more closely approximates the speed of verbal thought itself. And with respect to the letters – those are set by the ball in the machine or its keys. Editing now cannot be simultaneous with composition. It becomes a matter of revising, retyping, redoing. My suspicion is that the inclination to style here is more journalistic, more immediate, perhaps more casual.

Then let us develop one step more, the word processor – that is, the electric typewriter hooked to a visual screen which reproduces what is written, only later to be printed from a disc. Speed and shape do not change here, but editing does. In fact, from the labor of the retyping, the word processor makes editing simple. You can remove words, correct them, rearrange sentences, and in fact there is something of a shift in fascination. I have a colleague with a processor who remains fascinated with the project of rearranging (which appears on the screen like a movie in action) after two years. Whether this will result in the better-written book remains to be seen, but it clearly allows the book to virtually grow in all directions at the same time. We may see the return of Germanic tomes through the word processor (and since one can easily move entire footnotes at once, probably more heavily annotated works).

My point is now this – in each case, the different technologies of writing have subtle differences of action and differences of focus with which the writer is engaged, and thus a difference of inclination concerning which style emerges easily from the differently used instruments. *But* this inclination is not in itself a determination. Not only may the writer choose his instrument, but he can go counter to the latent inclination. Verbally one could write belles lettres with the word processor, but the process of composition and way of attaining this style would be different, and vice versa with respect to scholarly or journalistic styles.

However, to counter the latent inclination is also to move against the center of gravity, the point of ease which the machine most clearly allows. A kind of effort must be employed or discipline or habit. Thus when a type of instrument becomes common and widely employed, and when one considers vast numbers of users, it becomes less and less likely that overall or generally this resistance of direction will be more than the exception. At the social level inclination more closely approximates determination. Thus the border between inclination and determination is itself ambiguous. But the technology itself – and we must resist reification – does not determine although if used it may incline. It is here that we reach that fearful and yet challenging dilemma of the twentieth century.

The phenomenology of technology shows that our use of and choice of technology is fundamentally ambiguous. The very non-neutral structure of human-technology use is based upon the amplificatory-reductive aspects of artifact mediation. Yet, once chosen, there also emerge trajectories with latent inclinations, themselves ambiguous, but with more definable results and pathways. These pose both the promise and the threat of the twentieth century and the dilemma of technology which we simply cannot avoid.

There is no Eden, and by implication there can be no Paradise, because to be a historical, embodied human, is to be immersed in the essential ambiguity which we have seen to be an invariant feature of our engagement with technology. We are tied to our own fate and responsibility. We cannot reverse ourselves to a pre-technological culture since we have already too heavily populated the Earth beyond the Garden. And, indeed, by following the trajectories we have invented (and unleashed) in our technologies, we have also changed the face of the Earth itself. These changes are far from trivial, and the roadways, lights, and even changes in the balance of Nature which can be seen while traveling the Earth are real effects upon the global situation. There is a sense in which the Earth, now dominated by culture as it were, while dependent upon Nature, also contains Nature within its bounds.

In short, at the end of this meditation, we discover what the funny little cartoon character, an opossum named Pogo, claimed: "We have met the enemy, and he is us." And we have to add, "He is us with a big stick." The dilemma of technology is the dilemma of contemporary humanity. If we cannot come to grips with ourselves – not individually, but individually and socially and politically – we *will* find ourselves in the Frankensteinian fate. Not because Frankenstein has come to life, but because we have failed to see that it is we who are still pushing the buttons which give him the semblance of life. The same applies to the debate about the relationship between science and technology. Insofar as modern science is necessarily technological science in its very use of instruments, it cannot avoid the question of ontological non-neutrality. The Earth has been delivered to our care and we do not now dare avoid facing the critical ambiguity which belongs essentially to our situation.

PIAGET AND FREUD: TWO APPROACHES TO THE UNCONSCIOUS*

WOLFE MAYS (Manchester)

INTRODUCTION

Piaget is usually said to be primarily interested in the study of cognitive structures, and in showing how they influence the child's thinking at the various stages of its intellectual development. His theoretical position has therefore been described as a form of "structuralism," a view to which his own statements on this question in his later work have given some credence. Because of this his developmental studies have been regarded as radically opposed to the work of Freud who, among other things, emphasizes the way our conscious thought results from unconscious instinctual desires and feelings.

One must not, however, overlook that Piaget, at least in his younger days showed an active interest in psychoanalysis. His mother's mental ill-health made him, he says, intensely interested from the beginning of his studies in questions of psychoanalysis, and this helped him to achieve independence and widen his cultural background although he never felt any desire to involve himself deeper in this field, since he much preferred the study of normalcy and the workings of the intellect to that of the unconscious.

We know, for example, that Piaget studied Freud's writings, read the journal *Imago*, and that when he was in Zurich in 1919 he listened to Jung's lectures and was acquainted with Bleuler's work. Shakow and Rapoport throw some light on Piaget's early interest in psychoanalysis. Piaget, they tell us, was during the beginning of his crucial studies under the influence of Claparède, who was one of the out-of-town members of the Freud group formed in Zurich in 1907. In his early studies, they go on, Piaget shows the existence in children of those mechanisms of

* This is a shortened version of the Piaget Memorial Lecture, 1981, given at the Manchester Polytechnic and published by the Institute of Advanced Studies, Manchester Polytechnic, 1982, copyright Wolfe Mays.

Cho, K.K. (ed.) Philosophy and Science in Phenomenological Perspective.

ISBN 978-94-009-6115-9

motivated thought which Freud had inferred from the study of dreams, parapraxes, and neuroses of adults. Piaget continued to publish studies of this kind until the middle of the 1930s.[1]

Piaget states that when he first came to Geneva in 1921, he underwent a teaching psychoanalysis with a women who had herself been psychoanalyzed by Freud, and who had been sent to Geneva by the Société Internationale de Psychanalyse to disseminate its doctrines. This analysis occurred, he says, every morning at eight o'clock for eight months. Piaget has told us why he stopped being analyzed, although he would have liked to have continued.

"Everything I saw in it was interesting. It was marvellous to discover all one's complexes. But my psychoanalyst learned that I was impervious to the theory and that she'd never convince me. She told me that it wasn't worth while to continue."[2] "She's the one who stopped ... She felt that it wasn't worth wasting an hour a day on a man who couldn't accept the theory."[3] To the question put to him by an interviewer, "Essentially you were resisting it then?" Piaget replied, "Yes, but theoretically, not at all in the application of the analysis."[4]

What emerges from this little story is that after eight months of daily analysis, there was a resistance on Piaget's part not to the facts disclosed by the analysis, i.e., his own emotional life, but to psychoanalytical theory which the analyst used to explain these facts. One wonders, however, why this break occurred just then and not, say, earlier on. Piaget does not explore the alternative explanation, that negative transference – where a hostile reaction masks one of affection – may have occurred. This often happens when the analysis has continued over a period of time.

If this was the case, three possibilities arise: (1) the women analyst may have developed transference feelings towards Piaget and therefore broke off the analysis; (2) Piaget's theoretical resistance may itself have been a rationalization of his transference feelings towards her; or (3) the transference could have been mutual. One cannot, of course, entirely rule out the fact that there may have been a genuine difference of opinion.

Further, it is clear that Piaget's connection with the psychoanalytic movement must have continued for some time after this incident. Writing in 1956, he remarks that he had been honoured by being ex-

1. David Shakow and David Rapoport, *The Influence of Freud on American Psychology, Psychological Issues* 4, no. 1, monograph 13 (International Universities Press, 1964), pp. 121-22; 122, note 25.

2. Jean-Claude Bringeur, *Conversations with Jean Piaget*, transl. Basai Miller Gulati (Chicago: University of Chicago Press, 1980), p. 123.

3. Ibid.

4. Ibid.

pelled from the Société Internationale de Psychanalyse, presumably for nonconformity, some twenty years earlier, i.e., in the mid-thirties, just about the time when his interests seem to have changed.[5] He must therefore have been a member of the society for nearly fifteen years before his expulsion. He tells us that he had become a member when the society was in rather bad odour with the world of official psychology, implying no doubt that by the time he was expelled it had attained a measure of respectability. Despite the abortive psychoanalysis, it would appear from this that Piaget was successfully recruited as a member of the society.

In any case it is difficult to see how he could ever have been an orthodox Freudian. Before going to work in Geneva with Claparède, he had not only been influenced by the Bleuler school at Zurich, but also by Pierre Janet's teaching at the Collège de France. Of Janet's lectures there it has been said that they "were mostly attended by foreign visitors, by nonspecialists, and by very few students."[6] Piaget therefore would seem to have been among the few. It is from Janet that he seems to have derived his knowledge of what he terms the Royce-Baldwin law. This law, which has its roots in certain Hegelian doctrines (both Royce and Baldwin where Hegelians), states that self-consciousness and consciousness of the other are essentially social products. He also seems to have acquired from Janet the notion that behavioural schemes of action are to be regarded as equilibrium systems. And he refers to Janet as "My Professor."

We have Piaget's own statement (*The Language and Thought of the Child*, pp. xx-xxi), "M. Janet, whose influence will often be traced in these pages, familiarised me with a psychology of conduct which offers a happy combination of genetic methods and clinical analyses. I have also been deeply influenced by the social psychology of M.C. Blondel and Professor J.M. Baldwin. It will likewise be apparent how much I owe to psychoanalysis which in my opinion has revolutionised the psychology of primitive thoughts."[7] In the index of this book, Janet's name is listed ten times, whilst Baldwin's and Freud's appear only four times.

As Piaget admits, there are definite Freudian influences at work in his early studies, and these further show themselves in the Sorbonne

5. Cf. L. Apostel, W. Mays, A. Morf and J. Piaget, *Les liasons analytiques et synthétiques dans les comportements du sujet* (Presses Universitaires de France, 1957), p. 135, note 1.

6. Henri F. Ellenberger, *The Discovery of the Unconscious: The History and Evolution of Dynamic Psychiatry* (New York: Basic Books, 1970), p. 343.

7. Jean Piaget, *The Language and Thought of the Child*, 3d ed. (London: Routledge and Kegan Paul, 1959), pp. xx-xxi.

lectures of 1954[8] and in his later books *La prise de conscience*[9] and *Réussir et comprendre.*[10] In these two works he accepts the basic mechanisms of the unconscious and a doctrine of repression, and postulates a cognitive as well as an affective unconscious. These experimental studies are largely concerned with the behaviour of subjects when they are asked to solve simple problems of a practical kind, their aim being to show how our thought functions on an unconscious level when we perform such tasks.

Piaget believes that the questions raised by such unconscious cognitive functioning are paralleled by those which psychoanalysis raised in its studies of the affective unconscious. He has told us elsewhere, "I am persuaded that there will come a day when a psychology of cognitive functions and psychoanalysis will be fused in a general theory which by correcting each will improve one another."[11] But Piaget's psychology of cognitive functions and especially his views on the cognitive unconscious undoubtedly show the influence of his earliest psychoanalytical interests. One wonders therefore whether the general theory he has in mind will do more than reaffirm the parallelism he asserts between the cognitive and affective unconscious.

Although Piaget considers the facts of our affective life uncovered by Freud to be indisputable, he finds himself disagreeing with his general psychology.[12] This disagreement concerns such questions as: (1) the precise relation between the conscious and the unconscious – there is for Piaget no sharp boundary between them; (2) Freud's account of memory, which assumes that our memories remain stored unchanged through time in the unconscious; and (3) Freud's passive conception of consciousness as simply receiving the products of the unconscious and impressions from outer reality.[13]

What is needed, Piaget says, is a "genetic transposition of the Freudian doctrine through the elimination of those elements which make it too much a science of the permanent."[14] This criticism is directed not only to Freud's view of the unchanging nature of our memories, but also to the assumption that the child is thrust, as it were, into the world

8. Piaget, *Les relations entre l'affectivité et l'intelligence dans le développement mental de l'enfant*, "Les cours de Sorbonne," (Centre de Documentation Universitaire, 1954), hereafter referred to as AI.

9. Piaget, *La prise de conscience* (Presses Universitaires de France, 1974).

10. Piaget, *Réussir et comprendre* (Presses Universitaires de France, 1974).

11. Piaget, "Inconscient affectif et inconscient cognitif," *Problèmes de psychologie génétique* (Paris: Denoel/Gontheir, 1972), p. 36.

12. Piaget, *Play, Dream and Imitation in Childhood*, transl. G. Gattengo and F.M. Hodgson (London: Routledge, 1962), p. 184, hereafter referred to as PDI.

13. PDI, p. 185.

14. PDI, p. 186.

provided with a ready-made ego, and is immediately aware of objects and persons in much the same sort of way that adults are.

THE CHILD'S AFFECTIVE BEHAVIOUR

In his account of the development of affective behaviour Piaget emphasizes that it is closely bound up with the child's progressive socialization. From birth onwards, he tells us, the child enters into social relations with others and generally imitates his parents and particularly his mother. On the other hand, on Freud's view, Piaget points out, in such exchanges with others, we are simply concerned with an innate instinct such as the *Sexualtriebe* (libido), which during social intercourse becomes directed to other persons without its nature being radically changed.[15]

In order to evaluate Freud's account of emotional development, Piaget considers the earliest emotional attachment which the child forms, namely, that toward its mother. He notes that although the child responds to instinctive impulses, there is a considerable difference in its emotional behaviour according to the age at which it is expressed; it is very different in a child of three weeks, two months, or two years. Freud, Piaget points out, tries to explain this variation by saying that during the child's development the libido, for example, changes its objective, and in this way gives rise to the different stages in the child's emotional life.[16]

Freud has described three such stages; (1) where the libido is directed solely to the child's own body, which he divides into the anal and oral stages; (2) that of primary narcissism where it is directed to the body itself in general, as opposed to the later stages which occur between two-three years where it is directed upon the self; and (3) where the libido (or emotion) is transferred onto external objectives – to other persons and especially the person of the mother.[17] In this stage, according to Freud, various conflicts occur and specific complexes such as that of the Oedipus complex (the desire to possess one's mother and to kill one's father) are established. During these later displacements of the libido, the earlier stages become repressed but remain stored in the unconscious. They can, however, reappear in the case of regression to a more infantile stage in the adult, especially during neurotic and psychotic disturbances.

Piaget is clearly aware that Freud was a pioneer in recognizing that

15. AI, cf. pp. 33-4.
16. AI, p. 34.
17. Ibid.

the emotional life of the child passes through such well-defined stages. Nevertheless, he contends that Freud's views have much less of a genetic character than they are usually taken to have. For example, Freud tends to ascribe to the baby at the breast before the development of language, aptitudes characteristic of a much later stage; namely, that it possesses self-consciousness, has our kind of memory and other intellectual functions.[18] He further assumes, Piaget continues, that the young child initially perceives objects in much the same way as we do: that he lives in a spatialized universe peopled by substantial objects and by persons who have an emotional life of their own.[19]

Freud's position, which is a straightforward form of realism, is markedly different from Piaget's own constructivist approach. Piaget claims, in contrast to Freud, that the child throughout the first months of his existence lives in a universe lacking permanent objects. Even if we accepted Freud's doctrine of cathexis, namely, the transfer of the libido to different objectives, Piaget would still argue that before this could happen, such objects would first need to be constructed. According to him, this occurs through the child's sensory-motor activities as when, for example, he handles objects or puts them into his mouth. Only after the child has in this way arrived at some concept of a world external to himself, does he take it as made up of permanent objects and persons, which continue to exist when he is not perceiving them.[20]

Piaget contends that at the earliest stage of the child's existence, his affective life, has not yet been differentiated into self-consciousness and an awareness of others as persons. On the cognitive level, Piaget finds a close parallel here with what he terms the complete egocentricism of the first year, where the young child does not sharply differentiate between an internal and external world. When at a later stage such differentiation does occur, a radical transformation, he tells us, is produced in the child's outlook upon the world. This involves what Piaget describes as a dual decentration: (1) a cognitive decentration in which there is an elaboration of external space and the objects and persons located therein, so that the child becomes aware of an objective physical world; and (2) an affective decentration where the child no longer regards his feelings of pleasure and pain as a function of his own actions.[21] The social dimension begins to play an important role here; the child now takes other persons, particularly his parents, as the cause of actions which produce pleasurable or unpleasurable feelings. And these will lead, Piaget says, to the development of sympathies and antipathies

18. PDI, p. 185.
19. AI, p. 35.
20. AI, pp. 35-6.
21. AI, p. 36.

from which the moral sentiments will eventually arise. There is therefore, he argues, a close parallelism between cognitive and affective development – something he claims Freud ignores.[22]

Hans W. Loewald[23] has also criticized the Freudian concept of *cathexis* for assuming, as he puts it, a ready-made external world and a ready-made psychic apparatus to which some instinctual charge is applied. But he notes that Freud in some of his later writings (e.g., *Civilization and Its Discontents*), considered that the ego (subject) and external reality (object) differentiate and organize each other, instead of, as it were, being accomplished *ab initio*. He goes on to point out that the implications for the concept of *cathexis* were, however, not fully spelt out. But, unlike Piaget, Loewald does not specify further what this organizing activity consists of.

REACTION SCHEMES

Piaget is then critical of Freud's view that the child's emotional development results from *cathexis* – the transference of the libido onto different objects and persons. According to him, the basic determinants of our behaviour are what he terms "reaction schemes." These are essentially dispositions to behave in certain ways, and result from the way the individual interacts with his social and physical environments. He defines such a scheme as a *mode de reactions* reproducible on a new occasion and applicable (i.e., generalizable) to a whole range of such situations.[24] It has, he tells us, a greater flexibility than an instinct (or indeed a Kantian category) and also becomes related (by a process of assimilation) to other schemes to form hierarchical systems.

Piaget distinguishes two kinds of reaction schemes: (1) cognitive (intellectual) schemes, where the child's actions are directed toward objects (i.e., sensory-motor schemes); for example, when he attempts to balance objects or draw them closer to himself; and (2) affective (emotional) schemes, which are directed to other persons and which thereby introduce the social factor as a determinant of behaviour.[25] An individual will react, Piaget points out, to analogous situations according to his specific personality or character, and he defines a person's character as a set of affective reaction schemes[26] – the set of roles

22. AI, p. 38.
23. Hans W. Loewald, "Primary Process, Secondary Process and Language," in *Psychoanalysis and Language*, ed. Joseph H. Smith (New Haven and London: Yale University Press, 1978), p. 256.
24. AI, p. 95.
25. Ibid.
26. AI, p. 94.

that the individual plays in society. A reaction scheme then has, as it were, a certain duality about it. When we act on objects and persons, they in turn react back on us and modify our own actions. In essence then, Piaget is putting forward what in sociological theory is called a transactional (or social exchange) theory of behaviour.

To illustrate the way in which affective schemes manifest themselves in our conduct, Piaget cites the modes of reaction acquired by the child toward his parents. The child, he tells us, comes to react to a range of family situations in which reaction to authority and affection play an important part. And these modes of reacting he tells us, are readily transferable to new persons and social situations. In this way the politics of the family are, as it were, played out on a larger scale.[27] Affective (or emotional) reaction schemes then seem to play the same role on Piaget's account as do unconscious desires and complexes on Freud's.

On the Freudian view, Piaget goes on, it is assumed that these early feelings which the child has to his parents, as manifested, for example, in the Oedipus complex, influence him throughout his life. At a later date, he may behave in ways which are only explicable by reference to the early family constellation. Thus a man may throughout his whole life have loved only one woman, namely, his mother, whom he looks for under diverse forms of *imago.*[28] The libido can also be displaced onto ideal persons, as in the child's imaginative play. Sublimation may occur as in the case of intellectual creation; for example, in Schiller's poetry the theme of the battle against the tyrants reflects the revolt against the father.[29]

But, Piaget points out, when a particular feeling, such as affection for a parent, is transferred to some other person, its whole character may also be altered. It does not remain unchanged, as Freud assumes, in the unconscious. Thus even though the types of feeling a child may have to his father, who may be understanding, dominant, or cruel, may cause him in later life to react to others in a similar sort of way, his mode of reacting to them may also change. Similarly, though the love a child may have to his mother may make him love other women in the same kind of way, yet the content of this feeling may become modified when directed to a new person. One learns, sometimes speedily and sometimes tardily, not to expect to be treated by one's wife as one was by one's mother.

Piaget gives a number of examples[30] to show how the apparent con-

27. AI, p. 92.
28. Ibid.
29. AI, pp. 92-3.
30. AI, p. 93.

tinuity of feeling which an individual exhibits in similar circumstances may occur without our having recourse to the Freudian assumption that such feelings are permanently stored in the unconscious. One such example given by him is that of affection or love. Love itself, Piaget tells us, as great as it may be, is not always of the same intensity. One can have a very intense feeling, then an intermittance, and then it may reappear. The experience of love may also alternate with that of hate.[31] Piaget takes this as further evidence that such feelings do not necessarily persist in the unconscious between their respective manifestations.

Another example given by Piaget concerns the reactions of a young boy on his first day at school. He points out that, if the boy has rebelled against his father's authority, he may show the same attitude towards his teacher.[32] But this, he says, is not due to the boy unconsciously identifying him with the *imago* of his father. What has happened is rather that he has acquired a mode of feeling (or a reaction scheme) which he generalizes so that it is applicable to these later analogous situations.

The part played by parental authority in the early family situation in influencing our later life is, in Freud's more mature writings, assumed to be a function of the superego. This is said to arise as a result of children interiorizing the orders of their parents under the form of felt obligations. For Piaget, however, the superego is rather to be considered as a particularly simple example of an affective-reaction scheme, one arising from the continuous assimilation of our present situation to earlier family ones. Thus, he points out, the individual who has a strong superego imposes upon himself duties which are a function of the real duties he formerly gave his parents. In other words, he may be said to have a well-developed moral sense or conscience.[33]

THE UNCONSCIOUS

Although Piaget freely admits that he owes much to Freud's discoveries relating to the facts of our emotional life, he is, as we have seen, critical of the Freudian unconscious conceived as the storehouse, as it were, of our instinctive desires. Piaget's refusal to accept this concept in its undiluted Freudian form probably stems from his original philosophical training, which was largely in the Cartesian tradition current in the French-speaking universities of his day. This identified mental processes

31. AI, p. 94.
32. PDI, p. 189.
33. AI, p. 98.

with conscious awareness and knowledge with clear and distinct ideas. Descartes, who not only was a philosopher but also a mathematician, tended to take as his model for knowledge logical and mathematical ideas, much as Plato did. But as Piaget's early interest in the philosophy of Bergson shows, he also believed that our mental activities had a creative aspect about them. It is this other strand in Piaget's thought which no doubt made him sympathetic to Freud's findings concerning our emotional life.

Jean-Paul Sartre, who was brought up in a similar Cartesian tradition, talks of his intellectual shock when he first encountered the Freudian conception of the unconscious mind. It was completely alien to all he had previously learned as a philosophy student about mental life. He was therefore initially critical of psychoanalysis. Although he later came to accept its findings, he nevertheless interpreted them in terms of his own theory of existential psychoanalysis. In this theory he identifies the unconscious with prereflective experience, namely, with our actions upon the world before we have come to reflect upon them. Interestingly enough, in *Being and Nothingness* Sartre quotes Piaget's observations of the way children number successfully on a concrete level without knowing how they arrive at their results, as an example of prereflective experience.

Some of Piaget's objections to the Freudian unconscious can be traced to this initial Cartesian bias. For example, the reason he gave for the termination of his own analysis, even if it was a rationalization of the true facts of the situation, was his inability to accept Freud's theoretical position. Among other things, Piaget objects to the view that there exist actual feelings and complexes lurking, as it were, in the murky depths of the unconscious. These, Freud assumes, are the cause of the parapraxes of everyday life – slips of the tongue and other maladroit behaviour – of our dream life and psychopathological symptoms. And insofar as Freud takes the unconscious as being the primary reality from which conscious phenomena emerge, Piaget would say that Freud makes it into a real existant or thing, rather than taking it, as he would himself, as a set of potential dispositions.

If we look more closely at Piaget's theory of reaction schemes, we shall see reflected in it another aspect of Descartes' thought. Descartes, who was concerned with the universal character of logical and mathematical truths, believed that they were not present to our minds at birth, since he identified all knowledge with conscious awareness. Young children were obviously not immediately cognizant of the truths of logic and mathematics, and had to undergo suitable instruction before being able to understand them.

To deal with this problem, Descartes formulated his theory of innate ideas which were present at birth, and in which logical and mathematical truths occur in a latent form. As a result of suitable home and school environments, we were enabled to become aware of them at a later date in the form of clear and distinct ideas. These innate ideas might be compared to certain inborn tendencies to contract such diseases as tuberculosis, which only developed when the appropriate circumstances occur, for example, malnutrition, lack of sunlight, etc.

Piaget's reaction schemes bear some resemblance to Cartesian dispositions, although they have initially a more rudimentary and dynamic character. Their function is to explain why certain persistent ways of categorizing and feeling are manifested in our dealings with others and the public world of things. Piaget's position differs from that of Descartes, since he gives as much importance, at least theoretically, to our emotional life as he does to the cognitive realm. Descartes, however, regarded the emotions rather as a disturbing or distorting influence on our intellect; and his account of the mind is not only largely cognitive, but also egoistic, in the sense that he believes we are confined within the boundaries of our own self. To allay his doubts about his own existence and that of an external world, he had in his *cogito ergo sum* to posit the existence of the "I" as a doubting, thinking being. Piaget, for his part, emphasizes the social dimension – the role played by other persons in giving rise to self-consciousness (or *prise de conscience*): the self for him is essentially a social self.

Freud's conception of the unconscious may be traced back to an entirely different philosophical tradition mainly developed by such German thinkers as Leibniz, von Hartmann, and Schopenhauer, among others. They accepted the phenomenon of an unconscious mind which could desire, feel, and think and which was for Schopenhauer the source of the will-to-power. This approach to mental processes probably arose as a reaction to the philosophical views of Descartes and John Locke and their assumption that mental phenomena always involved conscious awareness – in the shape of clear and distinct ideas. As against the Leibnizian unconscious, Locke and his disciples had argued that every drowsy nod refuted this conception. Freud's postulation of an unconscious closely follows the former, more Romantic tradition.[34] He believes that psychical processes such as instinctive desire – for example, the sex drive – as well as remembering and thinking, are unconscious and not accessible to direct conscious perception. On the other hand, the perception of external phenomena and the experience of internal feelings such as pleasure and pain are directly conscious and so are the products of memory and thought.

The unconscious for Freud then consists of two parts:[35]

34. Cf. L.L. White, *The Unconscious Before Freud* (Tavistock, 1960).
35. *The Influence of Freud on American Psychiatry*, pp. 99-100.

1. The unrepressed unconscious: our original instincts and desires, from which under the pressure of external events most mental activity starts;

2. The dynamic or repressed unconscious: the ideational representations of our instinctive desires – ideas and feelings which have been found unacceptable and repressed. An example of the latter would be the Oedipus complex. Such repressed material can normally only enter consciousness if it first undergoes distortion by our mental defense mechanisms, one of the most important of these being the censor. Freud pictured the censor after the manner of a Central European police censor, monitoring all ideas welling up from the unconscious and preventing socially undesirable ones from entering consciousness.

The operation of these defense mechanisms is particularly to be seen in the case of the dream, which takes on a symbolic disguise so that the real mechanism is hidden from the dreamer.[36] On Freud's view unconscious symbolic thought, of which the dream symbolism is the example par excellence, is by its structure and function at variance with rational thought. It must therefore be differentiated from conscious signs, such as the words of our language, whose meaning is clear to us and which can be communicated to others. Unconscious symbolic thought, on the other hand, mainly occurs in dreams and daydreams and obeys the pleasure principle. It is through such symbolic disguises that our instinctive desires manifest themselves. In the case of dreams, which Freud considers to be wish-fulfillments, the real content of the dream (i.e., its latent content) is censored. It is distorted and transposed into symbolic form (i.e., its manifest content), which then becomes a symbolic representation of the repressed desires. Such distortion and transposition may also occur in our everyday conscious transactions with others.[37]

Although Piaget agrees with much of what Freud has to say about unconscious symbolism and the distorting character of the dream work, he thinks it unnecessary to postulate, as Freud does, the existence of the censor, which, as it were, prevents antisocial tendencies from entering consciousness, only allowing through suitably disguised ideas and feelings. The hidden (or latent) content of the dream can, Piaget believes, more readily be explained as due to the dreamer being unaware of all the tendencies which gave rise to the dream.[38]

Each symbol, Piaget tells us, may have in addition to its immediately apprehended meanings more remote meanings. He compares this to the way in which in conscious thought an idea may contain a set of implica-

36. PDI, p. 183.
37. PDI, pp. 183-84.
38. PDI, p. 191.

tions of which we may be partly or totally unaware.[39] In either case, whether we deal with an unconscious symbol or verbal sign, we are, he believes, unjustified in assuming that our ignorance of the range of meanings is due to the work of a censor.

Despite this caveat, Piaget admits that the unconscious dream symbolism will have undergone distortion and transposition, so preventing us from grasping its full implications. For Freud, this results from the process of condensation and displacement.[40] Piaget himself compares these processes with the cognitive processes of generalization and abstraction. He considers condensation (where a specific symbol may stand for a whole range of objects of a certain sort – say, a cat for the "class of females") to be a form of generalization, since it expresses through a common scheme (or class) a host of affective schemes involving real relationships to other persons.[41] In the dream, however, the scheme manifests itself through concrete (visual) images, rather than, as may be the case, in waking life in action.

For Freud, displacement (as when, for example, in the dream, elongated objects, such as walking sticks, pens, and pencils, take the place of the male member) also results from the operation of the censor. But once again Piaget contends that the hypothesis of a censor is unnecessary, as by its very nature the process of condensation always involves displacement – the meaning being displaced from the emotionally charged object to one not so charged.[42]

As an example of the operation of the mechanism of displacement which enables us to entertain dangerous thoughts in a disguised form, I may refer to an occasion at a certain university, when an eminent professor of French was addressing a staff meeting and criticizing what he thought to be the apparent unwillingness of the then vice-chancellor (who was somewhat short in stature) to institute reforms in the university. Without actually mentioning him, he quoted an old Chinese proverb: "When small figures begin to cast long shadows, the sun is setting."

Piaget claims that the connection between condensation and displacement, which is a feature of unconscious symbolism, is paralleled in conscious thought by the way in which all generalization involves abstraction. We cannot, he says, combine in a single image features borrowed from several objects without displacing the affective (emotional) stress.[43] Thus, for example, the schematic pictures used to illustrate social statistics, usually lack the robustness of the real objects they are

39. PDI, p. 172.
40. PDI, p. 210.
41. Ibid.
42. PDI, p. 192.
43. Ibid.

taken to represent. But despite Piaget's rejection of a censor, he does assume that condensation and displacement involve mental processes (albeit of an unconscious nature), just as generalization and abstraction do on a conscious level.

REPRESSION

Piaget, who, as we have seen, is highly critical of the Freudian censor, formulates his main objection to it as follows: How, he asks, can consciousness be the cause of ignorance, i.e., of unconsciousness, especially as a difficult repression requires the collaboration of consciousness for its completion? We may, he says, frequently wish to remain unaware of what we dislike, but there is no question of our being duped. "When, for instance we are tempted, and up to the last moment 'shut our eyes' to the nature of the tendency to which we finally yield, we are, nevertheless, really aware of what the outcome will be and consciousness is an accessory from the start."[44] It is interesting to note that Sartre objects in somewhat similar terms (no doubt reflecting their common Cartesian ancestry) to Freud's postulation of the censor, classifying it as a form of bad-faith or self-deception.

Conscious repression would then seem also for Piaget to be a form of self-deception, in which we choose, as it were, to turn a blind eye to unpleasant facts. We deliberately put out of mind certain tendencies which for one reason or another we find unacceptable and do not wish to face. Repression and volition can, for Piaget, be therefore regarded as two sides of the same coin. To explicate this relationship more fully, we need to look at the way Piaget considers volitional activity to occur in our everyday life. Such activity would seem at least to form the model for his concept of conscious repression.

Piaget gives the following example. I may, he says, be in my study writing a paper which I have promised to complete in a few days. I am attracted outside by the fine spring sunshine, and a friend invites me to go on a mountain outing with him. In order to resist this temptation I recall my past promise and anticipate my ambarrassment if the paper is not ready in time. As soon as I do this, he goes on, the momentarily strong tendency becomes weaker and is subordinated to values and feelings which have now become important for me.[45] Piaget therefore considers volitional activity to be of an affective rather than of an intellectual order, in contrast, for example, to the position of someone like Spinoza, who accepts the latter view.

44. PDI, p. 191.
45. AI, pp. 129-30.

Piaget's account of unconscious repression would therefore seem to be modelled on that of conscious repression. He defines it as "the blocking of inhibition for a tendency incompatible with others stronger than itself, because they are organized in stable assimilatory schemas."[46] If a tendency or an affective scheme conflicts with an already existing well-organized system of tendencies, it becomes, he says, impossible to assimilate it to the latter. It is therefore excluded from entering consciousness.[47] Thus, while socially acceptable tendencies will remain on a conscious level, antisocial ones will be rejected or repressed.

As an example of repression, Freud cited the case of a man who had apparently lost a book given to him by his estranged wife, and who had forgotten where it was until he and his wife had been reconciled again. Piaget would no doubt explain these facts by saying that a whole range of affective schemes involving the man's wife (including the possession of the book) had been blocked out by the man's negative attitudes toward her. When reconciliation occurred, the repressed, more-positive attitudes reappeared and with it the memory of the lost book.[48]

Piaget regards repression (and hence exclusion from consciousness of an affective tendency) as an essential factor in the organization of our personality.[49] Life would be intolerable, if we were unable to prevent unpleasant thoughts and feelings from entering consciousness at will. They are hence through repression relegated to a lower level in the hierarchy of tendencies making up the character of the person. But Piaget does not believe that this process of exclusion is unique to our emotional life. He proceeds to compare this process with that of the elimination of incompatible beliefs in the intellectual field, where we may reject propositions which conflict with some well-established system of beliefs, for example, the rejection of the Copernican theory by the church in the seventeenth century. This rejection, for Piaget, would seem to occur not only on a conscious level but also on an unconscious one. Indeed, he argues that a good deal of our day-to-day thinking occurs on such a level.

But this does not mean, Piaget points out, that we ought to try to explain every case, where we are unaware of the rationale underlying

46. PDI, p. 204 nl.

47. PDI, p. 209. In his later writings the function originally assigned by Freud to the censor is taken over by the superego. From this point of view the differences between Piaget and Freud as to the nature of repression are considerably reduced, since for Piaget the superego is itself a reaction scheme.

48. Sigmund Freud, *Introductory Lectures on Psychoanalysis* (London: Allen and Unwin, 1932), p. 32.

49. PDI, p. 209.

our own thinking, as being due to an intellectual censorship.[50] Similarly, he argues, we do not need to postulate the existence of a censor to explain why we fail to understand the hidden mechanisms (complexes, etc.), underlying our affective behaviour.

Piaget does not therefore believe that there is anything unique about affective repression. We can, he asserts, find plenty of analogies in the intellectual (cognitive) sphere. He gives the example of a child, or even sometimes a scientist, who holds strongly to a concept or system of ideas and will unconsciously repress any notion which conflicts with it. He may indeed, says Piaget, exert much effort to find reasons for this incompatibility, because he is only conscious of the results of the intellectual schemes he uses, and be unaware of his real reasons for rejecting a conflicting hypothesis.[51]

Piaget is fond of quoting Binet's remark that "thought is an unconscious process of the mind."[52] In keeping with this, Piaget contends that a very great part of our cognitive activities remains unconscious when our actions achieve their goal, or are successful. As a rule, he says, we only become conscious of the way we arrived at this result, well after the successful action has been performed. He is here, Piaget claims, in agreement with Claparède's *loi de prise de conscience*, which states: "The earlier and longer a relation has been in use, the later it is consciously perceived, consciousness only intervenes when action is obstructed."[53] In other words, consciousness only arises when our activities are prevented from achieving their particular objectives. Piaget's two books *La prise de conscience* and *Réussir et comprendre* are concerned precisely with explicating the phenomena described by Claparède's law.

A good deal of thinking and problem-solving, then, occurs for Piaget on an unconscious level, during which established schemes are reconstructed so that new systems emerge. And this process of reconstruction involves something like unconscious thought. As he puts it, "When in the field of reflective and even scientific thought a new problem is approached by way of uncritical transposition of habits of mind and ideas used in other fields, the assimilation is largely unconscious."[54] He notes that, for example, in Aristotelian physics, there is an unconscious assimilation of the physical facts of force to schemes of bodily origin – with our exertion of effort when we push against objects.[55]

For Piaget, creative thought in particular has unconscious roots; the

50. PDI, p. 208.
51. Ibid.
52. PDI, p. 172 nl.
53. "Edouard Claparède," *History of Psychology in Autobiography*, vol. 1, ed. Carl Murchison (Clark University Press, 1930), p. 80.
54. PDI, p. 208.
55. PDI, p. 172.

underlying preparation of original ideas is unconscious and hence unknown to us. Arthur Koestler, starting from similar psychoanalytical presuppositions, has referred to these unconscious thought processes as "games of the underground." They are, he says, "less rigid, more tolerant, ready to combine seeingly incompatible ideas, and to perceive hidden analogies between cabbages and kings."[56]

The distinction Piaget draws between conscious (reflective) thought and unconscious, more creative modes of thinking is already to be found in his account of the development of thought and language in his earlier work, *The Language and Thought of the Child*. In his introduction to this book, Claparède noted that child-thought occurred for Piaget on two planes. One, the lower, was the plane of subjectivity, of desires, games, and whims of the *Lustprinzip*, as Freud would say. "The upper plane, on the contrary, is built up little by little by the social environment ... It is the plane of objectivity speech and logical ideas, in a word, the plane of reality."[57]

Piaget's belief that creative thought can occur on an unconscious level would seem to introduce into his account of the human mind, if not an element of incoherence, at least one of dialectical tension. His acceptance of the facts uncovered by Freud of our emotional life fits uncomfortably onto a theoretical framework which, in part at least, gives to our conscious mind the task of the rational organization of experience. The tension would seem implicit in the parallelism he establishes between cognitive and affective schemes, though it is mitigated by his belief that the development of such schemes is dependent on the social context, which may be said to act, as it were, as a *tertium quid*.

RICŒUR'S OBJECTIONS TO THE FREUDIAN UNCONSCIOUS

As an example of the way philosophers, especially those brought up in the Cartesian tradition, have been critical of the Freudian conception of the unconscious, we may quote the work of Paul Ricœur.[58] He has made an extensive examination of Freud's writings and the literature relating to them. Although not unsympathetic to the Freudian position, he is nevertheless critical of some of his major assumptions, especially those concerned with the unconscious mind. Some of Ricœur's criti-

56. Arthur Koestler, *The Ghost in the Machine* (Hutchinson, 1967), p. 181.
57. Edouard Claparède, "Preface" to Jean Piaget, *The Language and Thought of the Child*, p. xii.
58. Paul Ricœur, *Freud and Philosophy: An Essay on Interpretation*, transl. Denis Savage (New Haven and London: Yale University Press, 1970).

cisms resemble Piaget's own, and both seem to stem from the initial acceptance of the Cartesian doctrine of clear and distinct ideas.

Ricœur has listed three main objections to taking the Freudian unconscious as a principle to explain the enigmas of consciousness. These are directed against the following:

1. Its realism, namely, the assumption that mental reality is made up of original drives and complexes of desires according to which the unconscious desires, images and thinks. As against this, Ricœur argues that we cannot directly experience the unconscious; it can only be reconstituted for a third person. Hence it belongs to the same category as the objective constructs of physics, which, though methodologically important, are metaphysically precarious.

2. Its causalism, which is implied in the mechanism of dreams and the neurotic work. Ricœur believes that we should replace this notion by that of the motivation of our desires. However, for Freud, human behaviour, at least in his later work, based as it is on instinctual desire, is always goal-directed. Further, insofar as, for example, in the dream our repressed desires are disguised by the dream-work before they are allowed to enter consciousness, motivation certainly plays some part here. The mechanisms, if they may be called such, of the dream and the neurotic work seem then very different from, say, the causal mechanisms of physics, and have a teleological character about them.

3. Freud's attempt to reduce genetically the psychic superstructure (i.e., consciousness) to the infrastructure (i.e., the unconscious). Ricœur makes the point that in Freud's view, the unconscious becomes the essence of the psyche, consciousness being included in it, much as a smaller circle is included in a larger one. But as we have seen under (1), Ricœur does not believe that the unconscious has the function of cognition and memory which Freud attributes to it. For his part, Ricœur identifies the unconscious with habit and action and argues that habit can only be understood in terms of motivation. On somewhat similar grounds, as we have seen, Sartre has identified our prereflective activities with the Freudian unconscious.

Ricœur, in proceeding to interpret the Freudian unconscious in terms of potentiality or habit, is, he tells us, following the example of Descartes, who conceived innate ideas as tendencies or dispositions ready to be called out on the appropriate occasion. But in identifying the unconscious with habit, Ricœur would himself seem to be postulating a hypothetical third person construct, namely a habit, to explain the contents of consciousness.

The essential difference between Ricœur and Freud arises from Freud's contention that the unconscious is the primary fact from which the conscious mind is derivative. Freud therefore sees no contradiction in an unconscious mind which perceives, has ideas, memories, volitions, and feelings. On the Freudian account, consciousness is that part of the psyche which possesses the additional attribute of consciousness. Ricœur, believing that such mental functions as thinking, remembering, and feeling always involve a measure of self-conscious knowledge, refuses to accept that the unconscious can exhibit such functions.

There are certain similarities between Piaget's and Ricœur's approaches to Freud's theory. This might be expected in view of the similar philosophical tradition in which they were brought up. Ricœur, like Piaget, believes that there is an element of construction involved in memory. They both also assume something like psychic traces, which are reconstructed in present experience. Piaget, too, identifies the unconscious with habit and action, but for him this would seem to apply largely to the early stages of development before the child has been able to internalize his performance in the form of thought-activities. When such internalization does occur, the psychic realm of thought and imagination becomes thereby constituted. As we have seen, during the child's development some of his conceptual and affective schemes are repressed, because they are socially undesirable or for other reasons, but they continue to influence him in the shape of "unconscious" dispositions or tendencies. And despite Piaget's belief that these repressed tendencies are purely potential and are not "complexes of ideas" in the Freudian sense, he accepts unconscious mentation of some sort, especially in the field of creative thought.

HUSSERL, FREGE AND THE OVERCOMING OF PSYCHOLOGISM

J.N. MOHANTY (Oklahoma)

In a letter to Marvin Farber, Husserl wrote, "External 'influences' are without significance ... Really, my course was already marked out by the *Philosophie der Arithmetik*, and I could do nothing other than to proceed further."[1] This self-interpretation on the part of Husserl is contradicted by a familiar account of Husserl's philosophical development. According to this latter account, Husserl began with a "psychologistic" philosophy of arithmetic in particular, but also of logic and epistemology. It was under Frege's influence, especially as a consequence of Frege's sharp 1894 review of his early work on the philosophy of arithmetic, that Husserl rejected his own psychologism, and was led to the conception of a *pure* logic. This widely accepted story has two further sidelights: in the first place, although eventually Husserl came to share Frege's anti-psychologism, unlike Frege he thought he could *logically* refute psychologism while Frege neither refuted psychologism nor thought any such refutation possible without begging the issue. Secondly, in spite of the zealous anti-psychologism of the *Prolegomena*, Husserl had not understood the full force and all the implications of Frege's philosophy of logic, and so, not surprisingly, relapsed into a version of psychologism which he dignified by the name "transcendental phenomenology."

I believe Husserl's own self-interpretation, as formulated in his letter to Marvin Farber, is substantially correct and the other story wide off the mark. Since I have elsewhere argued in detail why I consider that story incorrect,[2] for my present purpose I will only briefly indicate some important considerations in support of my thesis.

1. M. Farber, *The Foundation of Phenomenology*, Cambridge, Mass.: Harvard University Press, 1943, p. 17.

2. J.N. Mohanty, "Husserl and Frege: A New Look at their Relationship," *Research in Phenomenology*, V, 1975; Reprinted in J.N. Mohanty (ed), *Readings on Edmund Husserl's Logical Investigations*, The Hague: M. Nijhoff, 1977, pp. 22-32.

Cho, K.K. (ed.) Philosophy and Science in Phenomenological Perspective.

ISBN 978-94-009-6115-9

1. Is Husserl's *Philosophie der Arithmetik* guilty of psychologism? In responding to this question from our present perspective, it is first of all necessary to decide what Frege meant by 'psychologism' when he accused Husserl of it. Many scholars have, in this context, distinguished between weak and strong psychologism.[3] Weak psychologism is the thesis that the theoretical foundations of logic lie in psychology, so that psychological investigation into actual human thought processes constitutes necessary, but not sufficient conditions for enquiring into the foundations of logic. Strong logical psychologism takes logic to be a branch of psychology, and the laws of logic as descriptive laws of actual thought processes, making assertions about mental events – as a consequence of which psychological enquiry into actual thought processes would constitute both necessary and sufficient conditions for enquiring into the foundations of logic. Now Husserl's *Philosophie der Arithmetik* was guilty *at most* of weak psychologism, but certainly he did not ever espouse psychologism of the strong variety. Even in espousing a sort of weak psychologism, Husserl was not providing a 'foundation' for arithmetic in Frege's sense. He was 'clarifying' the sense of the fundamental concepts of arithmetic, in a rather peculiar sense of the word 'clarification.' The project may be ill-conceived, but the project neither presupposed nor asserted the thesis that numbers themselves were mental entities. The psychologism which Frege ascribed to Husserl is one which makes everything including numbers into "presentations". Not only did Husserl, in the *Philosophie der Arithmetik*, never regard numbers to be presentations; when he was speaking of "presentations," he understood that term in a manner that is very different from Frege's use of it. It is true that Husserl had not as yet been able to separate all the ambiguities in the word "Vorstellung" – a task he understood in the LI, but he never left it unclear even in that early work that numbers themselves are not representations in any sense.[4] Given the fact that one of the central theses of the PA concerns the distinction between symbolic and authentic thinking about numbers, it is unlikely that he could say that numbers were representations – not to speak of the complicating circumstance that he was using "Vorstellung" both in the subjective, Fregean and an objective, Brentanian sense.[5]

2. There is no doubt, however, that Husserl did reject some component of his early position, something that he, in the *Prolegomena*,

3. See esp. M. Sukale, *Comparative Studies in Phenomenology*, The Hague: M. Nijhoff, 1976, esp. ch. 1.

4. For example, in *Philosophie der Arithmetik* (quoted at PA below), Husserl wrote: "... the numbers in themselves, i.e. the actual numbers that are in general inaccessible to us." (p. 260). Also cp. *PA*, p. 223.

5. E. Husserl, *Logical Investigations*, English translation by J.N. Findlay, New York: Humanities Press, 1970, Vol. II, p. 652 ff.

characterized as "psychologistic" when he noted that he has moved beyond his earlier "psychologistic view of the philosophy of mathematics"[6] or when he recalled Goethe's statement to the effect that there is nothing to which one is more severe than the errors that one has just abandoned.[7] It is not as though he now came to see that numbers are not Fregean presentations, for he never had held such a view at any time. What he had now arrived at was a theory of *meaning* which ruled out the project of clarification of sense by going back to psychological *genesis* of that sense. I have shown in an earlier paper that already in 1891, Husserl had arrived at the near-Fregean distinction between *Vorstellung-Sinn*-object, a distinction which assured the objectivity of *sense*, and so made it possible for him to speak of a pure logic of meanings. But does the *Vorstellung-Sinn*-object distinction, by itself, assure an overcoming of psychologism?[8] I think, it does. There is overwhelming evidence in writings upto 1894, that Husserl had arrived at a non-psychological theory of meaning, and that meanings are characterized as 'ideal' already in a manuscript of 1894. The influence of Frege's review in all this must have been negligible.

Quite apart from his newly found objectivistic theory of meaning (at which he had arrived by 1891), Husserl also rejected a conception of logic which he had earlier held: the conception of logic as an "art" or "technology" of correct judging, and as D. Willard and J. Philip Miller have argued, it is this concept of logic and a certain theory of analysis that he held which he refers to by the later self-criticism.[9] In all this, it was not so much Frege's influence that worked on him, as Schröder's and Hilbert's.

What sense, then, are we to make of Husserl's remarks in the LI that he no longer thought his criticisms of Frege in PA to be valid?[10] Or, of his remark to Boyce Gibson that "Frege's criticism was the only one he was really grateful for. It hit the nail on his head"?[11] The former remark does not imply that Husserl now thought all his arguments

6. Ibid., Vol. I, Foreword to the First edition.
7. Ibid, Vol. I, p. 43.
8. Dagfinn Føllesdal asks this question in his response to my "Husserl and Frege," (see note 2 above); Føllesdal, "Husserl's Conversion from Psychologism and the Vorstellung-Meaning Distinction" in Dreyfus, ed. *Husserl, Intentionality, and Cognitive Science*, M.I.T. Press, 1982. For my response, see my *Husserl and Frege*, Indiana University Press, 1982, p. 133.
9. D. Willard, *Studies in Husserl's Early Philosophy* (forthcoming), and J. Philip Miller, *Numbers in Presence and Absence: A Study of Husserl's Philosophy of Mathematics*, The Hague, M. Nijhoff, 1982.
10. *Logical Investigations*, I, p. 179 fn.
11. W.R. Boyce Gibson, "From Husserl to Heidegger: Excerpts from a 1928 Freiburg Diary," ed. H. Spiegelberg, *Journal of the British Society for Phenomenology*, 2, 1971, pp. 58-83.

against Frege's concept of number to be mistaken. He certainly came to see that some of them were untenable. In particular, two of his criticisms would still be acceptable to him. One of these is that Frege's definition of "the number attaching to a concept F" as the extension of the concept "having the same number as the concept F" does not define the *content* of the concept of the number, but only its extension. Frege considers this intensionalism to be a consequence of psychologism. This indeed is strange, for Frege ought to be the last person to regard the meaning or sense (i.e., the content of the concept), which is what the intensionalist wants to define, as a psychological entity. That the extensional definition served all purposes of mathematics does not justify, for Husserl, the claim that a definition need not consider the sense at all. Secondly, Husserl argues that a number attaches, not to a concept as Frege would have it, but to an extension: of a concept, one may predicate the property of having a certain number, only indirectly. This issue then did not concern psychologism at all. Nor does the remark to Boyce Gibson suggest that it was Frege's review that changed his fundamental posture. What the review did in fact achieve was a recognition on Husserl's part of a real need for much greater clarity in his use of the concepts he had used, of concepts such as "act," "presentation," "content," "object."

3. It is also a component of the received account that under the influence of Frege, Husserl abandoned the psychologism of PA. If what I have said is true, the PA was not psychologistic in Frege's sense, and Frege's review had only marginal influence on him. But did, in fact, Husserl radically abandon the thesis of the PA and reject all relevance of psychology for logic and epistemology? This, by no means, appears to be the case. He rejects the thesis that the *concept* of number or even of a totality is derived from reflection on the *acts* of combination. A totality is *given* in an act of collective combination, now he urges, and neither the totality nor the *concept* of totality arises through reflection on such an act. This new thesis is then extended to logical categories, such as being, unity, plurality. He also drastically changes the concept of abstraction which, in the new theory, is not any longer a function of attention. The ambiguous concepts of "presentation" and "content" are sufficiently clarified as not to engender the misunderstandings they had given rise to. But, in the LI, the role of psychology in clarifying the foundations of logic and knowledge is never left in doubt. Only, now he still looks up to a Brentanian descriptive psychology to provide an adequate clarification of the essential concepts of logic and theory of knowledge.

All this shows that the received story is hardly borne out by the evidences at our disposal.

II

With this historical misunderstanding set aside, I now propose to turn to more systematic issues about overcoming psychologism as they were encountered by Frege and Husserl. Although the two men agreed in their opposition to psychologism as a theory of logic, they held different views about the nature of psychology itself, and, more importantly, about the concept of subjectivity.

From his rather scanty statements about psychology it appears that Frege thought of psychology as a *descriptive* science of actual mental processes. The laws of psychology are, for him, like laws of nature: they are universals in the mental realm.[12] Mental processes happen in accordance with these laws. The laws of psychology "give an average, like statements about 'how it is that good digestion occurs in man,' or 'how one speaks grammatically,' or 'how one dresses fashionably.' "[13] No such law has unrestricted authotity and is immune to change with time. There is no reason to believe that Frege wanted to belittle psychology as a science. What he wanted to reject is any intrusion of psychological explanations into the domains of logic and mathematics. I believe he would have agreed with Husserl that in sofar as psychology is a science, it must make use of logical principles, i.e., it must distinguish between what is true and what is simply taken to be true.

Husserl's views about psychology are far more explicit and well-worked out. His anti-psychologism did not hinder the continued growth of his concern with psychology as a science. The critique of psychologism in the *Prolegomena* was a criticism of the claims of *empirical* and *genetic* psychologies to provide the foundations for logic and knowledge. Around 1900-1, he was still thinking of a descriptive psychology, whose descriptions are "disembarrassed of all theoretical psychological interests" as being antecedent to such theories.[14] About 1903, he considers this descriptive psychology to be also eidetic. If a large part of the argument against psychologism makes use of the distinction between sciences of facts and sciences of essences, then *that* argument could not count against the claim of an eidetic psychology to provide clarification of the fundamental concepts of logic and knowledge. There is a third aspect to Husserl's resulting concept of psychology: the foundational psychology is to be descriptive, eidetic and also intentional (all three features, indeed, derive from his Brentanian ancestry).

12. G. Frege, *Der Gedanke* in G. Patzig, ed., *Logische Untersuchungen*, Göttingen, Vandenhoeck & Ruprecht, 1966, p. 30.
13. G. Frege, *Grundgesetze*, English translation by M. Furth, Berkeley, University of California Press, 1964, p. 13.
14. *Logical Investigations*, I, pp. 262-3.

Such a psychology shall describe the peculiar intentionalities proper to each type of mental act and, in accordance with Husserl's own understanding of intentionality, shall bring out the noesis-noema correlations that pervade mental life.

For Frege, as contrasted with all the above, the mental life consists of incurably private particulars, the science of it unavoidably inductive and statistical. But did Frege have a concept of intentionality? Some writers on Frege have thought he had.[15] It appears to me that if for a mental act to be intentional means merely that it must have an object, then that thesis itself would be devoid of any special significance. Brentano's point was not merely that every mental act has an object in that commonly acceptable sense, but something more. In the first place, *in* the mental act, there is a directedness towards an object, a directedness which obtains even when the object towards which the act is directed does not exist. This Brentano thesis is further enriched by Husserl with an account of why a particular act is directed towards a particular object in terms of a theory of the structure of that act: the sense or noema is the structure which makes reference possible. The Fregean sense had all the potentialities of providing such an account, but since the Fregean senses remain attached to signs, they at most provide an account of how a *name* refers to whatever it is a name of. The mental acts are intentional only by proxy. The mental acts grasp the senses, or exhibit some appropriate attitude towards them. That in an act one grasps an object does not yet amount to the intentionality of that act. One needs the concept of the sense *of* the act.

Thus Frege's remarkably sophisticated logical theory remains in sharp contrast with a rather naive philosophy of mind. Consequently, it is my contention, although he rejected psychologism and rightly so, he could not *overcome* it. With a concept of the mental according to which to be mental is to be a private particular, of course, the logical should be sharply sundered from the mental, but psychologism would not thereby be overcome. Here Husserl's efforts to overcome psychologism are instructive. Husserl's so-called relapse into psychologism is a continued effort to overcome psychologism by (i) ceaselessly reflecting upon the *origin* of psychologism, (ii) moving towards a richer conception of mental life which would permit (iii) a closer relation between the mental life and the objectivities that are grasped/presented in it, without falling prey to psychologism on the one hand, and naive realism on the other. In the next section, I will briefly explain these three points.

15. Cf. P.F. Linke, "Frege als Philosoph," *Zeitschrift für philosophische Forschung*, 1, 1946-7, pp. 75-79.

III

To begin with (iii). In a mental act one grasps an objectivity. In an act of reflection, one grasps a *sense*. For Frege, thinking is grasping of sense. The metaphor of 'grasping' certainly provides the initial, and, as a first approximation, correct description. Frege shows an awareness of the problematic character of this 'grasping', when he writes:

> But still the grasping of this law [the law of Gravitation] is a mental process! Yes, indeed, but it is a process which takes place on the very confines of the mental and which for that reason *cannot* be completely understood from a purely psychological standpoint.[16]

In a footnote to this text, Frege adds: "I should say that this question of grasping thoughts and recognizing them to be true is still far from being grasped in all its difficulty."

The same problem lies at the roots of Husserl's philosophy. In the foreword to the first edition of the *Logical Investigations*, Husserl formulates his worry thus:

> I felt more and more pushed towards general critical reflections on the essence of logic, and on the relationship, in particular, between the subjectivity of knowing and the objectivity of the content known.[17]

The "mystery" of this relationship – as he calls it in the draft of the foreword to the second edition of the *Logical Investigation* – remains untouched by the anti-psychologistic arguments. Natorp, in an influential review of the *Prolegomena*, pointed out that "A bond, a logical connection must be set up between the super-temporal being of the logical and its temporal actualization in the experience of the mind."[18] In lectures on logic, dating from the early twenties, Heidegger insisted on the provisional character of the *Prolegomena*, and on the need for overcoming the seemingly absolute separation between the real mental life and the ideal meanings. Heidegger recognized that, in Husserl's own thinking, the structure of intentionality provides such a unity within which the real-ideal distinction is made, but he wanted to go back to a more radical unity i.e., the unity of the *Dasein* whose mode of being is prior not only to that distinction, but to any subject-object distinction. Driven by the same problem, Husserl moved on to a transcendental

16. G. Frege, *Posthumous Writings*, Chicago, University of Chicago Press, 1979, p. 145.
17. *Logical Investigations*, I, p. 42.
18. P. Natorp, "On the Question of Logical Method." English translation by J.N. Mohanty, in *Readings on Husserl's Logical Investigations*. The Hague: M. Nijhoff, 1977, pp. 22-32.

philosophy with a theory of constitution of the objectivities in the acts which present them or bring them to 'givenness.'

But before taking such a transcendental turn, Husserl had to reflect on the very concept of psychologism. It is well-known that inspite of the careful, and often dramatic, arguments of the *Prolegomena* against psychologism, Husserl continued to worry about whether he had understood what psychologism really amounted to and where lie the roots of its incessant appeal. I think, in the long run, psychologism is founded on a phenomenon and an interpretation. The phenomenon is that such entities as judgements, sets, cardinal numbers "appear" within a thinker's mental life as "products," whose "production" takes place step by step following certain eidetic rules.[19] This much of phenomenon is, however, subjected to a naturalistic interpretation, the result of which is a wrong description of that phenomenon: it is thereby lost sight of, that entities such as a judgement, a set of numbers "appear" within one's mental life with the same claim to transcendence as things of the external world. The mundane locution of "production" is misleading. What is "produced" in an act of judging is not a *real* mental entity, but an *irreal* entity that can then be intersubjectively identified, recognized and re-identified.

Germane to psychologism is a naturalistic interpretation of the mental. The mental as such is not the psychological. It *becomes* the subject matter of psychology as a natural science by being, in that very thematisation, inserted into the causal order of nature. We can in fact distinguish between various levels of discourse about the mental, each level defining a certain concept of the mental. What psychologism and anti-psychologism of the common variety *both* share is a conception of the mental that is tied to a certain conception of psychological discourse. It is not necessary to deny that such discourse is legitimate or even to say that the mental is not a private particular. What I am insisting upon is that what makes psychologism possible in the first place is that interpretive framework within which the life of consciousness comes to be construed as the domain of private particulars or as the subject matter of introspective or even of scientific psychology. True *overcoming* of psychologism requires, not rejection of this interpretive framework, but first of all recognizing *that* it is an interpretive framework that passes for an ontological insight, and then asking *how* this framework itself is possible – eidetically as well as historically. Both require subjecting it to the famed *epoche*. We are thereby on the threshold of a transcendental philosophy.

Overcoming psychologism then does not require totally disconnect-

19. E. Husserl, *Formal and Transcendental Logic*, English translation by D. Cairns, The Hague: M. Nijhoff, 1969, paragraph 57b.

ing logic and science from the mental life. Such a severence owes its plausibility to an uncritical identification of the mental as such with the psychological, where 'the psychological' is understood in a sense that is derived from a definite, historically accomplished, theory. The obvious presupposition of such a *radical critique* of psychologism is a conception of consciousness as transcendental. 'Transcendental,' in this context, does not signify a domain that is, in any metaphysical sense, raised above the familiar, empirical, life of conscious experiences. There are not two domains: the empirical and the transcendental. There is only one, intersubjective and historically developing, life of consciousness. *As the source* of all those interpretive frameworks which make theories possible – those very theories which thematise consciousness as their subject matter, naturalistically or otherwise – the very same familiar experiences themselves are transcendental, while as inserted into a causal order or an explanatory order of a similar sort, they are "natural" or "empirical." Only by arriving at such a transcendental standpoint, we will be able to distinguish between the phenomenon (that every ideal, theoretical entity such as a proposition "appears" in one's mental life as a "product") and its naturalistic interpretation which alone generates the most pernicious variety of psychologism.

IV

We now come to realize why psychologism is a tempting theory to fall into, why a logical refutation, such as Husserl's in the *Prolegomena*, does not dispel its attractions once and forever. The situation is not unlike the status of speculative metaphysics in Kant's First Critique. Kant lays bare the 'origins' of speculative metaphysics in the structure of reason, and exposes its pretensions to be a science, but by no means claims to be able to eliminate its questionings. On the contrary, if Kant is right, metaphysical questions are unavoidable. To be able to see through their pretensions, is not to get rid of them, but to rehabilitate them, as questions, if not as bodies of cognition, securely in the necessary structure of reason. An analogous situation holds good of psychologism – possibly of other varieties of relativism and anthropomorphism. The transcendental point of view enables one to speak of the "origin" of psychologism, to see its mistakes as an ontological theory. Yet it does not permanently weed out its possibility. One gains an understanding of its possibility, by realizing that a "mundanisation" (of which 'naturalistic' interpretation is one variety) is a way in which transcendental subjectivity 'apperceives' itself, thereby construing itself as a private, inner, domain that is inserted into public, outer, nature.

Such an understanding of psychologism was not within the range of Frege's thinking. But he rightly saw – as contrasted with Husserl's overly optimistic critique in the *Prolegomena* – that psychologism could not be logically refuted in the strict and rigorous sense that Frege attached to 'logical'. This by itself could have, but did not, in Frege's case, led to a deeper reflection on the nature of the mental. Curiously enough, Husserl's early confident *critique* gave way to such a reflection, which proceeds, first, by outlining an eidetic, descriptive and intentional psychology (as opposed to the empirical, genetic and associationistic psychology in which classical forms of 'psychologism' were rooted), and then by a transcendental reflection which traces all theories back to their origin in the historically developing intentional life of a community of thinking subjects.

My immediate purpose has been only to throw some light on the differences between the approaches of Frege and Husserl to the problem of *overcoming* psychologism, and to controvert the criticism that Husserl, after his early critique of psychologism, fell back into it. If what I have said is right, the *refutation* of the *Prolegomena* still left room for, and it was philosophically incumbent on Husserl to seek an, *understanding* of psychologism in its origin and its reaches.

While I do not propose to examine the strengths and weaknesses of such a transcendental philosophy, one feature of it – a feature that immediately emerges from the above exposition – deserves some attention. If it is the same intentional act which under one interpretation is mundane, and as the source of *all* such interpretations, is the transcendental, then we have what Foucault so aptly characterises as the "strange empirico-transcendental doublet."[20] One may trace a route from the Platonic duplication of the world, through Kant's positing of a transcendental function parallel to, even if underlying, every empirical function (empirical association – transcendental affinity; empirical imagination – transcendental imagination; etc.) to modern phenomenology's contention that the empirical and the transcendental are one and the same life seen under two different perspectives. The implications of this, for transcendental philosophy in general, is far reaching.

20. M. Foucault, *The Order of Things. An Archaeology of the Human Sciences*, New York: Vintage Books, 1973, p. 318.

PHENOMENOLOGICAL REDUCTION AND THE SCIENCES

ERNST WOLFGANG ORTH (Trier)

Husserlian philosophy, known as Phenomenology, can be roughly characterized by pointing out two ways of proceeding:

1. phenomenological description, and
2. phenomenological, properly speaking, transcendental-phenomenological reduction.

These two procedures are often meant to signify chronological sequences in the development of Husserlian thought. But occasionally the problem arises, whether they are at all compatible with regard to essential and systematic criteria.

Ad 1. The proclamation of the descriptive method of phenomenology seems to mean a kind of methodical support of naivety. The theory offers a possibility to desist from methodical and theoretical complexity and indirectness and claims to appeal directly to the things themselves. The things themselves should be represented as they are, which means, as they appear. Supposing there were such a phenomenological philosophy, it could not stand for a critique nor even for a method of foundation of the positive sciences. One should rather assume that it would wholly replace the hitherto existing sciences by trying to fulfill their tasks. For this new philosophy seems to claim to investigate all possible fields of appearances, believing that thereby every scientifically essential task is fulfilled due to its belief that any theoretical account which could possibly follow should be, in any case, founded on the original and authentical descriptions which are practiced solely by phenomenology. In this conception phenomenology is held to be an allround method to master the most different themes in any single field of scientific research. It is not a foundation or a critique of single scientific disciplines but researches itself what the hitherto existing scientific disciplines had investigated. But according to its claim, it performs the investigations – in an especially thorough way, based upon a secure foundation.

Ad 2. In contrast, the theory of transcendental reduction seems to be

Cho, K.K. (ed.) Philosophy and Science in Phenomenological Perspective.

ISBN 978-94-009-6115-9

something new: no longer appealing to the things themselves, but turning away from objects completely – appealing to consciousness. This consciousness, named 'I,' is the first receiver of any appearance of things. With his theorem of phenomenological reduction Husserl seems to establish his approach on the traditional grounds of philosophical thought: philosophy as a philosophy of mind is the basis of every orientation in the world – in regard to single problems and on the whole. Thereby, it is also the basis of the sciences and so is competent to criticize the success of single scientific disciplines – in the sense of a critique of foundations. To be sure, Husserl does not appeal to a 'Bewusstsein überhaupt' in the Kantian sense – a kind of consciousness which is totally formal and cannot be interpreted as having any kind of ontological status. Husserl does not also appeal to concrete human beings in the sense of any psychologism, anthropologism, historism, or sociologism. The new basis is rather a so-called pure sphere of consciousness (reine Bewusstseinssphäre) which is formal as well as substantial: its ontological character is explicitly proclaimed. But here we are concerned with a character of being which has to be strictly distinguished from any other conception of being: it is the absolute region of pure transcendental consciousness.[1] The idealistic character of this philosophy is unmistakable, though Husserl again and again admonishes against identifying this idealism with any kind of traditional idealism.[2] However, from this point of view the function of philosophy as a 'Wissenschaftstheorie' or philosophy of science is guaranteed. This standpoint allows us to define single scientific disciplines concerning their deliminations and their fundamental methodical ways of proceeding, but this way of estimation seems to work in a way similar to traditional forms of philosophy of science.[3]

Husserl seems to turn away from his previous phenomenological descriptive philosophy by establishing his method of transcendental-phenomenological reduction, and seems to want to join the then widespread transcendental philosophical movement, i.e., Neo-Kantianism. Despite his change he seems to be willing to integrate essential elements of his pre-transcendental theory, i.e., phenomenological description, into the new transcendental position. (Husserl, having adopted the concept of intentionality from Brentano, used this concept for linking the two positions together.)

1. Hua III, 114 pp., 132 pp., 134.

2. Cf. also Husserl's conceptions 'transcendental' and 'a priori', Hua III, 73 pp., Hua I, 28; concerning idealism, especially the 'Nachwort zu den Ideen I', from 1930 (Hua IV, 138-162, of special importance, 150 pp.).

3. Regarding Husserl's relationship to Neo-Kantianism: Oskar Becker: Die Philosophie Edmund Husserls. In: Kant-Studien XXXV (1930), 119-150; Eugen Fink: Die phänomenologische Philosophie Edmund Husserls in der gegenwärtigen Kritik. In: Kant-Studien XXXVIII (1933), 319-383.

Regarding the state of affairs schematically, Husserl's argumentation provokes twofold opposition. On the one hand, he repeats an idealistic philosophy of mind which more and more turned out to be questionable. On the other hand, he tries to connect heterogeneous moments with each other, as mentioned above, to link the method of deliberately unaffected description together with a transcendental-idealistic philosophy of reflection.

The critical points of his method can be made even plainer, in this way of viewing the Husserlian conception, by pointing out that the transcendental-phenomenological reduction does in fact not add anything new. It has just changed the thematical focus: instead of describing objects the description deals with consciousness. The new claim is to work out consciousness in its pure structure, so to speak, its simplest form and, as a second step, to ascribe several functions to this consciousness, the principal function of which is to make understandable the constitution of world. This means to continue phenomenological description.

The fact that Husserl develops and modifies the concept of transcendental-phenomenological reduction (from *Ideas* from 1913) and adds other kinds of reductions (for instance the reduction to the life-world) has often been understood as a new revision or even as a series of revisions: Husserl is said to have turned away from his transcendental idealism – which is held to exist in a hybrid way – and is said to have turned, as a third phase, towards concrete human being.[4] But, in contradiction to this interpretation, Husserl himself continuously combined the descriptive method with the transcendental method in his late philosophy. The *Cartesian Meditations* from 1929 contain a remark which Husserl explicitly emphasized: "Hereby we come to the methodical insight that, besides phenomenological reduction, there is eidetic intuition as the fundamental form of any distinct transcendental method (that both of them thoroughly determine the legitimate meaning of a transcendental phenomenology)" (Hua I, 106.)[5]

However, 'eidetic intuition' means nothing other than the way of proceeding which Husserl calls phenomenological description. Already in 1907 he characterized 'ideierende Abstraktion' which is just eidetic intuition, as the initiation of the phenomenological reduction (Hua II, 8 pp). In this way the concept of phenomenological description already seems to involve a motivation for reduction.

4. It is important to avoid a misleading interpretation, which would tend to Heideggerian philosophy, here. Furthermore, we have to notice that concrete subjectivity can be considered in extremely diverging ways and from very different aspects.

5. Cf. 'Nachwort ...', Hua IV, 141 pp.

But all this means that a thesis which divides the development of Husserlian thought into three contradictory phases must be wrong. The difference between description and reduction turns out to be merely a relative difference. The one cannot be understood without the other.

In order to seize the methodical meaning of description adequately it is not very useful simply to define the term 'description,' as we know it from common language, as clearly as possible. The Husserlian concept of description is not defined so positively. It rather serves in a negative way to exclude any kind of methods of investigation and determination that work by indirect and derivative procedures. The Husserlian concept of description turns against construction which conceals the elementary views of a theme.[6]

In order to understand the meaning of phenomenological description we have to ask for Husserl's object of description. He does not describe this or that thing, but he does describe phenomena. And this means that understanding his concept of phenomenon is a precondition for phenomenological description. The concept of phenomenon is, by the way, not at all an expression of unaffectedness and ignorant plainness. For the understanding of the concept of phenomenon is already a manifestation of a kind of reduction which is sometimes called epoché by Husserl: To talk of appearance (or phenomena) means to be evading the actual, functional coherence of reality and to practice a kind of epoché which is beyond the normal perception which takes the objects for granted.

In *Ideas I* Husserl explicitly defines phenomenology as a science of phenomena ("Wissenschaft von Phänomenen") and explains afterwards: "There are other well-known disciplines of science, appealing to phenomena," (Husserl refers here to all fields of scientific research) and thereby to, "all sciences dealing with realities. However different the *meaning* of the term phenomenon might be in these contexts and whatever *meaning* might arise elsewhere; phenomenology, without doubt, is also concerned with all these 'phenomena' and according to all of these *meanings*. But phenomenology is related to all these phenomena in a

6. 'Description' is an operative term. The distinction between virtual ideas and mere symbolical views (eigentliche und bloss symbolische *Anschauungen*) fits here. It was originally drawn by Brentano, and was applied by Husserl already in 'Philosophie der Arithmetik' (1891), (Hua XII, 190-194). Thereby it is decisive that, in Husserl, description leads to essential relationships (Wesensverhältnisse, Hua IV, 87 pp.) through a reconsidered determination of the conception of 'phenomenon' (Hua III, 3). Wilhelm Dilthey had already aimed at a similar solution by means of his 'descriptive psychology'. Over against this, description had been para-ontological throughout the nineteenth century, i.e. description was meant to determine reality only provisionally.

totally different *attitude* than the traditional sciences show: this attitude *modifies* every traditional *sense* of phenomena in a certain way. Only in this modified sense do phenomena enter the *phenomenological sphere*. We have to understand this modification or, more properly speaking, we have to *perform the phenomenological attitude*. We have to elaborate reflectingly the particularity of the phenomenological attitude and thus of the natural attitudes and have to elevate them to a scientific consciousness. This is the first and by no means easy task, we must meet it totally in order to reach the bottom of phenomenology and in order to ascertain its particular character scientifically" (Hua III, 3).

At this point it is clear that by thematizing the concept of a phenomenon, which is the starting-point of any phenomenological description, a kind of reduction is already carried out. In the *Logical Investigations* Husserl had termed this process "ideierende Abstraktion" and later, in the retrospective view, he called it "eidetische Reduktion;" he also introduced the term "Epoché" for it, sometimes using it synonymously with reduction. The aim is to describe phenomena and this presupposes a certain attitude, namely to represent something which appears and to do so exclusively as it appears and to represent it within the limitations of its appearance (cf. principle of all principles, Hua III, 52). Thereby it is necessary to preliminarily exclude any additional theoretical interpretations and thematical coherences, etc., which are merely accessible indirectly.

To sum up: The precondition for transcendental-phenomenological reduction is the discovery of the concept of the phenomenon as based on a particular reductive attitude. This attitude is founded in a certain kind of human faculty of mental attitudes. Here we see that even in Husserlian pre-transcendental phenomenology the concept of consciousness is already implied in the concept of phenomenon.

> With regard to Philosophy of science and Sociology of knowledge this means that Phenomenology as Philosophy must be strictly distinguished from the so-called phenomenological or descriptive methods within the single sciences. The one who describes circumstances within the frame of a certain theme of a single scientific discipline and wants to clarify this special topic may perform an efficient work – but he remains scientist of a single discipline and does not become a phenomenologist in the sense of phenomenological Philosophy. To muddle these very distinct fields means both: on the one hand to ruin the Husserlian concept of Phenomenology and on the other hand to mistake the task of the scientific disciplines.

Indeed, Husserl does evolve his concept of phenomenon and consciousness step by step: Preparing the elaboration of the explicit method of reduction, he explains the attitude of epoché. Epoché is first of all nothing but the deliberate will to eschew certain popular prejudices and theoretical commitments. It is an attitude which cannot be called a fully developed method, but must be regarded as a minimum of methodical activity. Thus, epoché tends towards two directions: the one appeals to the contents of a phenomenon which now is regarded as a possible being or a kind of reality; the other refers to the subjective elements of apprehension.

It is one of Husserl's crucial decisions to take the subjective elements of apprehension as the subject matter of analysis in his next stage of consideration (on the level of *Ideas I*).[7] He studies those subjective elements, the absence of which is unthinkable in regard to any kind of orientation, and which remain evidently intuitive at any stage of inquiry. The method Husserl chooses for doing this examination is none other than eidetic intuition, which now is called eidetic reduction. It is called transcendental reduction because characteristics of consciousness is its particular subject matter. This consciousness – the life of acts (Aktleben) in the *Logical Investigations* – is intentional; it always turns out to be consciousness *of*, and is constitutive for what appears and thereby is urgently needed for any intelligibility of appearances.

As is well known, the general structure of this consciousness is defined by the reduction as ego – cogito – cogitatum. The determination of this constitutive region of consciousness tends to suggest that the transcendental-phenomenological reduction is an operation performed once and forever; and moreover, to characterize consciousness as a so-called absolute realm of being (absolute Seinsregion) marks phenomenology as an extreme idealism. This point has often been criticized by Husserl-philologists as the hypostasis of reduction.

But the relationship between intuitive, immediate description on the one hand and transcendental-phenomenological reduction on the other hand can be explained as follows: It is a matter of two extremes of a homogeneous continuum which I call orientation. The description represents something as a datum of perception or experience as it is given originally* – without any additional digestions and functions –, but it represents the object solely within the limits of its perception (cf. principle of all principles, Hua III, 52). In contrast to this, the reduction analyzes these very limits of the given in order to show up more precisely the context of this given. In doing so it, too, makes use of

7. J. Patocka's criticism of Husserl's conception of 'ego' is illuminating in this respect. Jan Patocka: Der Subjektivismus und die Möglichkeit einer 'asubjektiven' Phänomenologie. In: Philosophische Perspektiven. Ein Jahrbuch. Ed. by R. Berlinger and E. Fink, vol. 2, Frankfurt 1970, pp. 317-334. Jan Patocka: Epoché und Reduktion. Einige Bemerkungen. In: bewusst sein. Gerhard Funke zu eigen. Ed. by A.J. Bucher, et al., Bonn, 1975, pp. 76-85.

* (or seems to be given originally)

intuitive, immediate descriptions; and at the same time reduction is a kind of arrangement of such descriptions.

Disregarding for a while that this exposition concerns a very specific philosophical theorem, we can as well interpret it as a formal outline of the normal scientific proceedings: elementary experiences are unavoidably used as starting-points and are referred to again and again. But moreover, these experiences have to be handled operatively. The fulfillment of both parts of the task renders the possibility of giving clarifications of particular scopes of the theme in question; it even allows to dare predictions. For sure, transcendental-phenomenological reduction should not at all be a mere analogy to a characterization of scientific proceedings. The aim is rather to show by transcendental-phenomenological reduction how to found the possibility of science and to show why science can and even must be shaped so very divergently in different disciplines.

The above mentioned way of methodically arranging descriptions cannot easily be seen in the Husserlian concept of reduction. This indistinctness originates, in my opinion, from Husserl's assumption, which he held for a long time, that there were authentic, ultimate phenomenological matters of fact, which were made visible just by the transcendental reduction; only in his late philosophy does the supposition arise that ultimate matters of fact solely exist as matters which are reductively prepared. With that the connection of description and reduction turns out to be interrelational.[8]

According to these considerations the transcendental-phenomenological reduction must be freed from the aura of being a universal, allround method of miraculous power. Instead of talking about a singular reduction one should rather, for heuristical reasons, discuss a plurality of reductions. The reduction is (in the sense of its methodical function) reasonable only if it is understood as a multiple way of proceeding. Such an interpretation of the Husserlian method of reduction might be used in the sciences fruitfully, without spoiling the philosophical sense of the transcendental-phenomenological reduction.

8. The difference between reduction and description/resp. intuition proceeds iteratively. It appears continuously: Within the given, the differentiation of the given (Gegebenes) and the giving (Gebendes) emerges; they are mutually related. And also conversely: Within the giving (Gebendes) the giving and the given are differentiated and mutually related. The following scheme illustrates this circumstance:

```
Intuition   (description)                    Reduction   (consideration)
      /          \                                /            \
Intuition  –  Reduction                      Reduction  –  Intuition
 /   \          /   \                          /   \          /   \
I – R          R – I                          I – R          I – R
 etc.           etc.                           etc.           etc.
```

The task of the sciences is to fix and to clarify themes. Roughly speaking we could say that themes have to be made comprehensible[9] concerning two points of information: 1. what's the case? 2. what can (a) happen or evolve, or what can (b) be done? The precondition for any scientific approach is certainly a sensitivity for problems or, in other terms, a requirement for orientation which turns out to be a particular compound of knowledge and its lack, as well as of ability and inability.[10] It is a demand within the sciences that the determination and the exposition of a theme must be characterized by distinctness, which means that they must be worked out methodically, looking for solutions of problems step by step. Both, the determination and the exposition of a theme, have to be closely related: the character of structural consistency must accord with both, the theme as well as the method of proceeding. In the sciences this structural consistency means rationality. Nevertheless, rationality is not defined from the first, once and for all. Science always occurs as a partial rationalization. A manifestation of this is to be seen in the fact of the plurality of the sciences, which is nothing but an expression of different requirements for orientation, each of them being constituted by a certain situation. I call this the *dimensionality* of orientation. Scientific activities are channeled into many single disciplines, determined by certain situations, and in this way the anchorage of the sciences in so-called pre-scientific activities and the results of orientation come clearly into view. The position in the world, the state of knowledge, and the tendencies of the human will, required for orientation – Dilthey termed this "Weltstellung," "Erkenntnisstellung," and "Willensstellung" –,[11] are constitutive, pre-scientific starting-points for further orientations, and for types of orientation which are cultivated rationally and methodically in the sciences.

This state of affairs makes understandable the need to recur to pre-scientific forms of orientation on the occasion of conflicts of orientation within the sciences. This is to be understood in each case as an attempt to make fundamentally understandable again the aim of each scientific activity. Here the term pre-scientific is certainly ambiguous.

9. A quasi hermeneutical style of speech is noticeable here (cf. also the above quoted text from Hua III, 3) – Husserl was not aware of this. His definition of phenomenological theory of cognition (Erkenntnistheorie), as expressed already in the LU, tells that Erkenntnistheorie is not virtually a theory, because its aim is not explanation (Erklären), but rather comprehension (Verstehen) and clarification (Aufklären) (LU II/1, 20 pp.). No determined opinion can be presupposed from the beginning.

10. Thereby a rudimentary base of anthropology is involved in Husserl's philosophy; only in the late writings, he deals with it explicitly under the titel 'Anthropology' (Hua XV, 480 pp.).

11. Wilhelm Dilthey: Gesammelte Schriften, Bd. V, 159, 399, 401, 415.

On the one hand – as suggested here – it means factually and historically existing types of orientation; on the other hand, it might refer to elementary forms of orientation which are generally involved in any kinds of orientation whether it is scientific or not. First of all, Husserl tries to approach to the clarification of these elementary possibilities of orientation by using his phenomenological-reductive methods. When unfolding his philosophy he tries more and more to take into account the factuality of orientations, always seeking to avoid relativism, for instance in the form of historicism, naturalism etc.[12]

The meaning of Husserlian philosophy is to be found in just this way of asking for pre-scientific foundations of orientation; this is the sense of its claim to be a rigorous, meaning radical, science.[13] The principal task of reduction (we can also include epoché here) is to clarify the meaning of being concerned with a theme. Reduction provides awareness of themes and at the same time it shows us what it means to have a theme. Reduction does two things: it shows that we need fixed themes, and simultaneously it shows the need to transgress the limitations of the theme in order to understand the constitution of the theme in a wider context. Thereby it is a theory of the dimensionality of orientation. This means also that orientation always exists in a constellation or configuration and the same holds true of orientations about orientations. We can derive two principles from this: 1. There is no single theme which can guarantee in itself a sufficient and definitive solution of a problem, nor is there a sufficient way to pose questions (resp. how to constitute themes). 2. We cannot reasonably imagine the constitution of theories which were independent from themes.

We can replace the hitherto used term "orientation" with the Husserlian concept of "experience" which contains a deliberately wide field of meaning. "Every experience can be reduced phenomenologically" and even must be reduced in order for us to understand its obligatory character (cf. Hua XIII, 188 pp.).

Husserlian phenomenological reduction has turned out to be a complex method constituting the center of his philosophy (cf. Hua V, 140, epilog to Ideas from 1930), but it nevertheless has never been worked out coherently in one text. Let me distinguish three principal forms of reduction:

1. The reduction as epoché which presents a phenomenon as a

12. By the inclusion of concrete factors, Husserl did not mean to relate 'naively' to any single scientific discipline. He makes use of the factual 'pre' in order to determine the 'pre' in principle and generally.

13. In Husserl, rigorous science is actually not modelled on any present science. And philosophy exclusively could be worked out as a rigorous science, contrasting any single discipline on principle. Rigorous means radical.

theme. It defines first the sense of the phenomenological concept of phenomenon.

2. The so-called transcendental-phenomenological reduction.

3. The single thematical or functional reductions.

This triadic divsion signifies different levels for considering the complex method of reduction – in order to stress several distinguishable accentuations without destroying the coherence. At the same time this triadic division itself indicates the inner multiplicity of reduction. This multiplicity can then be shown in a more detailed way within the second type of reduction; the prominent so-called transcendental-phenomenological reduction turns out to be a way of proceeding which is itself structured in many different stages. The third concept of reduction substantiates the multiplicity of reductions in so far as we can number various single reductions here, each of which can be relatively isolated.

1. The first form of reduction which sometimes is also called epoché – Husserl did not use this terminology very stringently and continuously – consists in the stoppage of the execution of an experience or a judgment; this stoppage is in principle possible and actually performable. It is to suspend belief and to limit an actual problem's range, which is constituted as a theme, by asking. It "belongs to the realm of our perfect freedom" (Hua III, 64; cf. Hua III, 67). The human being's ability to freely orient himself, the original ability to pose questions (cf. Hua III, 67) is an immanent precondition of reduction. This moment of freedom, therefore must exist as an anthropological feature and must already be at work if the attitude of epoché with the aim of methodological clarification is to be applicable at all. Because of that the first form of reduction already turns out to be ambiguous and circular (cf. Hua II, 48 pp.): the actual possibility of epoché is the basis of the philosophical attitude of epoché.

Husserl connects the ability of reduction explicitly with the motif of attitude: "The educative character of phenomenological reduction also consists in the following: to make us sensitive to the perception of changes in attitudes" (Hua IV, 179). These attitudes of human beings cannot be objectified as such and are not denoted or ciphered. Epoché means attitude in general because it is actually shown as problematic here and thereby comes to thematical awareness. But the mental faculty of attitudes (for example, of epoché) is permanently in action, working on something, and in this way in epoché both are brought about in the same originality: the deliberate bracketing and the substantial theme; such that is grasped in the attitude as well as the state of being bracketed; that is to say the phenomenon as a "correlation" of the "appearance" and "the thing which appears" (Korrelation von "Erscheinen und Erscheinendem," Hua II, 14). The bracketing of the phenomenon, which does not at all mean an annihilation of the phenomenon, is accompanied positively and in the same originality by the constitution of a theme which itself turns out to be a phenomenon. The so-called usual phenomena ("übliche Phänomene") of the well-known 'natural' sciences ("längst bekannten 'natürlichen' Wissenschaften," Hua II, 3, 5 pp.) are merely possible as scientific themes because the sciences in question have already performed and continuously perform – unknowingly – a kind of reduction. The Husserlian characterization of epoché as an act of abstention from judging (also suspension of judgments) could be misunderstood: for it is at the same time to state a judgment in so far as the bracketed judgment is being constituted as a theme. With this the aim of phenomenological description becomes more intelligible. It means to trace back authentically an actual phenomenological attitude and not to attempt to copy something which is objectively given anyway.

The concept of the epoché is already implied in Husserl's concept of intentionality and in his concept of phenomenological intuition because any, so to speak, 'natural' human intention, posed as a theme, already involves a minimum of distance from the theme, the object in question. Otherwise, consciousness could never be aware of the theme – instead of an orientation there would be a mere process of meaningless functions.

The so-called "ideational abstraction" ("ideierende Abstraktion") which in the *Logical Investigations* meant phenomenological intuition is nothing other than an elementary form of applied epoché, even though epoché and methods of reduction are not yet discussed there. Epoché means to suspend the usual functions of orientation and, at the same time, a readjustment of orientation.

2. The second concept of reduction is, so to speak, the official one; the so-called transcendental-phenomenological reduction from *Ideas I* from 1913. It leads to the region of pure transcendental consciousness as that of an absolute being which enables to understand any meaning of being. The fundamental structure of this consciousness as a fundamental pattern of intentionality is: ego – cogito – cogitatum, respectively ego – noesis – noema.[14] Methodologically, this reduction is just the application of the possibilities pointed out concerning to the first type of reduction, to ask for the essence of knowledge or of orientation on the whole. It is the eidetical approach to consciousness as the ultimate resort of any orientation.

14. This represents at first, as it were, a horizontal pattern of the structure of consciousness. Husserl also takes vertical segmentations into account and analyzes these.

Even in *Ideas* this approach was not performed all at once. Moreover, the classical reduction from *Ideas* is also a multiple way of proceeding. Husserl says: "we are going to elaborate a method of phenomenological reductions" (Hua III, 5) in order to understand phenomena phenomenologically. The "operation" (!) which is called "transcendental εποχή" is "methodically" "dissected in several steps of 'suspension of judgment' and 'bracketing' and in this way our method will assume the character of a successive reduction. Because of that we are going to speak of transcendental or phenomenological reductions" (Hua III, 73; cf. p. 330). It belongs to the inner multiplicity of reduction, too, not to take each of its results for definite, absolute results, respectively not to hypostasize the results of reductions: "The transcendetal absolute which we did dissect (Husserl says 'prepared') (!) by the reductions is in fact not the ultimate; it is just something which is constituted by itself in a very particular sense of depth, originating from an ultimate and truly absolute". But this absolute again has to be interpreted and clarified, namely as the "horizon of time" (Zeithorizont) and "stream of experience" (Erlebnisstrom) (Hua III, 198). Husserl discovered in *Ideas* also that "all intentionality is structured by horizons" (Horizontstruktur aller Intentionalität) (Hua I, 86, FtL, 177). These are manifested for instance in acts of more distance from or nearness to the "I" (Ichferne oder Ichnähe, Hua III, 205). In consequence, he admonishes the reader in *CM* to be aware of "apodictical naivety" (apodiktische Naivität, Hua I, 178, 128). But this means that phenomenological reduction is not to be understood as a faculty of simply seeing or intuitiously viewing certain ultimate items, but to understand it as a process being methodically organized.

This is another indication of the particular meaning of Husserl's concept of description; and here is the motive for Husserl's creation of the peculiar term "synthetical originarity" (synthetische Originarität, Hua III, 377). In the reduction quasi vanishing points or extremes are discovered by dissection (preparing) in order to estimate intentionality and possible systems or complexes of intentionality.

Such vanishing points or extremes are: 1. the pure structure of consciousness ego – cogito – cogitatum. 2. the facticity of original temporality involving the mere ego-pole ("Ich-Pol"). 3. the so-called concrete transcendental intersubjectivity. Husserl reaches this latter type by further reductive procedures relating to his transcendental-phenomenological reduction, namely by reduction to the "primordial sphere of my ownness" (primordiale Eigenheitssphäre) by means of constitutive abstraction (Hua I, 125). This is characterized by purely methodical, operative, and dissective (preparing) features (cf. Hua XV, 3 pp., 189 pp.). The aim is to determine a concordant universe of subjectivities, each of them being the center of intentionality (or even worlds) which potentially guarantees compatible experience of world (cf. Hua XIV, 89 pp., Text no. 4 from 1921; cf. no. 5/6).

Already in 1910/11 Husserl explicitly required a kind of two-fold phenomenological reduction (Hua XIII, 189) which should analyse each, the self and the other, as centers of intentionality in order to establish a sufficient concept of subjectivity – and this turns out to be a concept of intersubjectivity.

Here another double has to be mentioned which Husserl does not show explicitly: The method of reduction in *'Ideas I'* does not appeal solely to so-called transcendental consciousness; correlatively, it dissects different regional ontologies and hereby tries to establish "a ... complete phenomenology of reason" (Hua III, 380) with regard to all possible "shapes of counsciousness" (Bewusstseinsgestaltungen, Hua III, 374).[15] "It is necessary to keep continuously in mind that all of our explanations ... (for instance these, concerning the constitution of things) ... have to be understood in the sense of a phenomenological reduction and in eidetical generality" (Hua III, 311).

The full sense of transcendental reduction is indeed reached with the elaboration of so-called concrete transcendental intersubjectivity. In the *Cartesian Meditations* this result is explicitly connected with the classical structure of consciousness: ego – cogito – cogitatum from *Ideas*. Yet, concrete transcendental intersubjectivity is nothing but a name (!) for the aim – which is the centering unity of all intentions and the reciprocal possibility to relate each of them to another. This universe of intentions is called concrete because it is by definition no longer in need of any further foundation. Husserl speaks, proceeding from the ego – cogito – cogitatum, of a "general system of typicality," a "general scheme" which is merely "designated" (Hua I, 87). Transcendental intersubjectivity is therefore not concrete because of the ability of some known, living being, for instance, a human being, to perform or to fulfill it authentically or originally.

What is, therefore, the ultimate or absolute which might be demonstrated as the result of transcendental-phenomenological reduction, accepting that the three above mentioned 'absoluta' are mere marks for orientation? In Husserl's late thought, especially when working out the *Crisis* a new reduction is offered: the reduction to the life-world (Lebenswelt, Hua VI, 123 pp.). It is the recourse to a concrete form of originally lived intersubjectivity which cannot be passed over. But in fact it may not be held for absolute, even though it can be

15. Concerning this point, cf.: E.W. Orth: Husserls Begriff der cogitativen Typen und seine methodologische Reichweite. In: Phänomenologische Forschungen Bd. 1 (Phänomenologie heute. Grundlagen- und Methodenprobleme), Freiburg, 1975, S. 138-167.

isolated methodically in a relative way. It serves to sharpen the whole transcendental reduction immanently, but not to dismiss it.[16] It is not an appeal to ultimate entities, but the attempt to find starting-points. Husserl does not revise his position here, but he makes it more understandable and practicable. His aim is to "interrogate concretely and analytically actual subjectivity, a subjectivity which concretely views and evaluates a world as an actual phenomenal world". "But Idealism has always been too quick with its theories ... it leaped over ... actual subjectivity" (Hua VI, 273). "The ego (Ich) which I reach by epoché is virtually called ego (Ich) by equivocation." "Designating it reflectingly I cannot help saying that it is me, I, who am performing epoché" (Hua VI, 188).

Thereby Husserl connects his problem of reductive foundation with the old theorem of occasional significations from the *Logical Investigations*. The transcendental foundation by the reduction and by each of the reductions is occasional, that is, it depends on each position within the system of intentionality which I, the interrogator, occupy. Because of that the self-determination of subjectivity must necessarily take a course through an equivocation – because it is involved intentionally. "I" (ego) in the reduction is an "equivocation for essential reasons" (Hua VI, 188). Such equivocations result unavoidably from "inner shiftings of intentionality which thereby are connected by essential coherences" (FtL, 158). The one who searches for orientation is always involved in intentional and intersubjective implications he cannot be fully aware of.

From this follows: "When phenomenology leads first by its reduction to ego cogito, this is an aequivocum – a beginning from an absolutely necessary equivocation" (1933 Hua XV, 586). It is occasional that the "ego of my epoché" (I, performing epoché) "can never loose its uniqueness and will never be declinable" (Hua VI, 188); but the ego, actively reflecting itself by performing epoché, is able "to decline itself transcendentally for itself" (Hua VI, 188). This means to be ready for transpositions to the vanishing points of reduction (structure of consciousness, temporality, transcendental intersubjectivity), and thereby to make itself and the whole system of intentionality intelligible in principle. The starting-point of investigation and orientation is indeed the concrete, personal human being: "every transcendental ego within intersubjectivity (participating in the constitution of the world) must necessarily be a human being within the world – that means: every

16. It has rightly been pointed out by H.G. Gadamer that Husserl did not want to give up transcendental philosophy by his theorem of life-world; on the contrary, it serves the refinement of the method.

human being bears a transcendental ego, not as a real stratum of his soul (...), but in so far as (!) it is the self-objectivation of each concerned transcendental ego which can be shown by phenomenological self-consideration" (Selbstbesinnung, Hua VI, 188 pp.).

By this line of argument Husserl rendered the proof that there must be many divergent lines of investigation and orientation which cannot be connected with at present (and should not be so connected; no relation should be proclaimed without tracing it back in 'synthetical originarity.' This is, also, the ethos of the individual disciplines). But at the same time a fundamental relating structure can be revealed. It is the human faculty of self-consideration which renders reductions possible and, as well, their evaluations.[17]

3. The third form of reduction is the pluralistic one. Operations are carried out here by many single reductions which can be relatively isolated. A theme can be prepared and structured in one way or another for scientific or any other kind of inquiry by reference to the tendency of the question, the aim of clarification, the state of knowledge, and the position of the interrogator. The above-mentioned single reductions concerning the transcendental-phenomenological reduction might be repeated here and be interpreted with regard to particular interests.

We can distinguish between two kinds of this third, pluralistic form of reduction:

a. The thematical and methodical elaboration of a certain field of investigation which is done on purpose and in awareness of strategies of investigation. It is the scientific single reduction.

b. To approach a theme or problem more or less unaware, assessing it by taking things for granted and reacting upon it correspondingly. It is the pre- or nonscientific single reduction.

A strict distinction between (a) and (b) cannot actually be drawn in every case. For, as long as the full meaning of the complete reduction is not seized, no scientific reduction can be sure not to drag in undetectedly beliefs or theoretical commitments which are not clarified yet. By the way, we cannot exclude from consideration that the so-called nonscientific orientations involve results from scientific orientations which had been accepted uncritically as mere materials (cf. 'abgesunkenes Kulturgut' : sunken cultural achievements, sedimentations). This is the reason why Husserl confronts the scientific together with the pre-, or nonscientific orientations, representing natural attitudes, with the philosophical (transcendental-phenomenological) attitude.

It is just the above-mentioned theorem of the occasionality of sub-

17. The insight, that the self-consideration (Selbstbesinnung) of factual, existing human beings is unavoidable, led Husserl to a fundamental phenomenological anthropology in his late philosophy.

jectivity which shows that the distinction of elements of the form (a) or (b) in pure culture is in fact impossible. Each reducing subject is as yet a very concrete, already determined individuality, a complex of intentionality, each of a special way of being interwoven in intersubjectivity – that is, the reducing subject realizes a perspective of its own.

The statuts of the result of reduction can also be differentiated into two types: A reduction can lead to (1) actually possible entities, and (2) mere hypothetical-problematic potentialities of being, the latter being exclusively characterized by the task of dissecting and preparing, and being useful solely with regard to methodical purposes.

All this has to be distinguished in concrete cases in order to avoid ontological suggestions and secondary rationalizations[18] in the sciences.

The reduction to the life-world (Lebenswelt), for instance, could be understood as a scientific procedure or as a pre- or nonscientific approach. To muddle both interpretations means to mistake Husserl's aims. His reduction to the life-world is not at all within the region of the life-world – and is not life-world-like. But there is life-world behaviour, of course, as a real possibility. The so-called abstractive reduction to the primordinal sphere of my ownness (Hua I, 125) is a purely scientific reduction; its result signifies a hypothetical-problematic potentiality of methodical purpose.

Admittedly, the mentioned single reductions are all integrally arranged in Husserl's transcendental-phenomenological reduction. But there is one example of a case where this arrangement is of no relevance: Single disciplines are explained here as formations of reductions. Husserl points out (FtL, 125) that a logician, focussing his investigations on problems of the philosophy of science performs a "reduction to the analytic of pure meaning" (Sinnhaftes). Therefore, "the actually logical, that is, scientific-theoretic intention" can be distinguished from that of "formal mathematics", even if this mathematics is enlarged so as to be a mathesis universalis. But this mathematics has "its legitimacy" on its own part "in the sense of that reduced unity", namely reducing from the meaningful (FtL, 125). The philosophy of science or, rather, logic of science, on the one hand, and mathematical logics on the other hand are distinguished from and confront each other according to the type of reduction that they represent.

Husserl's explication of the plurality of methods of reduction is of great importance for the practice of the philosophy of science and for judging the relationship between the sciences and culture in general. As has

18. I define 'ontological suggestions' as the subsequent positing of something as real which originally had been assumed on mere methodical, problematical, or operative purposes.

been shown, to carry out scientific tasks means always and necessarily to practice certain reductions, more or less consciously. Each of the sciences depends upon particular attitudes which in part have evolved historically and in part are performed consciously. Hence, we can explain the reproach of reductionism, which some sciences are confronted with, to be a very shortened argument. The fault is not reduction as such, but rather not to understand the sense of the respective reduction or not to realize this sense in performing the reduction. In order to understand the faculties and the nature of the liability of any science one must know its particular way of reducing. This knowledge is decisive with regard to reasonable applications of sciences to one another and to culture on the whole. For this, again, it is necessary to understand the remaining nonscientific (pre-scientific) dimensions of culture and their reductive foundations.

It is obvious that, based on this way of seeing, possibilities to determine the sciences arise which not only concern philosophy of science in a narrow sense but also concern the history of science and sociology of knowledge.[19] All this serves for a better understanding of the capacities of each single science.

Here a crucial problem arises: who or what can hold all these reductions together? Aren't the different single reductions, from which, for example, single sciences are evolved, in need of a, at least potential, general coherence?

This general coherence seems to be motivated by the demand for interdisciplinary co-operation which is expressed in individual sciences. A method and theme of a single discipline turns out to be unsatisfactory and is in need of filling up further horizons. From experience in the sciences we can at least state that certain groups of single sciences co-operate in the sense of mutually completing each other, for instance, the natural sciences, linguistics, comparative literature, the social sciences, etc. But this is merely a fact of the sociology of science and history of science. We do not off-hand know any fundamental reason for this.

There must be a 'logically' or 'theoretically' foundable coherence concerning the interdisciplinary research. The mere aim of establishing co-operation between different single sciences, because of thematical or methodical analogies and associations, or because of certain ideals of society, representing actual mentalities, can lead to unreasonable constellations.

19. The exterior influences of historical or social kinds are not so much concerned here, moreover, the consideration refers to the interior development and interaction in the sense of a phenomenological genesis.

> For example, following the remark that two different languages are of special efficiency with respect to the expression of each different field of experience, we could combine the use of both languages to establish a new one. Such combinations could not simply contain one half of language A and the other half of language B. Moreover, the new language has to reduce the two precedent languages to one common structure which could really combine their advantages. This common structure could not originally have been involved in any of the preceding languages. This means: interdisciplinary research needs more than co-operation among the participating sciences. It is again a question of a higher type of reduction.

Concerning such questions of philosophy of science, systems theory is an aid to solving this problem. Aspects of systems theory are also involved in Husserl's philosophy of reductions, especially when appealing to the consideration of transcendental intersubjectivity. But a theory of systems cannot be the last resort because it is in need of further qualifications. Husserl found intentionality and subjectivity to be these qualifications.

Intentional subjectivity, however shaped, is the ultimate vanishing point of Husserl's methods of reduction and the ultimate aim of any reductive proceeding. But Husserl's late philosophy indicates that this point may not be hypostasized. We cannot affirm a conclusive form or shape. This is the reason why the different reductions appeal to various aims which are oriented pragmatically to each of the aims of inquiry.

In everyday work as practiced in the sciences, the problem of the intended vanishing point of reduction is often not discussed at all. Single reductions are simply performed and are adhered to, when working out single points. If this pragmatic way of proceeding were merely practiced as a definite norm, the sciences would be abandoned to a residual of agnosticism.

If this agnosticism is practiced tacitly or undetected, it is an uncritical agnosticism. But it can also be consciously calculated; this seems to be the minimal position constituting the operative character of Husserl's philosophy of subjectivity. This is not at all an absolute position, but a critical one; all experiences, problem ranges, or solutions to problems are to be related to the subject who is in need of orientation – above all this means to be related to concrete human beings. This concrete human being is not simply the absolute ground of science; but the concrete human being is unavoidably the basis for starting any investigations in the search for clarifications which might possibly go beyond the level of concrete human beings. This means to take the possibility of self-consideration seriously and in that to assume responsibility.

VARIATIONS OF TRANSCENDENTALISM

NATHAN ROTENSTREICH (Jerusalem)

The transformation from the scholastic understanding of the concept "transcendental" to Kant's version of that concept is an established fact: scholastic philosophy conceived of transcendental predicates (and they differ from the position of the transcendent) as referring to concepts that, in terms of their universality, go beyond or above categories in the Aristotelian sense of that term, pointing to different *modi* of being. Hence, they were also called *praedicamenta*. "Transcendentalia" refer not to *modi* of being but to the being itself, and thus in terms of content amount to the predicates *unum, verum, bonum*.

The turn in Kant's philosophy is to some extent summed up by Kant himself, though, to be sure, that summary does not present all the nuances (and perhaps all the ambiguities) related to the concept. "I entitle *transcendental* all knowledge which is occupied not so much with objects as with the mode of our knowledge of objects insofar as this mode of knowledge is to be possible *a priori*."[1] The two aspects are interrelated: the belonging of the transcendental to the sphere of knowledge (not to being) and the position of the a priori as preceding experiential data (and not going beyond them). There exists a correlation in terms of the basic distinction between the transcendental and the empirical elements of knowledge. Because of that distinction we are placed within the orbit of critique of knowledge. Following the line of the distinction, it is even said that the distinction does not concern the relation of that knowledge to its objects.[2] We may wonder whether that statement exhausts the full position of the a priori elements. They are discerned or identified, not for the sake of a mapping out of the sphere of knowledge, but in order to identify elements of reason or understanding which apply a priori to data. In this sense, it is said that

1. Immanuel Kant, *Kritik der reinen Vernunft* B, p. 25; transl. Norman Kemp Smith (New York: St. Martin's Press, 1965), p. 59.
2. Ibid., p. 81; Smith, p. 56.

Cho, K.K. (ed.) Philosophy and Science in Phenomenological Perspective.

ISBN 978-94-009-6115-9

the meaning of the transcendental is only to make empirical knowledge possible.[3] Hence, the concept of the transcendental has a double meaning – one in terms of its position and the other in terms of its function.

II

There are several critical aspects accompanying the concept of the transcendental; some of them are important precisely when we hold before our eyes the transformation of the concept introduced by Husserl. The first aspect to be mentioned in this context relates to the "I" or the "Ego": "... I have no *knowledge* of myself as I am but merely as I appear to myself." "The consciousness of self is thus very far from being a knowledge of the self ..."[4] The negative or critical meaning of that statement is that the distinction between appearance and the thing in itself applies also (or let us say *even*) to the self-awareness of the consciousness. I appear to myself not as I am to the understanding:[5] the "I" is the mere form of consciousness.[6]

The second negative aspect is what might be called the exclusion of morality from the scope of transcendental philosophy: the notion of transcendental cannot be employed in or to the sphere of morality. This position may be seen as following from the limitation of the transcendental to the sphere of knowledge, that is, to the scope of reference of the a priori concepts to the empirical data, a reference activated in the sphere of cognition. Kant, in the explication of the cognitive aspect (in the negative or critical sense of explication), puts the confinement to knowledge in the following way: the empirical data are present within the horizon of morality as desires, urges, inclinations, search for pleasure, allurement, etc. Yet these empirical elements are not constitutive of morality; they are components of the empirical attitude, which have to be overcome within the scope of morality and because of the imperative grounded in reason as manifested in morality. In morality, there is no positive *reference* of reason and its *a priori* concepts to empirical data but rather an *overcoming* of the empirical data by reason and the imperative. Because of that position of the empirical data in the structure of morality, they are to be looked at as hindrances and not as correlative data. Hence transcendental philosophy is a philos-

3. *Prolegomena*, Anhang, etc. Kant's *Gesammelte Schriften*, ed. Preussische Akademie der Wissenschaften, Bd. IV (Berlin: George Reimer, 1911), p. 373 n.; transl. and introduction, Lewis White Beck (Indianapolis and New York: Liberal Arts Press, 1950), Appendix, p. 122 n.

4. *Kr. d. r. V.* B, p. 158; Smith, p. 169.

5. Ibid., p. 155; Smith, p. 167.

6. *Kr. d. r. V.* A, p. 381; Smith, p. 353.

ophy of pure and merely speculative reason.[7] "Speculative" in this context has to be understood, not as a purely speculative employment of reason,[8] but as theoretical in the sense in which the notion of rational science as purely speculative is applied to mathematics.[9]

There is an additional aspect, namely the characterization of transcendental philosophy as being unique in the whole field of speculative knowledge; no question which concerns an object given to pure reason can be insoluble for this same reason.[10] The meaning of that programmatic statement can probably be understood as follows: transcendental philosophy in its scope is delineated by the notion of the a priori both in terms of the position of the concepts or propositions as well as in terms of their application to the data. Since the notion of the a priori is applicable to data, whatever lies within the sphere of reference of the a priori to data is open to knowledge. Negatively speaking, whatever lies outside that sphere of the correlative applicability of the a priori is by definition outside the sphere of possible knowledge. The limitations inherent in the application of the a priori are, by the same token, the positive direction and solution of the problem or task of knowledge; open to knowledge is only that which lies within the scope of the applicability of the a priori.

When we anticipate, by way of resume, Husserl's version of the transcendental, pointing again to the basic features of Kant's version of it, the following can be said: the notion of transcendental has, for Kant, a meaning in the direction of application to data. The a priori qua a priori is independent of the data, but its validity is of a correlative essence. Once there is no correlation between the a priori and the data, the notion of the transcendental is not to be employed. The transcendental, having that function and position, cannot be regarded as being characteristic of reason or of consciousness as such. From here Husserl's version of the notion of transcendental can be understood.

III

Before proceeding to the next step in our attempt to identify the notion of transcendentality, an observation on the concept of evidence is appropriate. Kant confines the validity of evidence to the scope of mathematical knowledge, inasmuch as the proofs must always proceed under the guidance of pure intuition (*Anschauung*) and by means of a

7. *Kr. d. r. V.* B, pp. 28-9; Smith, p. 61.
8. Ibid., p. 669; Smith, p. 531.
9. Ibid., p. 508; Smith, p. 433.
10. Ibid., p. 505; Smith, p. 431.

synthesis which is always evident.[11] The demonstrated truth of mathematics is evident.[12] The reference to mathematics is essential in the context, since mathematics is a knowledge based on (or in) synthesis – to be sure, not a synthesis of sensuous data and a priori concepts or propositions, but a synthesis of forms of sensuality with the a priori form of thinking. "Even from *a priori* knowledge concepts, as employed in discursive knowledge, there can never arise intuitive certainty, that is (*demonstrative*) evidence, however, apodeictically certain the judgment may otherwise be."[13]

The following might be an interpretation of Kant's position and the rendering of the locus of the evidence as conviction in terms of the certainty related to a proposition: all knowledge is grounded in a synthesis between the conceptual element and the element of data present in the consciousness through the mediation of sensuality. From a structural point of view, a synthesis is a correlation between thinking and sensuality; from that viewpoint mathematics is a manifestation of the synthesis of forms of thinking with the forms of sensuality. Evidence can be attributed only to a synthesis taking place on the level of a synthesis of forms. Negatively: there is no synthesis where the element of the a priori attributed to forms of thinking occurs, and there is no corresponding element of the a priori related to the forms of sensuality. The sensuous sphere is present in the scattered data and not in the formal coordinates of sensuality. Hence, evidence and its position do not circumvent the essence of cognition as synthesis. It can be present only in its relation to the formal components of the synthesis and thus to the formal components of knowledge. But the synthesis is an act performed by consciousness or by thinking representing the active, qua spontaneous, component of consciousness.

IV

It is here that we may point to the first structural difference between Husserl and Kant in terms of their respective characterizations of consciousness and transcendentality. The basic issue for Husserl is not the synthesis between thinking and data delivered to consciousness by sensuality, but the intentionality of consciousness as such, whose characteristic feature is the interrelation of *noesis* and *noema*. The correlation between the two is not identical with the correlation established by synthesis between the a priori elements and the empirical ones

11. Ibid., p. 452; Smith, p. 396.
12. Ibid., p. 469; Smith, p. 406.
13. Ibid., p. 702; Smith, p. 590.

respectively. Intentionality in general, as the experience (*Erlebnis*) of consciousness of something (*von irgend Etwas*), is the very essence of consciousness. The synthesis for Kant is an explicit and deliberate act of consciousness; an act is performed for the sake of activating consciousness, which in turn is performed for the sake of arriving at cognition. To put it differently we may say: The synthesis is to be listed according to Kant with the teleology of consciousness, while for Husserl it belongs, by and through intentionality, to the very essence of consciousness. Moreover, the synthesis for Kant is taking place between heterogeneous elements – thinking and sensuality – whereas for Husserl the synthesis as a correlation between *noesis* and *noema* does not describe the character of the elements involved but their position within the structure of intentionality. Hence intentionality is present even when the *noema* is conceptual and not sensuous, as Kant's notion of synthesis would require. Therefore, for Husserl, intentionality in general and evidence belong essentially to each other. Evidence is a universal mode referring to the whole life of consciousness. Through evidence intentionality is endowed with universal teleological structure.[14] We are to arrive at it as an achievement or as a goal; in this sense it is of a teleological status. Coming back to our previous formulation, we may say that, whereas for Kant the synthesis is an achievement and thus points to the teleological structure of consciousness, for Husserl evidence is not an achievement. It points to the teleological structure of consciousness which is but a manifestation of the universal position of consciousness. Nominally, evidence is coterminous with a certainty that excludes every doubt.[15] Put phenomenologically, evidence is a mental seeing of something itself.[16] As such, it is related to the striving for knowledge, which amounts to the fulfillment of one's intention.[17] Hence, evidence is not related to a formal synthesis in the mathematical sense of the term, but to transcendental subjectivity.[18] It is the expression, the living evidence of the "I."[19] This aspect leads us to analysis of the notion of transcendentalism in Husserl and the difference between Husserl's version and Kant's.

14. Edmund Husserl, *Formale und transzendentale Logik. Versuch einer Kritik der logischen Vernunft* (Halle: Max Niemeyer Verlag, 1929), p. 142.
15. Husserl, *Cartesian Meditations. An Introduction to Phenomenology*, transl. Dorion Cairns (The Hague: Martinus Nijhoff, 1960), p. 15.
16. Ibid., p. 12.
17. Ibid.
18. Ibid., p. 22.
19. Ibid., p. 23.

V

In our attempt to understand Husserl's version of the concept of the transcendental lodged within the universal structure of intentionality we may go another step. Husserl sees his relation to Kant's version of the transcendental in the following way: "Kant never permitted himself to enter the vast depths of the Cartesian fundamental investigation, and his own set of problems never caused him to seek in these depths for ultimate groundings and decisions."[20] At this point we may insert an observation that is meant to reinforce Husserl's resume, using Kant's own description of his viewpoint. Kant employs as a description of "depth" (*Bathos*) the following: that my place is the fertile bathos of experience.[21] One may juxtapose the depth of experience with its prescription of the synthesis in which the transcendental element is involved and the depth of the "I" in its pure and "living subjectivity"; "a transcendental philosophy is the more genuine, and better fulfills its vocation as philosophy, the more radical it is and ... comes to its actual and true beginning, only when the philosopher has penetrated to a clear understanding of himself as the subjectivity functioning as primal source ..."[22] Kant's philosophy is on the *way* to this (and we could add *only* on the way to it) or is a step in the right direction. To be sure, it is a philosophy opposed to prescientific and scientific objectivism. It goes back to the knowing subjectivity as the primal locus of formations of sense and ontic validities. Kant's philosophy is "a truly universal transcendental philosophy meant to be a *rigorous* science ..."[23] We notice here that Husserl imposes, as it were, his early concept of philosophy as a rigorous science upon transcendental philosophy (which is a philosophy of science and not science). Kant's rendering of that philosophy is the first attempt in that direction.

Yet we cannot be oblivious of the fact that what Husserl tries to establish is a kind of synthesis or integration of the Cartesian direction with the Kantian one. Hence he relates transcendentality to the motif of the knower's reflecting upon himself and his knowing life. "Working itself out radically, is the motif of universal philosophy which is grounded purely in this source and thus ultimately grounded. This source bears the title *I-myself*, with all my actual and possible knowing life and, ultimately, my concrete life in general."[24] The application of

20. Husserl, *The Crisis of European Sciences and Transcendental Phenomenology. An Introduction to Phenomenological Philosophy*, transl. David Carr (Evanston, Ill.: Northwestern University Press, 1970), p. 99.
21. *Prolegomena* (edition cited in note 3), p. 379 n.; Beck, Appendix, p. 123 n.
22. Husserl, *Crisis of European Sciences*, p. 99.
23. Ibid.
24. Ibid., pp. 97-8.

the notion of life to the context of the ultimate subjectivity is not accidental. It can be explained not only by way of an extrapolation or sublimation of the concept of our concrete life. Since we are immersed in life and life is ultimately grounded in the radical subjectivity, it follows that subjectivity is bound to be viewed as "life." The reasoning starts from the opposite angle – namely, that, reflecting phenomenologically, we discern life within the radical subjectivity. The life characteristic of that level cannot be erased on the level of our concrete existence and life.

What could "life" connote on the level of radical subjectivity? Husserl speaks about a dimension of the living spirit.[25] The discernment of that dimension is open to theoretical self-evidence.[26] It is a matter of spiritual functions that exercise their accomplishments in all experiencing and thinking. Though Husserl refers in the context to the distinction between transcendental subjectivity and the soul,[27] it is obvious that Kant maintained that distinction, since otherwise he could not, among other things, present the paralogisms of rational psychology. Kant (and this is not said by Husserl and is a consequence of our previous exploration) deals with the concept of the transcendental in terms of its position within the cognitive synthesis, while Husserl attempts to characterize the transcendental in its own inner structure. This is here called "life." The functional aspect in Kant does not provide room for the *Gestalt* aspect phenomenologically presented by Husserl. Husserl tries to combine the discernment of subjectivity with the realization of the demand for apodicticity. This is related to the position of evidence, not in terms of the apodicticity of a presupposition as one of the modalities of judgment as Kant had it, but in terms of the findings of self-reflection. Hence, Husserl refers to the Kantian and subsequent transcendental philosophy as a philosophy "in which the transcendental primal active ... the motive which arises out of the demand for apodicticity, is still not aroused."[28]

What is "life" that is attributed to subjectivity? In a sense, the systematic position of the *Cartesian Meditations* is to be placed in that context. We refer to the flowing conscious life in which the identical Ego lives, to its conscious life, to its sensuously perceiving and imagining life, or to its asserting, valuing or willing life to which the Ego can at any time direct its reflections: "he can contemplate it and, in respect of its contents, explicate and describe it."[29] There seem to be two

25. Ibid., p. 118.
26. Ibid., p. 119.
27. Ibid., p. 118.
28. Ibid., p. 339. Cf. *Cartesian Meditations*, pp. 14 ff.
29. *Cartesian Meditations*, p. 31.

levels of "life," the first being the sum total of the intentional acts in one's character on the one hand and the process of flow on the other. The second level is reflection, which is the upper scale of intentionality concerned with the variety of acts.

The first level is the concern of descriptive psychology, while the second level is the concern of transcendental phenomenology of consciousness in the strict sense of that term.[30] Natural reflection belongs to our everyday life, while in the phenomenological reflection we are engaged in a transcendental experience whereby an essentially changed subjective process takes the place of the original one.[31] "Consequently I, the transcendental phenomenologist, have objects ... solely as the intentional correlates of modes of consciousness of them."[32] Consciousness is reflective or deliberate, that is, is accompanied by consciousness being aware. But at the level of consciousness and discernment, the intentionality characteristic of consciousness is explicated. Hence, we identify objects as correlates of consciousness, not as constructs of propositions by way of a synthesis, but as given correlates that cannot be isolated from the acts of *noesis*. Husserl moves from synthesis to correlates or from propositions to acts. In a sense he is closer to those parts of the *Critique of Pure Reason* in the first edition that Kant omitted in the second because they were concerned more with acts and less with the logical structure of propositions. Husserl implicitly refers to the first edition of the *Critique*, without explicitly mentioning it.

VI

In the first place, intentionality (*intentionelle Mitbeziehung*) is mentioned in the context of the synthesis of recognition, which applies to every external objectivity though it cannot be said that that synthesis exhausts the full performance of "external experience."[33] Further, reference is made to "reproductive" consciousness, which connotes the consciousness directed to an object as one perceived in the past at which I am now again. The statement is about to convey the notion that there is no perception that does not imply the step as a performance by consciousness. To put it differently, there is no receptivity of perception unless the activity of consciousness is presupposed and made manifest in it. At this juncture we have to mention that recognition appears in the first edition of *Critique of Pure Reason* as the "Syn-

30. Ibid., p. 32.
31. Ibid., p. 34.
32. Ibid., p. 29.
33. *Formale und transzendentale Logik*, p. 141.

thesis of Reproduction in Imagination," preceded by the synthesis exhibited by the "Synthesis of Apprehension in Intuition," and followed by the "Synthesis of Recognition in a Concept."[34] It is essential for Kant that even the elementary mode of cognition – that of apprehension – is grounded in a synthesis, or *is* a synthesis. If this is so on the elementary level, then a fortiori the synthesis is present on higher levels of awareness – in imagination and concepts. Each one of the levels is imbued with a mode of synthesis characteristic of it: apprehension, reproduction, and recognition. Though Husserl refers in quotation marks to "synthesis of recognition," he does not mention the other acts present in Kant, let alone the levels of awareness to which Kant refers. But the affinity between the active character of consciousness as understood by Kant and Husserl's interpretation of the activity is a telling example of the affinity that pertains at this point between his conception and the Kantian one.

Parallel to that "positive" relationship to Kant is the expression of Husserl's reservation, namely, that Kant confined his philosophy of the a priori or primacy of the activity of consciousness to experience. Husserl sees that confinement as a reaction to Hume or as an expression of Kant's reactive dependence on Hume. Since Hume was concerned with experience, Kant, in his attempt to solve Hume's problem, remains within the boundaries or "depth" of experience without going into the position of "ideal configurations," that is, the ideality of logical configurations within the scope of consciousness or the intentional and correlative characteristic of consciousness with reference to that which is ideal and not empirical. Hence, Kant's understanding of the a priori character of logic did not lead him to conceive the proper meaning of the ideality of the logical forms. Could he conceive of that, he would identify a motive for transcendental questions.[35]

This is a programmatic statement both in its negative reference to Kant and its positive interpretation of transcendentality: if transcendentality does not connote, only, the a priori condition grounded in thinking but relates to the very structure of consciousness and its acts, transcendentality cannot be confined to the employment of empirical data. Wherever there is the correlation between *cognitio* and *cogitatum* and that relation is not confined to the sphere of data and their presence in consciousness (for example, through the act of recognition), there exists a transcendental structure and grounding that pertains also to ideal or logical configurations which are *noemata* and thus have to be seen within the scope of the intentionality of consciousness. The transcendental problem of objective logic is parallel to the transcendental

34. Kant, *Kr. d. r. V.* A, pp. 98 ff.; Smith, pp. 131 ff.
35. Husserl, *Formale und transzendentale Logik*, p. 231.

problems of the science of the real (*Realwissenschaften*).[36] Hence, the transcendental inquiry amounts to the inquiry of the phenomenological subjectivity. In this sense the Kantian manifestation of transcendental philosophy and its neo-Kantian followers are to be listed as significant early stages (*Vorstufen*) of genuine transcendental philosophy.[37]

As a matter of fact, this statement serves as a kind of resume of the axis of the difference between Husserl and Kant, not only in terms of the scope of the transcendental inquiry (that is, whether it is limited to experience or has to be enlarged to encompass also the sphere of ideal configurations) but also whether transcendentality has to be seen in the context of the conditions of knowledge, empirical as well as logical, or whether it has to be seen in the context of an attempt to identify the essence of subjectivity.

A cognate subject to that of the different interpretations of the concept of transcendentality is that of the concept of constitution. In Kant constitutive principles are, by definition, principles related to empirical employment; only understanding is endowed with such principles while reason is not. The principle of reason is only a rule and "is not a principle of the possibility of experience and of empirical knowledge of objects of the senses ..."[38] Thus we could say that the notion of constitution is a concrete rendering of the overriding notion of transcendentality.

We do not need to elaborate on Husserl's version of constitution, which is a central theme of some of his late writings.[39] In accordance with the general trend of his thought, he refers to "constitutive subjectivity." The universal problem of transcendental philosophy and, in this context, of logic and theory of science are brought under the same heading.[40] The reference to spontaneous activities[41] enlarges the scope of the constitutive acts; hence the ideal configurations, to which we referred before, are to be included within the scope of constitution.[42] Coterminous with that rendering of the notion of constitution is possibly the inclusion of experience within the range of evidence:

36. Ibid., p. 233.
37. Ibid., pp. 234-35.
38. Kant, *Kr. d. r. V.* B, p. 537; Smith, p. 450.
39. I dealt with the issue in "Ambiguities of Husserl's Notion of Constitution," in *Phenomenology and Natural Existence. Essays in Honor of Marvin Farber*, ed. Dale Riepe (Albany, N.Y.: State University of New York Press, 1973), pp. 151 ff.

An illuminating explanation of Husserl's motives for his idealistic version of phenomenology is to be found in Roman Ingarden's article in the same volume, "About the Motives Which Led Husserl to Transcendental Idealism," pp. 95 ff.

40. Husserl, *Formale und transzendentale Logik*, p. 205.
41. Ibid., p. 235.
42. Ibid.

"Experience in the ordinary sense is particular evidence."[43] This is so since there are no opaque data to which transcendental concepts or principles are to be applied "from above." Experience ceases to be understood as an encounter and becomes an *Erlebnis* in the different levels of it: "we have ... a transcendental idealism that is nothing more than a consequently executed self-explication in the form of a systematic egological science...." Husserl rendered a resume of his own position when he introduced the notion of the a priori in "the second sense" of that concept, namely, the assertion (*Feststellung*) of the form through the modes of giving to itself (*Selbstgegebenheiten*).[44]

The paradoxical development of this turn to self-giveness, which is characteristic both of the concept of transcendentality as well as of the concept of constitution, is Heidegger's rendering of transcendentality which amounts, in a sense, to the reintroduction of what might be described as the vector of going out. Thus, it is a return to the Kantian version within the structure of the philosophy of existence: "every opening of the being (*Erschliessung*) as transcendence is *transcendental* knowledge. *Phenomenological* truth (openness of being) is *veritas transcendentalis*."[45] The outgoing character of the transcendental is a symmetric response to openness of the transcendent (*Erschliessung*). Though the element of the outgoing has a Kantian innuendo, the element of transcendence removes, instead of replacing, the concept of transcendentality from the structure as identified by Kant. Husserl's self-giveness becomes the reference to being and its openness.[46]

43. *Cartesian Meditations*, p. 57.

44. Husserl, *Die Idee der Phänomenologie, Fünf Vorlesungen*, ed. Walter Biemel, Husserliana XI (The Hague: Martinus Nijhoff, 1950), p. 52.

45. Martin Heidegger, *Sein und Zeit*, Erste Hälfte (Halle: Max Niemeyer Verlag, 1929), p. 38. The English edition, *Being and Time*, transl. John Macquarrie and Edward Robinson (Oxford: Blackwell, 1967), p. 6, uses the word "disclosure" for *Erschliessung*.

46. For additional reference, consult Husserl, "Kant und die Idee der Transzendentalphilosophie" (1924) in *Erste Philosophie* (1923-24) *Erster Teil, Kritische Ideengeschichte*, ed. Rudolf Boehm, Husserliana VII (The Hague, Martinus Nijhoff, 1956).

On the two systems, consult I. Kern, *Husserl und Kant, Eine Untersuchung über Husserls Verhältnis zu Kant und zum Neukantianismus* (The Hague: Martinus Nijhoff, 1964).

THE IDENTITIES OF THE THINGS THEMSELVES

JOHN SALLIS (Chicago)

I want to propose a certain critical orientation – that is, to begin measuring out the space of a critique of Husserl's phenomenology. "Critique" I understand as an establishing of limits, as a reflection which exposes a position as circumscribed and determined by certain positings. It is a matter of a reflection that would transgress the Husserlian position, that would exceed it in such a way as to expose certain positings as constituting its limits.

The spirit of such critical reflection clearly is not foreign to Husserl's thought. Phenomenology could not even pose as fundamental science if it simply took itself for granted, if it failed to incorporate a dimension of self-reflection. Husserl well recognized that phenomenology must take seriously the need to reflect upon its own determinations, upon its own constitution as the fundamental scientific discipline. It is this need that installs within phenomenology a recurrent movement of return to beginnings and that makes of the phenomenologist a perpetual beginner.

It is, then, such phenomenological self-reflection, such reflection on the phenomenological position and the project it generates that I want to resume here. However, this resumption will not be a mere continuation of the Husserlian reflection. One might call it, rather, an archaeology, using in a quite different sense a name that has repeatedly been applied to phenomenology itself, to the actual practice of phenomenology. Now it is a matter of an archaeology to be practiced on the Husserlian reflections in and through which phenomenology as such is constituted, an archaeology to be practiced in such a way as to uncover beneath phenomenology as constituted in those reflections a supporting ἀρχή. More specifically, I shall review certain fundamental determinations of phenomenology that were developed in Husserl's reflections, review them, however, in such a way as to expose beneath them a series of ontological positions that do not become explicit in Husserl's texts. Still more specifically, I want to expose beneath the determinations of

Cho, K.K. (ed.) Philosophy and Science in Phenomenological Perspective.

ISBN 978-94-009-6115-9

phenomenology a series of positings, each positing pertaining, though in different ways, to the *identity* of the things themselves – thus, a series of identity-positings. And though I regard the structure generated by the entire series of positings as tacitly underlying phenomenology as determined by Husserl, I want especially to suggest that one of these positings serves in an extraordinary way to give to phenomenology a basic solidarity with the history of metaphysics; on the other hand, I shall also suggest that the peculiar way in which this particular position functions within phenomenology serves to distinguish phenomenology from the history of metaphysics – or, rather, to render phenomenology the realization of that history, that at which it aims, its *telos*, its end.

It goes almost without saying that such archaeological critique is subversive. To expose the ἀρχή, to uncover the underlying identity-positings, is to deprive the position of its aura of self-evidence. It is to gain a certain leverage by which that position and the vast project of research that it prescribes can be decisively displaced.

Let me take the *Logos*-article of 1911 as the primary text in which to circumscribe the relevant determinations constitutive of the concept of phenomenology as such. This concept is expressed in its title: Phenomenology is to be philosophy as rigorous science. From the outset Husserl stresses the traditional character of this ideal. It is an ideal that was repeatedly resumed in the course of the philosophical tradition, even if never fully achieved:

> Such a fully conscious will to rigorous science dominated the Socratic-Platonic revolution in philosophy and also, at the beginning of the modern era, the scientific reactions against Scholasticism, especially the Cartesian revolution. Its impulse carries over to the great philosophies of the seventeenth and eighteenth centuries; it renews itself with most radical vigor in Kant's critique of reason and still dominates Fichte's philosophizing.[1]

And yet, precisely because of its will to rigor, phenomenology cannot merely resume, merely take over, anything – not even the conception of what is required in order for philosophy to be constituted as rigorous science. Philosophy as rigorous science can be achieved only if, in Husserl's words, "we accept nothing given in advance, allow nothing traditional to pass as a beginning, nor ourselves to be blinded by any names however great, but rather seek to attain the beginnings in a free dedication to the problems themselves and to the demands stemming from them" (PSW, 70). To this extent phenomenology must be non-traditional, must detach itself from the tradition for fear of being

1. Edmund Husserl, *Philosophie als strenge Wissenschaft*, Zweite Auflage (Frankfurt: Vittorio Klostermann, 1965), p. 11, hereafter cited to as PSW.

blinded to the problems themselves. Traditional philosophies, the history of metaphysics, must be set out of action, brought under what Husserl later calls the philosophic ἐποχή. Phenomenology must isolate philosophical problems from philosophy – that is, from the preestablished contexts and formulations that would otherwise come inadvertently into play.

Thus the separation would be complete and definitive: on the one side, phenomenology would resume the ideal of philosophy as rigorous science, the sheer ideal, nothing more, not even the most general traditional conceptions regarding the realization of that ideal; on the other side, this very ideal would require of phenomenology that it be disengaged from the history of metaphysics, that it set that history out of action, allowing history at most only that marginal role to which Husserl refers when he grants that past philosophies can "work on us as an inspiration" (PSW, 70). The two sides of the relation of phenomenology to the tradition would thus be well-defined: The traditional ideal would be resumed; and yet, the constitution of the discipline in which that ideal would be realized, the constitution of phenomenology, would be carried out in total disengagement from the tradition. The division would border on the clarity and distinctness of a division between form and content. There would be no remainder of form in content, no residue of content in form, no mixing across the line separating the ideal of phenomenology from phenomenology itself.

How, then, is phenomenology to be constituted as rigorous science? What is to constitute its rigor? Husserl's formulations are well known – for example, the one, already cited, according to which phenomenology is to be dedicated "to the problems themselves and to the demands stemming from them." Again, Husserl writes: "The impulse to research must proceed not from philosophies but from things and problems [*von den Sachen und Problemen*]" (PSW, 71). And yet, this opposition, the opposition between philosophies and problems, is hardly suited for sustaining the separation that Husserl would institute. Almost as soon as one speaks of problems he is referred back to the tradition and compelled to grant to the tradition a role much greater than that marginal one to which Husserl would limit it; for philosophical problems simply do not fall fully formulated from the heavens but rather exist only against the background of a philosophical tradition in which they have arisen and from which they have received their means of being formulated. Hence, if phenomenology would genuinely set the tradition out of action, its rigor cannot consist simply in dedication to problems.

It is not, then, so much a matter of problems but rather, as Husserl frequently expresses it, of the things themselves. Let me recall just two among those many passages in which Husserl directs phenomenology *zu den Sachen selbst*. The first occurs in the Foreword to the second edition of the *Logical Investigations*. Referring to the *Investigations*, Husserl writes:

> They are attempts at genuinely executed fundamental work on the immediately envisaged and grasped things [*Sachen*]; and even where they proceed critically, they do not lose themselves in discussions of standpoint, but rather leave the last word to the things themselves and to the work on them [*den Sachen selbst und der Arbeit an ihnen das letzte Wort belassen*].[2]

So, phenomenology is to attend to the things themselves as they are immediately envisaged, as they show themselves in their intuitive presence. The other passage occurs in *Ideas I*:

> To pass rational or scientific judgment upon things [*Sachen*] means being guided by the things themselves, getting away from talk and opinion back to the things themselves, questioning them in their self-givenness, and laying aside all prejudices alien to them.[3]

This return to the things themselves is to play the determinative role in phenomenology. It is to limit the operation of the tradition, limit it to a merely marginal role. Phenomenology will thus be able to demand of itself "die vollkommenste Voraussetzungslosigkeit" (*Ideen*, section 63).

In this requirement of rigor, in this injunction "to the things themselves," one can discern the workings of the first of those positings which I have proposed to uncover, the first of the identity-positings. This injunction, if taken at its highest level of generality, prescribes a certain reflexive operation of the principle of identity: The phenomenologist is to be "guided by the things themselves;" he is enjoined to let the thing itself show itself from itself, in contrast to a procedure in which something different from the thing itself would obtrude into the showing. And yet such an injunction can be coherently heeded only if there is a thing *itself*, only if the thing is so united with itself that all intrusion of otherness can be set out of action, only if the thing is constituted in a fundamental identity with itself, a self-identity. Thus, beneath the requirement of rigor there lies a positing of the principle of identity, a positing of the identity of the thing with itself, of its self-identity. The phenomenological position, as rigorous, presupposes a positing of the field of things *as* a field of self-identity. This is, then, the first of the underlying identity-positings.

The determinative role to be played by the return to the things themselves is formulated by Husserl as the principle of all principles:

2. Husserl, *Logische Untersuchungen*, Fünfte Auflage (Tübingen: Max Niemeyer Verlag, 1968), Erster Band, p. x.

3. Husserl, *Ideen zu einer reinen Phänomenologie und phänomenologischen Philosophie*, Erstes Buch (The Hague: Martinus Nijhoff, 1950), section 19, hereafter referred to as *Ideen*.

> No theory we can conceive can mislead us in regard to the principle of all principles: that every originary dator intuition [*jede originär gebende Anschauung*] is a legitimizing source of knowledge, that everything originarily (so to speak, in its bodily actuality) offered to us in "intuition" is to be accepted simply as what it is presented as being, but also only within the limits in which it there presents itself (*Ideen*, section 24).

This principle expresses the source from which all other principles must draw their legitimation, and this is why Husserl calls it the principle of all principles. But it is not a principle *of* phenomenology, not a principle which phenomenology itself would uncover, formulate, and elaborate, but rather is the principle by which phenomenology is itself constituted as a discipline. Furthermore, it is a principle which, by referring all legitimation of knowledge to originary intuition, disrupts the very concept of principle. It withdraws from all principles their traditional function, their grounding function, by placing them all under the demand for legitimation by reference to intuition. The principle of *all* principles is the principle of *no* principles – that is, it is a principle which is not a principle, a principle which is not itself, something different from itself. And what of the grounding function that would belong to the principle of all principles itself? Would it not withdraw this function from itself too, cancelling itself as a principle and yet, in that very cancelling, functioning precisely as a principle? It is a matter of a principle whose very inscription in Husserl's text is at the same time its erasure. It is a matter of something which is not identical with itself, something different from itself, or, to speak more precisely, a matter of utter self-differencing.

One could distinguish, then, two positings which together would comprise the position of rigor, that is, would posit the return to the things themselves as determinative for phenomenology. On the one hand, there is the positing of self-identity which underlies the very concept of things themselves. On the other hand, there is the positing which issues in the principle of all principles. What is decisive is that the second positing, a positing which unfolds into an utter self-differencing, is itself a violation of that self-identity posited in the first positing. Thus, within the complex positing by which phenomenology would be constituted as rigorous, there is a fundamental opposition, an opposition so fundamental that it could disrupt our very concept of the fundamental, i.e., our concept of ground, and indeed our very concept of concept. This opposition serves to remove the entire dimension of this positing, the dimension of phenomenological self-reflection, from that field of self-identity in which phenomenology would otherwise secure itself.

Rigor is not, however, the only fundamental determination of phenomenology. According to the text *Philosophy as Rigorous Science*, phenomenology is to be determined not only by its directedness to the things themselves but also by another directedness, another determining moment. Husserl identifies this other moment near the end of that text, at a point where, having referred to the moment of rigor, he continues thus:

> Philosophy, however, is essentially a science of true beginnings, of origins, of *ῥιζώματα πάντων*. The science of what is radical must from every point of view be radical itself in its procedure (PRS, 71).

Thus, phenomenology is to be not only rigorous science but also *radical* science: It is to be directed at the root of things, at the true beginnings, at the original things, at things in the original. Husserl offers a negative indication of the meaning of this radicalness. Referring again to the phenomenological return to the things themselves, he continues thus:

> But one must never abandon one's radical lack of prejudice [*radikale Vorurteilslosigkeit*] and identify such 'things' [*Sachen*] with empirical 'facts' [*empirische Tatsachen*], thus remaining blind to ideas, which are, after all, to such a great extent absolutely given in immediate intuition (PRS, 71).

Thus, the radicalness of phenomenology requires that one avoid simply identifying the things themselves with empirically given things; and so, to construe phenomenology as empiricism is precisely to miss its radicalness, its directedness to the originary. As radical, phenomenology is to avoid prematurely or dogmatically identifying the things themselves with anything; it is to bring the identity of the things themselves into question, to ask which things are things themselves in an originary sense.

Here again there is an underlying identity-positing, the second in the series of positings. In order to be radical, phenomenology would bring into play the question of the identity of the things themselves, the question as to which things are things themselves in an originary sense. But in bringing this question into play, one would already have posited a certain identity-structure, one more complex than in the previous case. Specifically, one would already have posited that identity-structure according to which there would be some things self-identical in a sense that would surpass the simple self-identity underlying the demand for rigor; these things would have the self-identity *of an original*, that is, an original self-identity in contrast to the self-dispersion, the difference, belonging intrinsically to everything having the character of an image. In other words, the identity-structure would install in the field of things the contrast between original self-identity and various degrees of imaginal self-difference. In short, it would structure the field of things according to the dyadic structure of image and original. In bringing into play the question of the identity of the original things themselves, one would then be undertaking to order things with respect to this already posited identity-structure. Therefore, beneath the requirement of radicalness there lies a positing of this identity-structure, this image-original schema. The phenomenological position, as radical, presupposes the positing of the field of things as a field of originals and images.

These are, then, the determinations of phenomenology according to the text *Philosophy as Rigorous Science* and the identity-positings which underlie them. According to the Husserlian text, phenomenology is essentially constituted by the demands for rigor and for radicalness. And since each determination serves to limit and specify the other, it is especially in their interplay that this constitution is effected.

And yet, as soon as phenomenology is placed at the intersection of these two determinations, its alleged disengagement from the history of metaphysics becomes suspect; for throughout this history, at its most critical junctures, at its moments of profoundest self-reflection, philosophy has reverted to this intersection and demanded of itself that it be rigorous and radical; repeatedly philosophy has undertaken the radical return to the things themselves, undertaken the return so radically as to bring into question the very identity of the things themselves. Thus, the solidarity of phenomenology with the history of metaphysics decisively exceeds the mere sharing of the formal ideal of scientific philosophy; and there is a mixing across the line which Husserl would like to draw between the ideal of phenomenology and phenomenology itself.

Let me trace in merest outline some of those junctures in the history of metaphysics at which the radical return to the things themselves is undertaken anew.

Consider, first, the turn inscribed at the beginning of metaphysics, the Socratic turn presented in Plato's *Phaedo*. Here Socrates relates his own history; he tells of how, having repeatedly failed in the investigation of things by the methods of his predecessors, he finally resolved not to study things directly, for fear of such blindness as befalls those who look at the sun during an eclipse. Instead, he says, "I thought I must have recourse to λόγοι and examine in them the truth of beings."[4] This turn from immediately presented things to λόγοι is of course what eventually became the ascent from sensible to intelligible.

Despite some similarities with the turn by which Husserl would found phenomenology – for example, the break with predecessors, the fear of a kind of blindness – the Socratic turn seems, in its fundamental intent, to be almost the opposite of the phenomenological turn; it

4. Plato, *Phaedo*, 99e.

appears to be a turn away from the things rather than a return to them. It is a turn away from immediately presented things, a turn to λόγοι and eventually to εἴδη. And yet, the turn away from the immediately presented things appears as a turn away from the things themselves *only if* it is assumed in advance, dogmatically, that the immediately presented things are to be identified as the things themselves – that is, only if the question of the identity of the things themselves is not really allowed to come into play. If, on the other hand, the Socratic turn is regarded within that Platonic context in which in fact the question of the identity of the things themselves is in play, then it becomes clear that the Socratic turn away from things as immediately, sensibly presented is a turn back to them in their originary presence. It is a turn away from things in their immediate presence to those things in their truth. It is a turn from the remote images of things to those things themselves in the original.

The Socratic turn determines the entire history of metaphysics. In that history it is reenacted again and again, reenacted at the most critical junctures of that history. In Aristotle it is reenacted in the determination of first philosophy as the turn to, the looking toward (*θεωρητική*), the first beginnings and causes (*τῶν πρώτων ἀρχῶν καὶ αἰτιῶν*). In Descartes it is reenacted as a turn ultimately to the subject. As with Socrates, its Cartesian presentation is autobiographical – as in the following passage from the *Discourse on Method:*

> This is why I gave up my studies entirely as soon as I reached the age when I was no longer under the control of my teachers. I resolved to seek no other knowledge than that which I might find within myself, or perhaps in the great book of the world.[5]

Giving up his studies at La Flèche, Descartes broke with the traditional scholasticism represented there; like Socrates, he broke with his predecessors. Instead of their theories inscribed in the books of tradition, he turned to the great book of the world, to things themselves; he set out, in his words, "to reflect on the things which present themselves [*à faire telle réflexion sur les choses qui se présentaient*]." But the radicalness of his questioning led finally to that which (in a special sense) underlies things, to the *ὑποκείμενον*, the *subiectum*; and thus the turn was consummated in the turn to the subject.

The turn is again reenacted in Fichte. Here philosophy begins almost immediately with the turn back to the subject, now understood more radically as the I. This is the original thing itself, and the task of the philosopher is merely to attend to it as it shows itself. Thus Fichte

5. René Descartes, *Discours de la méthode*, Première Partie.

writes that the object of philosophical thought is "a living and active thing which engenders insights from and through itself and which the philosopher merely contemplates."[6]

Finally, in Hegel the demand to turn to the things themselves is explicit; no less than with Husserl, this demand determines the project designated by the title "phenomenology." The demand is issued again and again in the Preface to *Phenomenology of Spirit* – for example, in the passage in which, referring to the kinds of discussions usually included in prefaces, he writes:

> For instead of dealing with the thing [*Sache*] this kind of activity is always away beyond it; instead of tarrying with it and losing itself in it, this kind of knowing is forever grasping for something else; it remains preoccupied with itself instead of being preoccupied with the thing [*Sache*] and surrendering to it.[7]

Thus, at all of these junctures it is a matter of the same turn, the turn which then Husserl too would reenact in and as the beginning of phenomenology. A solidarity is thus exposed within the metaphysical tradition and between phenomenology and that tradition: Always it is a matter of the radical return to the things themselves.

Underlying this solidarity, underlying the project of the radical return to things themselves, there is another identity-positing, the third in the series, in many respects the most consequential from an archaeological point of view. This position and its consequential character can be most easily exposed and formulated by bringing into play the concept of presence and by thematizing the solidarity in terms of this concept. What metaphysics and phenomenology have in common is that both accord a peculiar privilege to presence. For both it is a matter of attending to things *as they present themselves*, that is, in their *presence*. And it is a matter of attending to them in their *original* presence – that is, in that genuine presence that is to be contrasted with such presence as is had by images, with presence permeated by a differentiating absence. Thus, a certain privilege of presence is posited beneath the project of the radical return to the things themselves, the project shared by phenomenology and metaphysics.

This position can be thematized more precisely. Whether in the form of metaphysics or phenomenology, philosophy appeals to the things themselves in their originary character, directs itself to things as they present themselves in their originary presence. In other words, philosophy binds itself to a certain discipline, the discipline of presence. What philosophy takes things to be is governed solely by the presence of

6. J.G. Fichte, *Zweite Einleitung in die Wissenschaftslehre, Werke*, I, p. 454.
7. G.W.F. Hegel, *Phänomenologie des Geistes* (Hamburg: Felix Meiner), p. 11.

those things; their being is philosophically determined solely in reference to their originary presence. But this is to say that an *identity* is posited *between being and presence*. The positing of this identity of being and presence is what underlies the radical return to the things themselves; and this identity-positing is what is shared by metaphysics and phenomenology, what constitutes the solidarity at its deepest level.

And yet, despite the solidarity, there is something distinctive about the phenomenological renewal of the radical return to the things themselves, something which distinguishes phenomenology from metaphysics and makes it more than a mere rehabilitation of the tradition: despite the mixing across the line that Husserl would draw between the traditional ideal and its phenomenological renewal, there is something to give genuine content to Husserl's proclamation in the text *Philosophy as Rigorous Science* that philosophy "is not yet a science at all, that as science it has not yet begun" (PSW, 8). To develop this problem adequately, to exhibit fully that surplus by which phenomenology exceeds metaphysics, would require that one resume certain of Husserl's central-most reflections, among them those concerning phenomenological reduction. Such a centering would perhaps eventually be necessary for a genuinely sustained movement toward the edge of the text; but here I am attempting only a fragmentary sketch of that movement. Let me, then, merely focus again on the text *Philosophy as Rigorous Science* and undertake by means of a contrast drawn in it to circumscribe as directly as possible that character by which phenomenology exceeds the sphere of solidarity that has been sketched.

The relevant contrast is drawn in the following passage:

> Psychical being, being as "phenomenon", is in principle not a unity that could be experienced in several separate perceptions as individually identical, not even in perceptions of the same subject. In the psychical sphere there is, in other words, no distinction between appearance and being... (PSW, 35).

Though this contrast harbors of course a host of problems that Husserl elsewhere elaborates, it is presented here in very straightforward terms. The contrast is between the experience of two different regions of being. On the one hand, the experience of external objects (or physical being) is always by way of several partial perceptions. Such an object transcends every partial appearance in such a way that there is necessarily a distinction between being and appearance – that is, a difference between being and presence. On the other hand, the experience of psychic being, inner experience, does not involve any such separate partial perceptions or profiles. A mental state is not a unity given in and through various appearances but rather is something immediately given, directly present. In this region, therefore, there is no distinction between what something is and what it appears as, no distinction between what it is and how it is present, no distinction between being and presence. With regard to the region of psychic being, there is identity of being and presence.

Phenomenology is, then, distinctive in that it carries out the appeal to the things themselves in a way that is fundamentally linked to the region of psychic being – to this region regarded, not psychologically, but rather as the locus of the identity of being and presence, or, at the level of the Husserlian formulation, regarded as pure or transcendental consciousness. So, what is it that differentiates phenomenology from that metaphysical tradition? What is it that renders phenomenology so scientific that it can claim to accomplish that beginning of scientific philosophy which the tradition never succeeded in making? Whereas metaphysics, turning radically to the things themselves, does indeed posit the identity of being and presence, phenomenology goes still further with regard to this underlying identity-positing: Phenomenology attaches itself to a region in which this identity is *necessarily* posited, necessarily in force, a region in which this identity subsists necessarily, by the very nature of that region. Phenomenology enforces that discipline of presence which it shares with the metaphysical tradition, enforces it by orienting itself to that special region in which is realized necessarily the identity of being and presence, that is, the very identity that defines the discipline.

This self-orienting by which phenomenology is installed within the position of the identity of being and presence is of course simply what Husserl calls the phenomenological ἐποχή. In the Husserlian formulation, the ἐποχή is that procedure which allows the intentional object to present itself *as intentional*, as a *noema*, as irreal. To this end, the ἐποχή takes the form of neutrality-modification, neutralizing whatever real existence the object might otherwise be taken to possess, especially that unanalyzed objective existence that things in the world are naturally taken to have. By undergoing the reduction brought by the ἐηοχή, objects come to be taken as *being* precisely insofar as they *present* themselves in an intentional experience – that is, as *being* precisely insofar as they are *intentionally present*. Thus, the effect of the ἐποχή is to neutralize every form of being other than intentional presence, to exclude *every form of being that exceeds presence*. It is thus that it enforces the identity of being and presence and installs phenomenology within the position of that identity. To be installed in that position is, in the Husserlian formulation, to adopt the transcendental or phenomenological attitude.

It is also to engage oneself in the radical return to the things themselves, to do so in a way that decisively exceeds the history of metaphysics, exceeds it in precisely such a way as to realize its intent and be thus its end. And yet, this excess is linked to another, and it is only in relation to this other excess that phenomenology's exceeding of the history of metaphysics can be theoretically unfolded. But through this other excess, which I have sought to expose as a series of identity-positings, phenomenology is itself exceeded.

HUSSERL'S TRANSCENDENTAL PHENOMENOLOGY AND HISTORY

ELISABETH STRÖKER (Cologne)

Husserl's "transcendental phenomenology and history" is not a new subject, but it is a young one. Only in the last decade have Husserl scholars given it greater attention. For a long time it may have seemed that Husserl's philosophy had nothing to do with history, that history could not be its subject, since his transcendental phenomenology was concerned primarily with insights into general structures and ultimately into the essential structures of transcendental subjectivity and its world-constituting achievements.

Historical problems apparently could come up only as the counterpart of what was phenomenologically important: as the mere factual in contrast to the essential; as the singular in contrast to the general; as the growing and passing in contrast to what remains; as what is changing and varying in contrast to what is constant and unvarying. Above all, history could evidently appear only as that which I, as a natural human being, am involved in – not as something that belongs to me as a transcendental ego.

Husserl made several remarks that support this view, principally in *Ideas I* (1913). They occur particularly in such contexts where Husserl, misleadingly, described the decisive methodical step of his phenomenology the transcendental reduction – in terms of "suspension" or "overthrow" of the world or putting it "into brackets." This misconception, to which Husserl contributed his share, could not be overcome, it seems, even by Husserl's factual performance of the reduction. But the transcendental reduction was undoubtedly meant to be something quite different from "suspension" of the world; it was the objectification of the world – in such a way however that the world was "reduced" to its phenomenon in the transcendental consciousness. Yet this meant nothing else than that the world's being and existence, taken for granted in the natural attitude (but usually not thematized in it), could become subject to the transcendental phenomenology as a world "meant as" being and existing. Thus it could be taken seriously in its claim of being.

Cho, K.K. (ed.) Philosophy and Science in Phenomenological Perspective.

ISBN 978-94-009-6115-9

It was Husserl's goal to clarify this "claim of being," to explicate the "sense" the world has for all of us – that is, to explain phenomenologically what we mean in saying that the world exists.[1]

It is undeniable that the subject too forms part of the world. Yet as a human being in the world, he is not only part of corporeal nature but a historical being, and the world-as-world of his actions and creations is a historical world.

Nevertheless, it is not history but nature to which Husserl gives his full attention when, in the transcendental attitude, he investigates the world as "meant as being."

Husserl did not disregard the fact that in the world there are not only natural things but also those he called "cultural objects," created and formed by human social activities. In the first decade of this century Husserl realized, from his conversations with Dilthey, that the sciences are also products of historical life. Could not one have expected then that, from the beginning, history (like nature) would become the object of Husserl's phenomenological study?

Husserl analyzes nature in detail again and again; he orients himself almost exclusively on mathematical and physical determinations of things, their spatio-temporality, their causality. Science that has to be explained phenomenologically is for him, quite naturally, natural science.[2]

Hence, it is a surprise to find that Husserl, in *The Crisis of European Sciences and Transcendental Phenomenology* (1936), gives prominence to the idea that we are historical beings, *heirs of the past*; that holds true particularly for philosophers, their concepts, problems, and methods. Historical reflections are now necessary for a radical understanding, not only of our own selves but also of philosophy.[3] That historical reflection belongs essentially to the business of philosophy is Husserl's decisive insight in his later years, and is the source of his often discussed "turn" to the life-world. As a matter of fact, it is Husserl's concept of history that is basically new in *Crisis*.

Husserl had dealt with history earlier, for example in his 1923 lectures on "First Philosophy," wherein the history of philosophy introduced the systematic part. Yet in this separation between the his-

1. Cf. Elisabeth Ströker, "Das Problem der Epoché in der Philosophie Edmund Husserls," in vol. 1, Analecta Husserliana, ed. A.T. Tymieniecka (Dordrecht: Reidel Publ. Co., 1971), pp. 170-85.

2. Cf. Ströker, "Edmund Husserl's Phenomenology as Foundation of Natural Science," in vol. 2, Analecta Husserliana, ed. A.T. Tymieniecka (Dordrecht: Reidel Publ. Co., 1972), pp. 245-57.

3. Edmund Husserl, *The Crisis of European Sciences and Transcendental Phenomenology*, transl. David Carr (Evanston, Ill.: Northwestern University Press, 1970), pp. 17, 71-2.

tory and the system of philosophy, history did not form an integral part of "the things themselves" (*der Sachen selbst*) that Husserl was concerned with. Hence, it has rightly been pointed out that in the *Crisis* Husserl took history seriously in quite another and new way.[4]

In connection with this, a number of problems arose for phenomenological scholarship. Could it be that a new – that is, a historical – foundation of phenomenology was brought into being by Husserl's *Crisis*? The methodological question has been raised: whether Husserl's phenomenology, while being concerned with history, can still be understood as transcendental phenomenology in the sense developed by him after 1907, or whether with the historical questions in *Crisis* something totally new came into being in his phenomenology (suggesting that Husserl's later work broke with his previous thought).

I call attention to these questions, but they are not the subject of this paper. I shall return to them only insofar as they touch upon the problematic issues I want to take up. The hints so far perhaps illustrate that history plays a peculiar role in Husserl's thought; this applies to his transcendental phenomenology on the whole, not only to its later phase.

II

First, I shall briefly present the idea that Husserl's transcendental phenomenology was concerned with history at a relatively early stage – earlier than Husserl himself expressly dealt with it. In other words, I want to show how, in Husserl's development of his phenomenology, there gradually crystallized a concept of history that came fully into its own in *Crisis* and there takes final shape (insofar as one can claim, in view of the fragmentary status of Husserl's last work). This attempt is given direction by the question of what is meant when Husserl talks of "history."

Second, I want to address the questions of what Husserl's concept of history offers to phenomenological understanding, what is going on in the discipline of history, and what historians are concerned with when they do historical research.

As to the first question, going into further detail seems unavoidable, since examining Husserl's conception of history only in *Crisis* would be too narrow a point of view. Other philosophers have realized this.

Yet it is my *thesis* that Husserl's concept of history underwent a

4. See principally David Carr, *Phenomenology and the Problem of History* (Evanston, Ill.: Northwestern University Press, 1974); also, Ludwig Landgrebe, *Phänomenologie und Geschichte* (Gütersloh: 1968).

certain development and made its way gradually from rather inconspicuous beginnings – and this, according to the progressive differentiation of his method. Or to put it more precisely, I hope to show that Husserl's turn to history, as explicitly found in *Crisis*, cannot be understood otherwise than as an intrinsic consequence of the procedure Husserl inaugurated when founding transcendental phenomenology. This "thesis of continuity" may seem to be a rather bold thesis, but I expect to show that Husserl, when coming to terms with history, does not turn his back on his former approach to transcendental phenomenology. Rather, it is to be regarded as the final demand on possibilities implied in Husserl's transcendental phenomenological method from the start.

Let us remember that Husserl's starting point was the question of *how* the world is presented in consciousness. It was no problem to him *that* the world exists; this is a mere fact that has to be admitted. Husserl would later (1932) term this fact the "original historicity" (*Urhistorizität*) of the world. Rather, it is its *mode* of givenness Husserl is puzzled by. This puzzle is grounded in the transcendence of the world. That the world is not merely a content of consciousness but is outside it and that nevertheless its transcendence cannot be found elsewhere but as a transcendence "given to" consciousness (that is, "*meant as* transcendent" to it) leads Husserl to the transcendental attitude for asking how this can be conceived.

The constitution of the transcendent world in consciousness that, in respect to its world-constitutive achievements, has to be seen as transcendental consciousness thus becomes Husserl's main theme. It served as a guide to permanently refining the phenomenological method, which finally arrived at a stage of intentional analysis and brought about "constitutive phenomenology." It is in the precise meaning of the term that this form, typical of Husserl's transcendental philosophy, shows something no longer as merely "given" to or "intended" by consciousness, but as basically being a transcendentally instant product, resulting from manifold transcendental syntheses of sense-constituting activities (*Sinnstiftungen*), which, however, are never to be completed. It is not an accident that Husserl's program of constitutive phenomenology in the mid-twenties thus developed from a static to a genetic phenomenology.

Where, in this kind of phenomenological approach, does history occur?

In his early analyses Husserl found a state of affairs he described by the term "horizon." Anything given presents itself in surroundings of other given things that form its "external" horizons. Yet it has also further fundamental characteristics, which in a certain perspective remain unknown but which nevertheless exist. In this case, Husserl speaks of its "internal" horizons. Having these twofold horizons is an essential feature of all givenness.

The correlative on the side of the act is a surplus of meaning: the given is always meant to be more than that which it is as actually given; such a surplus is at the same time a principal possibility for further investigation and for transforming the potentially "co-meant" into something actually meant.

Thus, phenomena like *actuality* and *potentiality* in all givenness enter the "horizon" of Husserl's phenomenology. Being regarded simply as different modes of consciousness of objects, they still belong to investigations of the static sort, which Husserl himself would criticize before long, since actuality and potentiality characterize certain relations of acts among themselves.

But these relations are primarily *temporal relations*. In the earlier "Phenomenological Analyses of Internal Time Consciousness" Husserl investigated the temporal structure thoroughly. Yet now the temporality of consciousness gains a special impact on Husserl's method of intentional analysis. What in the static analyses was differentiated simply as potentiality and actuality now leads deeper into the specific temporality of all givenness – and that, thanks to a peculiar temporality of the transcendental consciousness. That *anything* given (and to be given) to consciousness is *temporal* is the first discovery of genetic phenomenology.

That does not, of course, mean that any object is given "within" the time, since we, in the natural attitude, experience it as a sequence of states and processes in objective time. Rather, the principal temporality of all givenness means that everything given is identifiable and determinable as a certain being (*Seiendes*) only in continually progressing syntheses, in such a way, however, that the temporal structure of the acts that constitute its sense of being (*Seinssinn*) is different from any sequence of time as it is normally understood.

Penetrating into the internal horizons of a given object is not only transforming that which "now" is potentially co-meant in a "then" actually self-given, and former actual givenness as "now" past as simply being left behind. Rather, in any temporal phase of givenness is that which "has been" given in a preceding phase preserved in a certain way. That which on the side of the object actually emerges and in the course of objective time again disappears, to give way to new actual givenness, is not extinguished in consciousness but leaves behind "sediments" that can be reactivated under certain circumstances.

Consciousness, continually existing in constitutive acts, is not simply in the "stream of consciousness" of *Ideas I* in which acts *in* the time endlessly come and go; rather consciousness structures itself at the same time according to the past, the present, the future, and in such a way, indeed, that each of these phases is permanently under the influence of the others. It is by no means paradoxical that, for example, the present and even the future can co-determine the past, since they do not do that as merely temporal phases of consciousness that were to be conceived in a time being already pre-given to consciousness. Rather, it is the temporal self-structuralization of consciousness as something transcendental, thanks to which a world of objects can be constituted at all.

That means that all constitution is now genetic constitution, motivated from a background of constitutive achievements in the past, which also co-configurate the anticipation of any actual present in the future. Any object whatsoever is no longer the identical objective "pole" of intending acts, nor is the subject the corresponding subjective "pole" of acts and merely the source of origin, as was the case in static phenomenology. Husserl rightly emphasized in his *Formal and Transcendental Logic* that such genetic phenomenology only then leads to concrete phenomenological analyses.[5] Its concreteness does not, of course, only concern the constitution of objects. Closely with it goes the self-constitution of consciousness that also turns out to be genetic. That means that the ego has to conceive itself as a unity of a temporal structured consciousness in all its sedimented acquisitions, including all those to be potentially acquired in the future. It is this concrete "habitualized" ego which Husserl calls "monad."

It is not an accident that Husserl, in this connection, speaks of the *history of the ego*. As early as 1921 he stated (and I believe this is the first passage of this sort) that "every community of absolute egos, of absolute subjectivities – in full concretion to which belongs the constitution of the world – has its *'passive'* and *'active'* history and *exists* in this history only. *History is the great fact of absolute being*; and the last questions ... are totally the same with the questions about the absolute sense of history."[6]

To understand this adequately, it should be noted that the passage

5. Husserl, *Formal and Transcendental Logic*, transl. Dorion Cairns (The Hague: Martinus Nijhoff, 1969), sections 60-4. For earlier stages of Husserl's genetic phenomenology, cf. his *Zur Phänomenologie der Intersubjektivität*, ed. I. Kern, Part 2, Husserliana XIV (The Hague: Martinus Nijhoff, 1973), pp. 34-42.

6. Husserl, *Erste Philosophie*, ed. R. Boehm, Husserliana VIII (The Hague: Martinus Nijhoff, 1959), p. 506: "Absolut betrachtet, hat jedes ego seine *Geschichte*, und es ist nur als Subjekt einer, seiner Geschichte. Und jede kommunikative Gemeinschaft von absoluten Ich, von absoluten Subjektivitäten – in voller Konkretion, zu der die Konstitution der Welt gehört – hat ihre *'passive'* und *'aktive' Geschihte* und *ist* nur in dieser Geschichte. *Die Geschichte ist das grosse Faktum des absoluten Seins*; und die letzten Fragen ... sind eins mit den (Fragen) nach dem absoluten Sinn der Geschichte." As to the last statement, see also Ludwig Landgrebe, "Meditation über Husserls Wort 'Die Geschichte ist das grosse Faktum des absoluten Seins,'" *Tijdschrift voor Filosofie* 36 (1974), pp. 107-26.

just quoted is the very last in a manuscript of ten pages, whose subject is nothing less than the phenomenological reduction and the regress from the natural world to transcendental subjectivity. That may seem strange at first, but it is illustrative of Husserl's concept of history.

According to several later corrections, Husserl attached great importance to this essay from 1921. For us who know the later development of Husserl's transcendental phenomenology, it is relatively easy to recognize in this manuscript the kernel of a problem that Husserl explored to a remarkable extent in *Cartesian Meditations* (1931) and *Crisis* (1936). Both works form stages in Husserl's conception of history.

1. The first stage is noted when Husserl says in 1921: "According to this, it is only the egos in their communicative relationship that are absolute beings. They are, in their community, the absolute supporters (*Träger*) of the world ..." They are "absolute" insofar as all being is transcendentally to be referred back to the being of egos, which in their plurality constitute the world. So it is *intersubjectivity*, whose importance Husserl became aware of when he talked of history for the first time.

It would be going too far beyond our subject to deal with Husserl's theory of intersubjectivity more closely. Of immediate interest for us may be only what we miss in it: to recognize that that which we miss is nevertheless implicated in Husserl's theory of intersubjectivity and that it becomes, at least partly, prominent in the *Crisis*.

It is well-known that Husserl dealt with the problem of intersubjectivity especially in the fifth of his *Cartesian Meditations*. Its intentional analysis results in the mutual self-constitution of the plurality of egos, each of which acknowledges the other egos qua transcendental egos and so are able as a transcendental community to constitute an objective world.

But how does the existence of other egos and my insight into their belonging to a social community effect my history? Husserl's exposition of the transcendental intersubjectivity is awkward, to be sure, for our problem, in that the analyses in the Fifth Meditation mainly remain static and that the possibility of genetic investigation is not taken advantage of sufficiently.

The static form of analysis as to the givenness of other egos in terms of "appresentation" and "apprehension" has its grounds in Husserl's all-too-narrow, scarcely adequate starting point. Besides the fact that Husserl investigates intersubjectivity according to the model of communication between two egos only, he makes them appear primarily through mutual perception in exclusively spatial connections, whereas the temporal dimension is not exposed there.

In fact, what had been regarded abstractly only as my ego, as my monadic life of acts in all its horizons of the past, present, and future, as my transcendental acquisitions and habitualities, is now, in the context of the transcendental community of monads, methodically transcended. Everything potentially given and co-meant in what is given to me is now to be understood as something which, although not explicitly given to me, can nevertheless be meant by me as possibly given to others. What is lacking in my actual experience can principally be experienced by others, can be "borrowed" by me, and can, as borrowed, become my possession, by whatever complex syntheses this may be brought about.

Nevertheless, each ego keeps its own monadic (and thus abstract) temporal structure of consciousness and consequently its monadic history. The other egos in their temporal self-constitution are not even taken into account. In other words, the problem of "horizon" in the *Cartesian Meditations* was mainly limited to the spatial horizons of the objective given outside the egos, whereas Husserl does not take into consideration those horizons in which they are already founded, namely, the horizons of temporally structured consciousness and the "melting" of genetically constituted horizons of the egos in their transcendental community.

Closer examination reveals, however, that the genetic analysis in the Fifth Meditation is only put aside by Husserl's special problem – the constitution of the objectivity of the world.[7] But Husserl clearly did not want it to be overlooked. "The ego constitutes itself in, so to speak, a unity of a 'history,'" Husserl states, even in the *Cartesian Meditations.*[8] Yet there is, to be sure, a "history-so-to-speak;" Husserl was careful to put the term in quotation marks, evidently aware that this kind of history was only an abstract one, as long as it was not grasped phenomenologically as history of transcendental intersubjectivity.

2. There are, it must be stated, no Husserlian investigations that penetrate deeper into the intersubjectivity until it is more finely elucidated in its historicity. However, we find another determination of Husserl's concept of history in the *Cartesian Meditations* that comes to prominence later in the *Crisis*.

For history, in its full Husserlian sense, is the history of the transcendental intersubjectivity. We must keep in mind that, so far, we have had

7. For a while Husserl cut off, so to speak, a methodical procedure he had already prepared for assuring primarily the objectivity of the world by intersubjective constitution. (Cf. my essay cited in Note 1 above.) Husserl dealt more with newly arising difficulties in performing the transcendental reduction than with the problem of the historicity of the monadic community. Hence, the latter was left uninvestigated.

8. Husserl, *Cartesian Meditations*, transl. Dorion Cairns (The Hague: Martinus Nijhoff, 1960), section 37.

to deal exclusively with *history in the frame of the transcendental reduction.*[9] That is also the meaning when Husserl says in *Crisis*: "History is, from the very beginning, nothing else but the vital movement ... in original sense-formation and sense-sedimentation."[10] Neither procedure is to be understood as a mundane activity of human subjects *in* the world. What Husserl proposed here is nothing less than the thesis that it is the original constitutive activities of transcendental intersubjectivity from which the world has, and permanently gains, its sense. This sense, however, is to be comprehended historically as far as transcendental intersubjectivity becomes phenomenologically clear in its history – that is, in its history through exerting the influence of the egos, each on the others, by which the abstract "history" of the single ego is completed and made concrete.

As already mentioned, the mutual constitution of the egos-qua-historical-egos, and therefore its concrete self-constitution as well as the transcendental-historical constitution of social communities, remained a program for Husserl. One can only see in which direction it should have been followed, since it would have been a matter of Husserl's intentional analysis in his genetic phenomenology that had to be worked through further to an *intentional-historical* analysis.

Only by this kind of analysis could Husserl's phenomenology become genetic phenomenology in its full sense. We can see that Husserl did not truly arrive at it in his last work. We meet it in transcendental intersubjectivity being understood in its historical-genetic constitutions of objects, but it is presupposed rather than phenomenologically analyzed.[11] The meaning of history that Husserl comes to terms with in the *Crisis* remains, at that point, restricted.

However, Husserl even then did not overlook the historical genesis of transcendental intersubjectivity as a problem left open to analysis, nor did he overlook the consequences of a historically conceived transcendental intersubjectivity for its constituted world. What he finally had in mind was a more differentiated world than one which was only transcendent and objective.

9. For this meaning of history, cf. Ströker, "Geschichte und Lebenswelt als Sinnesfundament der Wissenschaften," in *Lebenswelt und Wissenschaft in der Philosophie Edmund Husserls*, ed. Ströker (Frankfurt: 1979). For Husserl's term "transcendental historicity," see the following text.

10. Husserl, *Crisis of European Sciences* (1936), Appendix 6, p. 371.

11. The problem is not only the transcendental genesis of the constitution of objects, as Husserl has investigated in the *Crisis* (and remarkably enough in the case of geometry and its nontemporal formations). (Cf. *Crisis*, pp. 353-78.) This fine analysis is, to be sure, a case of "intentional history." But it remains so in a one-sided sense, as long as it is not developed as a historical-genetic self-constitution of the transcendental intersubjectivity.

This leads to our second question: How are the relations between Husserl's transcendental phenomenology and history as a science to be understood? This is, of course, a risky question, since Husserl – though not totally silent on it – could not work it out further, and therefore encouraged our own speculations on this issue.

III

According to Husserl's suppositions, it must be regarded as almost trivial that a world, being constituted by a historical, structured, transcendental community of subjects, cannot be constituted otherwise than as a historical world, if Husserl's concept of constitution is not to lose its meaning. Husserl expressed this clearly in an unpublished manuscript he wrote in 1932, immediately before starting the essays in *Crisis*. He says that "the world thus bears in itself an *essential historicity* prior to the question for the factual history." He finishes with the remarkable proposition: "That is phenomenology which discovers *worldly* historicity as a *product of* transcendental historicity."[12]

It is hardly surprising that Husserl did not leave any remarks that treat in more detail this late discovery of his phenomenology. I wish to offer some suggestions that go further than Husserl's work on this issue.

Can one, for example, using the quotation above, regard transcendental phenomenology as a foundation of historical science in the same sense that it was and has continued to be claimed for natural science? This would mean that the possibility of history becomes transparent from specific constituting performances of transcendental subjectivity and that the remembering, tradition, and reconstruction of past events in the world can be understood through transcendental phenomenology.

Husserl added to his statement of the essential historicity of the world the question of this historicity proposing itself *still prior* to that of factual history. Husserl expressed a state of affairs when he spoke often about the *historical a priori* of the world. In our consideration it turned out as an a priori of the transcendental monadic community which the world, as a historical world, is able to constitute only by its

12. Husserl, Manuscript A VII, 11 (unpublished as of 1982): "... dass die Welt somit eine wesenmässige Historizität in sich trägt, *vor* der Frage nach der faktischen Geschichte ... Das aber muss transzendental verständlich gemacht werden ... Das ist die Phänomenologie, die von der vorgegebenen Welt zurückfragend *weltliche Historizität* als *Gebilde* der *transzendentalen Historizität* entdeckt."

own being constituted, that is, by mutual self-constitution of the egos, each of which has its own history.

This process, however, is accompanied by the ego's own self-apperception of the ego-qua-ego *in* the world. Husserl calls this the "self-objectivization," in consideration of the fact that I as a subject can make myself an object *in* the world. Yet as such, the I is as much a corporeal as a conscious being. The structure of its human consciousness is, of course, none other than that of its transcendental consciousness, and its transcendental historicity appears in the mundane self-apperception of the ego as the historicity of its natural consciousness.

Transcendental historicity is, for its part, the transcendental condition that something like history can actually exist in the world. For history is, in contrast to nature, not something that could be ascribed to the world or something that could exist without a human being, because, in principle, there can be no nature without history. Historical events, facts, and processes are generally bound to memory, with its conservation through language and writing. All history is basically human history. (What we call "natural history" is, of course, a different case.)

The notion that history is human history is, however, comprised of two parts:

1. It means, on the one hand, that history is bound to a typical structure of consciousness in such a way that historical facts and their contexts can be intended in a way similar to that of other objects and processes. Historical events can be objectivated like natural events, but not in exactly the same way.

2. History is history of human beings not only as something purely objective, which like something exterior to consciousness can be identified. It is as if historical insight would only serve to increase the store of objective knowledge. For we do not, as subjects, stand outside history as something merely past; we are at the same time in it. For it is the history of our actions and passions, our doings and leavings; it is history we are "involved" in, in almost a literal sense.

Historians have to investigate both points: history as the objective context of past events and at the same time history that the subjects (and even as researchers of history) are affected by – and who only then come to recognize history as well as themselves. It is this which Husserl refers to as "worldly history." (But is it to both points that Husserl can provide a phenomenological fundament?)

Husserl's intentional analysis, since it was refined to genetic analysis, certainly uncovered transcendental intersubjectivity as *transcendental-historical*; and since anything given results from genetic sense-constitutions which are essentially co-determined by past constituting achievements, it includes a "store of sense" from the past that is sedimented in it. Accordingly, we can comprehend something "meant as being," whichever sense is currently ascribed to it, only to the extent of how it succeeds in reactivating its sediments from the past.

This Husserlian insight involved the methodical program of "intentional history" which, as the transcendental-historical form of intentional analysis, the reactivation of former sense-sediments had to carry through. Besides, it implied Husserl's self-critical requirement to reverse all his earlier abstractions and suspensions of history, and consequently this also holds true for the history of philosophy. It must now be grasped as the sense-fundament of Husserl's own phenomenological philosophy and must be "intentionally-historically" (*intentionalhistorisch*) rehabilitated.

We must ask, however: Should mundane history be conceived as a transcendental product of sense-constituting subjectivity, permitting it, in a strict sense, to be the mundane equivalent of Husserl's intentional history? If so, this would mean that history would be essentially nothing else but history as the "previous" to something "now" given (*dessen "Vorgeschichte"*). Historians would be obliged only, in the case of something presently given, to search for the past stages of its development and to bring these into the present. In other words, it is the "bringing into the present" of the "been" of a "now" that would be the precise mundane equivalent of those re-activations of sense-sediments by which Husserl's transcendental history is to awaken the original sense-constitution of the given.

However, one can doubt whether Husserl's phenomenology and its concept of transcendental history, as history of the sense-constitution of the given, can yield a phenomenologically secure foundation for mundane history as a whole and its scientific treatment. I would like to close with two considerations on this point.

1. History does not exhaust itself by being simply the previous of something now given. In this case it only would be seen conversely through a mirror from my own point of view. Opposed to this, however, the historical-critical method of the science of history requires that the past as past should be taken seriously. It is to be understood not only as past that for us no longer exists, but also as once-present that has had its own open future that, however, was as hidden from itself at its own time as our future is for us today. Historical understanding can respect this "past future" of the past only if it takes the past on its own terms. How this is possible by present means of knowing is the special problem of historical hermeneutics.

Husserl's conception of history seems to me, however, to be too one-sided as a backward look at history. In it there always lurks the danger of anachronistic distortions of history. Its consequences are often a false teleology. That Husserl was not aware enough of this danger can be seen from the example of his contributions to the history of philosophy. This appeared to him as a development which from the beginning indicated transcendental phenomenology. That is undoubtedly inadequate, but corresponds, as I see it, precisely to his methodical program of intentional history.

2. Was it accidental that Husserl often spoke of "sediments" and "sedimentations," thus using an archaeological vocabulary, when he was concerned with the reactivation of past sense-history? Husserl once conceded that he would have liked to have spoken about the "archaeology of consciousness" if this expression had not already been lost to another science.

Archaeology is not, however, history. If the historian does his research, then he knows (if he is a good historian) that he does not merely expose past sources of events that are waiting to be discovered in order to teach us once and for all what the past was like. Rather, he selects and evaluates the documents from the viewpoint of his own historical situation to construct historical conclusions from them. Standing in history, being influenced and concerned by it, he *makes*, at the same time, history; he is no different from anybody else who is both subject and object to history. It is only in this twofold relationship to history that he can be identified as a historical being and that history can be comprehended.

In Husserl's transcendental history, however, I do not find a clear point of entry that takes sufficient account of man's twofold historical relation. The method of intentional history regards man, it is true, as a subject of history although it does not elucidate how he stands in it and shapes it by his doings and leavings, thereby finding himself.

Certainly, Husserl has shown us that we are heirs of the past. He has shown us how we are possible at all. But how we really are and have to be heirs in the world seems to be somewhat open in Husserl's thought. At any rate, his phenomenology is the only transcendental philosophy that takes the problem of history seriously and can come to terms with it. This is Husserl's lasting achievement. It also sets a new task for phenomenology in the future.

MARVIN FARBER'S CONTRIBUTION TO THE PHENOMENOLOGICAL MOVEMENT: AN INTERNATIONAL PERSPECTIVE*

HELMUT R. WAGNER (Geneva, N.Y.)

The prime source for this paper should have been the files of Farber; however, they are inaccessible and may remain so indefinitely. Consequently, I had to rely on a secondary source of great relevance: the voluminous correspondence between Farber and Alfred Schutz. Farber himself assured me in 1975 that, between 1939 and 1959, Schutz had been his foremost collaborator in major organizational and editorial work.[1]

* I am deeply obliged to Professor Kah Kyung Cho, who offered me the opportunity to present this paper to the Buffalo conference and made available supporting materials and the draft of an exposition of Farber's philosophical development, which enhanced my understanding considerably. (Dr. Cho's manuscript was published in 1982; *see* References, Cho.)

Further, I owe particular thanks to two founding members of the International Phenomenological Society; Herbert Spiegelberg, the philosopher and historian of the phenomenological movement; and Richard H. Williams, the first secretary-treasurer of the journal, *Philosophy and Phenomenological Research*. Dr. Williams provided technical information about the original structure of the International Phenomenological Soceity which was missing in my sources. Professor Spiegelberg offered access to his important correspondence with Farber; in personal communications he clarified many details on which my other sources were hazy; finally, his publications served as an additional source of information.

1. Farber informed me in 1975 that, during the first period of his journal, he had three main collaborators. They were, next to Schutz, Felix Kaufmann and Herbert Spiegelberg. In addition, there is reason to assume that, at least for the first year, Cairns played a role in the affairs of the journal and, for a longer period, also V.G. McGill, a fellow student of Farber at Harvard, who remained a close friend of his. Since November 1982 the literary estates of Kaufmann and Cairns, at the Centre for Advanced Phenomenological Research in Waterloo, Canada, are again accessible; preparations for their consultation are underway. So far, my efforts to learn something about the preservation and the whereabouts of McGill's literary estate have been futile. Spiegelberg's correspondence with Farber was made available only after the gist of the present paper had been presented at the conference in Buffalo at the end of March 1982. As mentioned in my introductory remarks, it served me in checking the general lines of the present expositions, but its exploitation in all its details will have to wait.

Cho, K.K. (ed.) Philosophy and Science in Phenomenological Perspective.

ISBN 978-94-009-6115-9

The Schutz materials convey a detailed picture of factual development and trends of the first decade of the American phenomenological movement, which had its tangible center in the journal *Philosophy and Phenomenological Research*; they also cover main aspects of the second decade. After this paper was drafted, Herbert Spiegelberg generously made available his correspondence with Farber, which was as lengthy as that between Schutz and Farber. While adding new details, these sources largely confirmed the major lines. The final version of my paper reflects the enlightenment gained from these exchanges.

Along with other collections of correspondence (Spiegelberg and Schutz, Schutz and Aron Gurwitsch, and a few others), "official" unprinted documents in the files of Spiegelberg and Schutz, and available printed sources, the documentation of this paper is broad but not complete.[2] I am confident that my representations will stand up, as far as they go, when compared with additional evidence contained in three or four source collections not available at this time to anyone. It may take a long time before the definitive history of the first two decades of Farber's journal and of the International Phenomenological Society can be written.

I

In this paper I will deal with Farber's contributions to the international phenomenological movement. I will try to give a simple and historical account of his activities that would tie his name to the invisible international fraternity of phenomenologists even if he had not written *Phenomenology as a Method* and *The Foundation of Phenomenology*.

These activities were centered upon the founding of the International Phenomenological Society (IPS) and the establishment and first period of *Philosophy and Phenomenological Research* (PPR). They reached their peak between 1939 and 1948, although they continued on a diminishing scale at least up to 1959, a period in which it became clear that Farber was placing more and more distance between himself and Husserl – to paraphrase Professor Cho. These activities had lasting effects: not only did they make phenomenology a going concern in the United States but they also supported the phenomenological movement in Latin America and helped keep European phenomenologists alive

2. This incompletion is aggravated by the fact that copies of a number of possibly relevant letters by Schutz were missing from his files and would have to be located in Farber's collections. In contrast, Schutz's and Spiegelberg's files contained a considerable number of handwritten letters by Farber, mainly covering the years in which he had no secretary.

(even though these activities played only a moderate role in reviving phenomenology in Germany).

These effects outlasted Farber's serious engagement with phenomenology for a simple reason: essentially they were indirect. It would be difficult to imagine the founding of IPS and PPR withouth the influx of European refugee scholars or that the refugee phenomenologists would have gained much influence in the United States without Farber. To become or remain effective in an international framework, they needed the relative security they eventually gained in America. When we speak of Farber's contribution to phenomenology in an international perspective, we speak largely of what Farber did for, with, and through the European refugee phenomenologists – partly in agreement with his own intentions, in part simply in consequence of the latter.

II

Together with Dorion Cairns and Charles Hartshorne, Farber shared the distinction of representing the second generation of North American philosophers who studied with Husserl. The first was represented by Winthrop Bell and William Ernest Hocking;[3] both may have had a hand in steering the three toward Husserl. Farber's dissertation, *Phenomenology as a Method and as a Philosophical Discipline* (1928), placed him, like the others, in the position of a phenomenologist existing outside the mainstream of American philosophy. A man of action who wanted to bring phenomenology into the mainstream, he was biding his time, buried in Husserl's writings and working stubbornly on the truly monumental undertaking, *The Foundation of Phenomenology*.

Since 1933 a number of phenomenologists had come to North America. It is not known to me whether, but unlikely that, any of them knew much about Farber or whether he tried to seek them out. A definite change occurred in 1937, when Schutz was on a four-week business trip in the United States. Husserl had suggested that Schutz look him up, and he took a side trip to Buffalo in order to do so. They both came into immediate philosophical exchanges and took a great liking to one another, a friendship which later should survive occasionally quite substantial differences in editorial and philosophical views. The encounter with Schutz was a shot in the arm for Farber. When the

3. It is of interest to note that of the five, four obtained their Ph.D.'s from Harvard, and the fifth did part of his graduate work there. The latter was the Canadian, Bell, who did his doctoral work in Göttingen under Husserl. This is no accident; it is due to the strong influence of William James and Josiah Royce and the tradition they had created at one of the leading universities in the United States.

death of Husserl occurred (April 1938), he was ready for the preparation of a memorial volume. As contributors he mobilized eight Americans, four of them students of Husserl, and eight thinkers of Central European origin. Of the latter, six lived already in the United States; the other two – Gurwitsch and Schutz – were still in Europe.

In July 1939, Schutz arrived in the United States and found Farber already on the move. The latter quickly involved him in his activities. Their joint efforts reached one of two immediate goals in a few months. In December 1939, a small number of phenomenologists gathered at the New School in New York and founded the International Phenomenological Society: eleven Americans and six refugee scholars. Another three Europeans became founding members in absentia; Malvine Husserl was named a honorary member. Farber was elected president,[4] Cairns vice-president. The council of the society consisted of two Americans (McGill and John Wild) and five refugee scholars (Gerhart Husserl, Felix and Fritz Kaufmann, Spiegelberg, and Schutz), plus three Europeans (Gaston Berger, Fink, Landgrebe). In addition, six ex officio council members were appointed in absentia (Allport and Perry, US; Banfi, Italy; Brunschvicg, France; Hicks, England; Romero, Argentina).

The composition of the council showed that the founders of the IPR took the designation, international, serious. During the preparatory phase, Farber corresponded with "our friends in Louvain" (Schutz); the nomination of Fink and Landgrebe resulted from these efforts. Schutz, on his part, wrote to Gurwitsch in Paris, asking him to contact French thinkers who could be invited to cooperate with the American group; he named Gaston Berger, Raymond Aron, Jean-Paul Sartre, Jean Hering, and Alexandre Koyré. In view of the immense difficulties, it is remarkable that Berger could be reached and agreed to be placed on the list of the council members of the IPS.

It seems that this international orientation was limited to the axis North America and Europe: on one end the US and Canada, on the other end Germany, Austria, and France. The original plan to publish the journal of the IPS in English, French, and German, had to be shelved for technical reasons. If Spanish was not mentioned, it was because, with one exception, none of the founding members was aware of the philosophical potential of the countries "south of the border" of the US. Only Farber saw farther. It was he who made certain that

4. In a letter to Gurwitsch, written six weeks before the meeting in New York, Schutz treated the question of the first president of the society as an open but delicate one. He himself favored a European thinker and mentioned Emile Bréhier, professor at the Sorbonne and author of a history of German philosophy. Schutz asked Gurwitsch to inquire discretely whether Bréhier would accept an offer of the presidency of the IPS. But he added: "The whole question should be directly decided by Farber."

Francisco Romero was added to the list of ex officio members of the IPS council.

The aim of the IPS was "to further the understanding, development, and application of phenomenological inquiry as inaugurated by Edmund Husserl." Phenomenology is "no special school or sect;" it wants "to maintain philosophy in the ancient sense, as an exact, descriptive discipline, at the same time bringing it to bear on the problems of the modern world." Three practical objectives were established: the organization of meetings; the establishment of national divisions "wherever possible," and the publication of a journal (PPR I, 1940: 126).

In retrospect, it is easy to see Farber's hand in the two characterizations of phenomenology: to be "an exact descriptive discipline" and "to bear on the problems of the modern world." I think that nobody among those present at the New York meeting could have possibly objected to these formulations. And nobody, I assume, was impolite enough to point out that the two points, undefined as they were, could be subjected to all kinds of interpretations. Farber, it appeared later, would consider their initial acceptance as the blind sanctioning of his own interpretations. That meant, for instance, that he ascribed to philosophy as an "exact-descriptive discipline" a much broader range than that imagined by his most tolerant European collaborator, that is, by Schutz.

From the outset, Farber thought of the IPS as an organization of philosophers from the whole spectrum of exact-descriptive philosophies, as viewed by him. In another passage of the mentioned letter to Gurwitsch, Schutz explained: "The intention is not to confine the activities of this society upon phenomenology, even though the phenomenological school is supposed to form the core of it. Beyond it, every true thinker is welcome. Of course, the American positivists will not be directly invited to collaborate; they have already several organizations. But, at the moment, opinions about this point are still divided."

It is doubtful that the New York meeting discussed conditions and criteria of, or procedures for, membership acceptance. The question was buried, it seems, by the practical suggestion to elect a secretary and treasurer who would take care of both membership in the IPS and the finances of the journal to be launched in the following year. Richard H. Williams, a sociologist from the University of Buffalo, was chosen for the position and served in it up to 1946. Recently, he informed me that the fees for all individual subscriptions to the journal were automatically counted as membership dues for the IPS. Subscribers from other countries were double-counted in the same fashion. Institutional subscriptions, however, were registered separately. It follows that the membership lists published up to 1949 annually in the journal were identical with the lists of individual subscribers to PPR.

This system, if recognized as such, was intriguingly simple and thus accepted without ado. Yet it eliminated any philosophical criteria for membership in the IPS, replacing it by a financial one: membership was automatically obtained with payment of the subscription price for the journal. I doubt that Farber and his close collaborators had figured it that way; but this membership criterion guaranteed the realization of Farber's idea that the society be completely open to philosophers of all convictions. I have no evidence that, during the first decade of the IPS, anybody had second thoughts about the implications of the practice. But this is not surprising since the IPS, for all practical purposes, was hardly a going concern. Spiegelberg had second thoughts, but he voiced them only during the fifties.

To begin with, the war in Europe and the entrance of the United States into it made it difficult to pursue international organizational objectives; it even hampered the organization of meetings in the United States. Originally, it had been decided that the US members come annually together on occasion of the meetings of the American Philosophical Association (Eastern Division). The aim was to get a phenomenology section on the program of the association, and to arrange a business meeting afterward. The first of these meetings took place in 1940. The phenomenology symposium did produce a set of outstanding papers. However, what was to set the tone for future meetings, turned out to be the "high-water mark" in the history of the organization – as Spiegelberg called it. The subsequent business meeting of the IPS was not well-attended. After a lecture by Felix Kaufmann, the members who were still present attempted the formulation of "a common platform for this new society" yet "came to nothing" (Spiegelberg, 1976 II: 628). There may have been informal luncheon gatherings of IPS members at the APA conferences during the next years, but another meeting of the IPS was announced only for February 1945. It too had to be postponed on account of severe travel restrictions imposed by the government on private citizens and particularly "enemy aliens," a classification fitting most of the refugee scholars who had joined the society. The second meeting of the IPS, finally, convened in April 1946, well after the end of the war, at Hunter College in New York. To my knowledge, it was also the last meeting of the society.

In contrast to the sad fate of the IPS as a scholarly association, the annual reports of the growth of its membership were rather encouraging. But it cannot be gainsaid that they reflected a growing interest in the largely invisible society; it is only certain that they expressed the growth of individual subscriptions to the journal, a recognition of its high quality. The first list, in 1941, comprised about 190 names; the last, in 1949, an even 400. North American subscribers more than doubled; holding roughly more than three-quarters of the first as well as the last list. In 1941, there were 31 European subscriptions in 10 countries; in 1949 there were 45 scattered throughout 13 countries. Four years after the war, it was clear that the Americans would not make substantial inroads into the ranks of Europeans sympathetic with phenomenological philosophy. Of some interest was the growth of Latin American subscriptions from 7 to 35. This was still a modest number. Yet, it was impressive enough as an indicator of an unexpected potential. For a period, the journal published its articles with appended extracts in Spanish.

Whether an active IPS would have been able, during and after the war, to establish durable contacts with Latin American phenomenologists in the sense of its initial programmatic intentions, is difficult to say. The fact remains that the society had no "secretary for Latin American affairs" and that connections were editorial rather than organizational. Farber was successful in gaining good Latin American contributors and could pride himself on publishing about eight papers offered by South American thinkers at the First Inter-American Conference of Philosophy, which convened at Yale University in 1943. All were brought in their original language, but some English translations and comments were added. But this achievement, again, was that of the editor, Farber, and not that of the IPS.

After the meeting of 1946, the society itself was completely deactivated; Farber relinquished all efforts to revive its annual meeting program after the severe restrictions of the war years had been lifted. When he, three years later, ceased to publish new membership lists, he merely underlined the fact that the IPS was no longer a functioning organization. There is no shred of evidence that the officers of the society and the members of its council, after their confirmation in 1940, were ever democratically confirmed, reelected, or replaced. Eventually, of the original seven refugee scholars of the council, only two maintained an active interest in the IPS. Both were quite uneasy about its state of affairs or, rather, the absence of any affairs. But it took far into the fifties before each of them, separately and at different times, mailed polite inquiries to Farber. Nothing changed on account of them.

If the name of the society was not erased with the cessation of its activities and if it maintained the semblance of a continuing existence, this was so because it lived on in the person of its first and only president who imperceptibly had become its president for life. Farber, it seems, was quite adamant in maintaining this presidency and asserting it, whenever the occasion arose. Essentially, that was no longer the case in the realm of the United States. For all practical purposes, Farber reserved it for matters of "diplomacy" and "foreign policy" – that is, for the relative rare cases of "negotiations" with Herman Van Breda of the Husserl-Archives in Louvain, or with groups of European phenomenologists who aimed at organizing their own phenomenological societies.

Today, some of the early refugee members write off the IPS as a total loss. Yet, in its first years, they gained from it a sense of recognition of philosophical objectives which were dear to them, and it helped them overcome the sense of intellectual isolation which, for many, was the most characteristic result of their "American experience." If the society failed to become a permanent rallying ground for them, it at least served as one occasion which set them socially and intellectually in motion again. From scattered instructors of undergraduates in courses which had little to do with their own philosophical concerns, they became again part of a movement, the phenomenological movement on American soil.[5] The name of the IPS, I gained the impression, became the symbol of their new feeling of belonging, of a we. It was for this reason that their reaction to the actual course of the society – and the journal – was fraught with strong emotions.

The early activities around the IPS, also, brought some of the Europeans in contact with Americna phenomenologists. For them, the movement broadened. In addition, the early activity plans of the society led to their admission to the American Philosophical Association[6] and thereby offered them opportunities to encounter some outstanding American philosophers they otherwise would not have met. To mind come, in the case of Schutz, such names as Mandelbaum and Ducasse. Schutz, for one, appreciated this very much; he was set to step out of the splendid isolation of his intellectual refugee existence into the realm of American intellectual life.

III

The only objective on the program of the IPS that was successfully realized was the establishment of the journal, *Philosophy and Phenomenological Research* (PPR).

Schutz's files contain the draft of an announcement of the pending publication of the journal. To all appearances, it is a final version with the exception of the naming of a few planned articles and the signature of the members of the editorial staff. It seems to have been set up by Farber possibly in May or early June of 1940. It opened with two

5. The correspondence, which Schutz conducted with a number of other refugee scholars in the U.S. contains evidence of this statement.

6. This was not a matter of signing an application and sending a dues check. It involved scholarly decorum: each applicant had to be sponsored by well-reputed members of the association.

paragraphs which contain a clear statement of the philosophical basis and the philosophical objectives of the new undertaking.

> This new journal ... is the successor of Husserl's *Jahrbuch für Philosophie und phänomenologische Forschung...*
> The Philosophy of Edmund Husserl constitutes the point of departure for the publication. Edmund Husserl, one of the most important and productive thinkers of the modern period, has exercised a great influence on the present generation. The organization of those who are influenced by his thought marks an event of outstanding importance in contemporary philosophy. No student of philosophy can afford to ignore this literature, and its significance for numerous fields of scholarship, including psychology, art, law, psychiatry, mathematics, and natural science.

The letterhead of the announcement contained already that additional formulation which would become the trademark of PPR: "Published for the International Phenomenological Society ..." As publisher was named the University of Buffalo. However, it would have been justified to change this byline to: "published ... by Marvin Farber with the assistance of the University of Buffalo."

In the trite economic, yet practically decisive, sense of launching a new philosophical journal as well as in the sense of shaping its content editorially so as not only to secure its financial survival but also to make it into one of the nationally and internationally most respected philosophical periodicals, PPR is overwhelmingly the achievement of Farber.

There is no room here to substantiate this in detail.[7] With regard to the editorial preparation of each issue alone, the correspondence between Schutz and Farber and Spiegelberg and Farber contain overwhelming evidence that – at least during the crucial first three to five years – Farber literally worked to the utmost limits of his physical capacities in order to bring each issue out as scheduled. Unofficially, he had set up an acting editorial committee consisting of him, Schutz, Spiegelberg and, most likely, Felix Kaufmann. The closest of his co-opted editors lived in New York City, more than 650 railway kilometers away from Buffalo. All business had to be conducted by letter. Farber, for years without a secretary, wrote most of his messages and comments by hand. The exchanges occurred with highest frequencies. To keep up with this correspondence taxed Schutz greatly and was

7. In addition to the characterization of Farber's editorial activities in the text, I will mention further that Farber alone gained and maintained the administrative support for his undertaking from the chancellor of the University of Buffalo, and that he single-handedly secured the needed financial support not only for the start but also the continuation of the journal, which he steered successfully through severe financial crises.

quite a burden to the others. Yet, Farber often dealt with each of his remote editors separately and involved them in different matters. His workload was that of the others combined.

In 1948, years after Schutz divested himself of the greatest part of his editorial obligations, he told one critic of Farber's editorial policies: The European members of the editorial board have to restrain themselves, and must understand what he is contributing: "Believe me, ... the journal stands and falls with Farber; its whole existence and dissemination, its deserved reputation, are exclusively due to his incredible devotion to his undertaking."

Later, when it had become painfully obvious that Farber's interest in phenomenology had been markedly reduced, Schutz maintained that the phenomenologists still had a "little homestead" in the journal. Maybe he should have said that Farber's house had many mansions and still contained guest quarters for the descendents of Husserl.

It is not easily to describe concretely an intellectual movement; and it is difficult to draw a picture of the social in contrast to the "literary" function of a journal. Clearly, the European phenomenologists among the subscribers and contributors of PPR wanted it to be the exclusive voice of phenomenological thought; and they wanted it to be a living center as well as a tangible symbol of the phenomenological movement at least in North America. They tended to judge its content – and that means its editor – by the deviations from the first principle with an emotional severity dictated by the second expectation. The editor pursued philosophical objectives at variance with those of the phenomenologists, when he insisted that phenomenology is a philosophical method among others and slanted the overall content of the journal accordingly. He bolstered his editorial policies with weighty "realistic" arguments, which Schutz once translated into the statement: "In America, one cannot make a journal with European Philosophy alone". Since Farber had complete control of the journal and in every case decided whether to follow the advice he had requested from others, he was in an autocratic position which fitted well with the strong autocratic tendency in his personality. And since he had his ego invested in this enterprise, he too displayed strong emotions and answered any criticism of his policies with unrestrained sharpness.

Farber's editorial policies and his personality would have been completely irrelevant if the refugee phenomenologists had considered the matter opportunistically: PPR was one, if not the only, outlet for phenomenological articles. But since they had agreed, as founding members of the IPS, that PPR was the official journal of this society, they considered it *their* journal. Farber, who alone had secured the funds and did the crucial editorial work, considered it *his*. From the outset, this spelled "conflict." If it remained hidden for long years, so for two reasons: At first, the refugee scholars were not sufficiently acquainted with Farber's actual philosophical position which, ultimately, guided his editorial policies; later, they misread the signs of his growing distance from phenomenology as isolated lapses and errors. They did not see the trend; thus, they were shocked when it was finally revealed to them.

If the refugee scholars accepted a degree of philosophical tolerance in PPR, so obviously in the sense of making room for thinkers whose positions were relatively close to phenomenology. But Farber pushed the tolerance limit far beyond their worst expectations. In 1945, he offered the following programmatic statement: "The central interest of the publication is in philosophy as a descriptive discipline, which includes the epistemological and philosophical studies of scholars who are far removed from transcendental phenomenology as a universal philosophy, but who nevertheless have much in common with its descriptive program." The tremendous leeway expressed in the undefined term "descriptive program" notwithstanding, Farber added that PPR "also aims to be hospitable to the entire field of philosophical scholarship in all countries ..." (PPR 6, 1945: 2). What he meant here had become clear in and after the fourth volume of the journal, when leading logical positivists (Carnap, Nagel, Neurath, Reichenbach, etc.) made their appearance. For the Europeans, this was a step from non-phenomenologists to anti-phenomenologists, and they were disturbed. In the paper of 1945, Farber also expressed his intention to restrict dealings with Scheler and Heidegger to severe criticism. He reiterated this opinion in a letter to Schutz and suggested a stand against existentialism, lest we "will be swept away by the growing trend of logical analysis." Schutz responded simply: "I think that Phenomenology could find, by far easier, an understanding with philosophers of this kind than with Neo-Positivists." Farber maintained his philosophical convictions; yet, as editor, he gave in to Schutz.

These matters of editorial policies must be distinguished from Farber's philosophical development away from phenomenology. It would be possible to find the roots of his tangential movement already in his doctoral dissertation and in the *Foundation of Phenomenology*. It found occasional and progressively stronger expressions in his other publications, papers and essays, which appeared up into the sixties.[8] Before 1949, however, some of these articles may have remained un-

8. In a recent "report," actually a well-researched paper, Professor Kah Kyung Cho not only confirmed but substantiated these conclusions in detail. See his "Marvin Farber (1901-1980) in memoriam. Sein Leben und Wirken für die Phänomenologie in USA." *Phänomenologische Forschungen* 12 (1982): 145-72.

known;[9] others may have caused the bewilderment of some of his phenomenological readers, but seemingly did not induce stronger reactions, not even such voiced in private correspondence. In any case, none of these publications had prepared any of the refugee scholars for positions Farber revealed in 1949 and 1951.

In 1949, Farber, in coeditorship with Roy W. Sellars and McGill, brought out a symposium volume entitled, *Philosophy for the Future* with the revealing subtitle, *The Quest of Modern Materialism* (Macmillan, 1949). Its concluding part was Farber's contribution, called "Experience and Subjectivism." I think that this essay contains outlines of the essentials of Farber's philosophy as it became known in his books after 1960. The term "materialism" is used in about the sense which it had acquired in the writings of the later Marx, complete with its evolutionary aspects. The phenomenological search for the "given" in experience is a false problem: appeal to experience is appeal to observational fact and logical methods. Phenomenological methodology, in its transcendental aspects, is "methodological solipsism." Only the early work of Husserl – at best up to the first volume of the *Ideas* – remains acceptable; Husserl's later idealistic position is "fatal." Phenomenological reduction, stripped of its subjectivistic connotations, remains acceptable as auxiliary method next to other "objective" descriptive methods: "Every sound descriptive proposition in phenomenology can be asserted within the framework of a naturalistic (realistic, or materialistic) philosophy."

For Spiegelberg, this essay was "the main shock"; forthwith, he considered Farber a thinker outside the ranks of the phenomenologists. I do not know whether other of the Europeans read Farber's essay.[10] No reaction to it, other than Spiegelberg's, has come to my attention. In any case, it was clearly an expression of Farber's philosophical views, to which he was entitled and which had no direct bearing on the editorial picture of PPR. It was different with the paper of 1951. He named it "Experience and Transcendence" and published it as the lead article of volume 12 of PPR. Thus, he brought it forcefully to the attention of his readers, and notably the refugee phenomenologists. In its opening section, he proclaimed Haeckel's "cosmological theorems" (*Riddle of the Universe*, 1899) as "effective statements of important truth" and suggested complementing them by a set of "cultural theorems," confirming "the dependence of man on conditions causing cultural evolution –

9. So in the report, "Aspects of Philosophy in the USA, 1940-1946," which appeared first in a French and later in a German translation in a French and a German journal, respectively.

10. This is most unlikely in the case of Gurwitsch and Schutz. Had one of them come across it, he would almost certainly have mentioned it in their frequent correspondence.

economic, social, and psychological, as well as material factors of the environment." He repeated and enlarged his critique of idealistic-subjectivistic phenomenology and stressed again his counterposition.

This time, Schutz received reactions from several sides. Spiegelberg wrote to him again, protesting this "neo-materialistic music" and wondered whether "we can let this pass." Schutz replied that the paper was "as much a shock to me and many others as it was to you." He recommended he write "a counter-article which Farber certainly would accept." However, he did not consider the paper "a programmatic statement of the future editorial conduct of the journal." As long as Farber is willing to print phenomenological papers, his own articles must be seen as contributions by a philosopher "who accidentally is also the editor." (By the way, no "counter-article" appeared in the journal.)

Gurwitsch, like Spiegelberg, one of the original members of the editorial staff, had largely kept aloof of discussions of editorial matters. Now, however, he directed a letter to Farber which led up to the question: "Is this the voice of the philosophical author Marvin Farber or that of the President of the International Phenomenological Society and the editor-in-chief of *Philosophy and Phenomenological Research*?" Having been assured that Gurwitsch did not want to challenge his privilege as "philosophical author" to express his views and to criticize Husserl, Farber responded shortly but not unfriendly. He answered Gurwitsch's key question by saying: "Naturally ... I wrote as an individual" and added: "My fidelity to E(dmund) H(usserl) remains – *after my fashion*, which is now no different from what it was when I was his admiring student." In order to show that his editorial policies were unchanged, he pointed out that he had lined up various phenomenological and even existentialist "materials" for future publication.[11]

It is not known to me – but unlikely – that other European members of the editorial board approached Farber in matters of this article of 1951. To my understanding, the refugee phenomenologists preferred to restrict their contacts with Farber to matters concerning their services as editorial readers of incoming papers or else to exchange about contributions which they submitted themselves. For voicing their opinions on Farber's editorial policies, they directed themselves to Schutz, a trusted colleague who had close contacts with Farber, who would listen to their complaints and, if need be, was willing to negotiate difficulties with the editor-in-chief. As far as they were involved, then, the circle was rather an ellipse with an official and an inofficial

11. The reference to existential papers is particularly important because, in his article, Farber had written a quite sweeping attack not only on Scheler but especially on all existentialists from Heidegger to Sartre and from Jaspers to Marcel.

focal point. This, indeed, gave Schutz a quite unique position within the social and personality constellation of this "group."[12]

In their personalities, Schutz and Farber were quite different. I am tempted to say that Farber was ready to attack and make enemies at the drop of a hat, whenever he felt challenged in his policies. Schutz, by contrast, captivated people by his friendliness, openness, and sincerity. Thus, he inspired trust in everyone he met. In case of practical differences, he tended to give people the benefit of the doubt and did his utmost to find conciliatory solutions.[13] Yet, he had a keen practical sense and was a skilled negotiator and arbiter. Farber esteemed him highly for his human qualities, his scholarship, and his practical advice. Next to Felix Kaufmann, who died in 1949, Schutz was the only European in the PPR-circle to whom he listened. Had it not been for the friendship between the two, I imagine, the early history of the journal would have been characterized by frequent open conflicts between refugee phenomenologists and editor. As it was, Schutz usually convinced Farber not to follow his first reactions against critics; and he convinced his Central European acquaintances if not to accept then to tolerate Farber's editorial policies.[14]

This arbitration "system" worked satisfactorily until the start of 1947, when Helmut Kuhn mounted a campaign against the editor in the form of letters to Farber and members of the editorial staff. He protested the acceptance of papers by logical positivists, the policy of allowing replies and replies to replies in the journal, and publication of papers by Soviet-Russian philosophers. The first point evoked sympathy from the European members of the circle. The second was

12. I put the term "group" in quotation marks to indicate that it is used very loosely. For once, I do not know what Farber's relations to his American collaborators were. Only McGill, a close friend of his, may have been in the same close contact with him as Schutz. Without access to the early files of the PPR-correspondence, a comprehensive sociological description of the "circle around PPR" will be impossible.

13. Those who have known Schutz will know this; but they will also know that, in matters of his central theoretical and philosophical concerns, he was quite adamant.

14. The existence of this kind of personal mediation between Farber and refugee scholars is clearly attested in the correspondence between the former and Schutz. This does not exclude the possibility that other refugee scholars did not turn to Schutz but settled their differences with Farber directly. It would take the inspection of the whole set of correspondence files of Farber to ascertain whether such cases occurred. My conviction is that, if they exist, they would not be very numerous. In this, I am basing myself on further evidence from the Farber-Schutz correspondence. In the cases on record, it was usually Farber who took the initiative by reporting his difficulties with others to Schutz. To me, this is a clear sign that he was seeking Schutz's comments before he made his own decisions and, at least in this sense, appealed to him as one would to a mediator.

picayune, and the third hit a pet project of Farber: the participation in the "Russian Translation Project" of the American Council of Learned Societies, for which he published, in PPR, translations of articles by Soviet philosophers.[15] Kuhn was grossly misinformed about this project[16] but persisted and managed to isolate himself completely. He resigned from the staff of the journal and, shortly thereafter, returned to Germany.

This conflict prompted Farber to draft a new policy statement for the members of his editorial staff. In it, he treated the Kuhn issue as a result of changes from the "rather narrow program" of the start to "our present policy of tolerance and representation of all movements." Having reconfirmed his commitment to pay "due attention to phenomenology," he received positive responses from other staff members. In reaction to it, he spoke of his intention "to hold staff meetings at regular intervals."

The alliance between Farber and the refugee scholars had been reaffirmed. I found no evidence that even one meeting of the editorial staff of PPR was called at any time between 1947 and 1959.

During the second decade of the PPR (for present purposes to be seen as its second period) several occasions for conflict arose but remained under control.[17] When Schutz died in 1959, the end of the PPR federation between American and European scholars was in sight. Matters of editorial policies aside, the journal had been americanized. If it still served as a "homestead for phenomenology," this was so for a later breed of phenomenologists.[18] The refugee thinkers went their own way. Schutz, I am sure, would have welcomed this. In principle, he had viewed his American activities, including those connected with ISP and PPR, as attempts to help create a permanent place for phenomenology within the realm of North American philosophy: a clearly distinguishable current in a larger river, not a pond on an isolated reservation.

15. The articles themselves were selected by American experts from Russian journals written for inner-Russian consumption.

16. Kuhn had assumed that the materials were handouts from the Soviet Embassy and, as such, were written for propaganda purposes.

17. During the fifties, several occasions for severe rifts between Farber and refugee philosophers arose. Among the attested cases reported in Schutz's files are two that involved Spiegelberg in 1953 and Schutz himself in 1958.

18. Thus, Gurwitsch no longer published anything in PPR. Spiegelberg resigned from the editorial board in the early sixties, mainly in reaction to Farber's book, *Naturalism and Subjectivism* (1959). But facts of this kind belong to the story of the third decade of PPR, synonymous with the third period of the history of the journal.

IV

Most of my presentation so far seems to be at variance with my topic. It sounds like a description of the influence of European phenomenologists upon PPR and, indirectly, American philosophy. At best, it may be taken as a sketch of the history of the journal during its first decade.[19] Yet, due to a particular dialectic in the indicated developments, we can see the opportunities and impulses for Farber's influence on the international phenomenological movement, or at least on that in Central and Western Europe.[20]

In part, Farber's contributions were of an elementary kind; he helped keep phenomenology as philosophy alive by helping keep phenomenologists alive. Whatever he may have done in this respect prior to 1939, Schutz involved Farber – as he involved anyone he knew well – in efforts to bring European thinkers whose lives were endanged by Hitler to safety in the United States. These efforts were successful in the case of some who had found a temporary refuge in France, among them Aron Gurtwitsch, who entered the US as late as 1940. By exploiting I do-not know what connections, Farber became instrumental in rescuing Jean Wahl from Vichy France. Upon an appeal from Malvine Husserl, he tried – though unsuccessfully – to get her out of German-occupied Belgium and into North America. Shortly after the war, he effectively organized regular collections of funds in order to mail food packages to philosophers in starving Germany; among them were Husserl's students of the later period, notably Fink and Landgrebe.

Today, it may be difficult to appraise the importance of those humanitarian efforts, as little as they were in the face of the enormity of the human tragedies set in motion by Hitler.[21] During these years, they expressed the meaning of the term, international, in the byline of the journal's title page.

Turning from the concern for phenomenologists to the concern for phenomenology, Farber's role in the main consisted in the creation of a platform from which the refugee phenomenologists could speak: a foreign group with outlandish ideas who otherwise had little chance to

19. In a letter to me (dated 1/14/80), Marvin Farber assured me that "the PPR history ... has been planned for some time." I can only hope that his literary estate contains the plans and the materials for its execution.

20. Farber's interest in Eastern philosophy is known and manifested by the presence of Eastern scholars on the present editorial staff of PPR. They are in the best position to tell us whether, through their mediation or otherwise, Farber has gained influence in Southeast Asia, etc. In addition, I do not feel qualified to appraise the possible influence of PPR on Latin American phenomenologists.

21. Both Gurwitsch and Schutz were most heavily and for a long period involved in efforts of this kind, referring to them as "passiology."

be heard. Farber, of course, created this platform for phenomenologists, period, regardless of national origin. As it turned out, however, it was evenly populated by American and European-born phenomenologists and philosophers in the vicinity of phenomenology.

This assertion pertains up to the ninth volume of 1948-1949. I pointed out previously that, for present purposes, the first decade of PPR was crucial. This is confirmed by a scrutiny of contributors and contributions to the journal during this period. The Husserl Memorial volume of 1940 included, Farber published more than 300 articles from about 150 authors. To reach a basis for a viable comparison, I will have to omit about 40 papers from 30 authors residing in other countries, mostly in Latin America.[22] This leaves about 270 papers from about 120 authors living in the United States. Not quite 100 authors were native Americans,[23] 22 could be identified as recent German, Austrian, and French refugee scholars. The first category contributed 200 papers, the second about 70, a distribution rate of better than 3 to 1. With the exception of *Social Research*, established by Alvin Johnson for his University in Exile, there is no journal in the United States which could claim to have offered refugee scholars such a generous portion of its editorial space.

Regardless of title and programmatic statement, PPR was from the start a high-quality philosophical journal, which preferred and, in any case, hosted a respectable number of phenomenological contributions. During the nine years under consideration, they amounted to about 110, or 35 percent of all papers published, or 40 percent of those published by authors residing in the United States. This contributor group counted 40 persons, equally divided between native Americans and refugees. The latter group, however, had slightly more articles to their names.

If I resort to numerical illustrations, I do so for a simple reason: it is the quickest way to make my point. Insofar as the phenomenological movement in the United States was set in motion with the founding of the IPS, it counted on a small array of Americans, such as the veteran William Hocking, the trio of Dorion Cairns, Marvin Farber, and Charles Hartshorne, and such reenforcements as Curt John Ducasse, John Wild, and to a degree Roy Wood Sellars. The leading Europeans were Gurwitsch, Felix and Fritz Kaufmann, Kuhn, Schutz, and Spiegelberg, plus the French senior phenomenologist, Jean Wahl. At the time, the group

22. The argument of this paper is not affected by this omission. However, I have to point out that, in any case, I would not have been able to place the bulk of these contributors philosophically.

23. Some of them may be immigrants of long (pre-Hitlerian) standing. There are a good number of German names, which I could not identify as those of refugees, in the sense in which the word is used in this article.

of about 40 phenomenologists and related thinkers gathered around this core of fourteen and the journal PPR easily qualified as the strongest ever assembled for the furtherance of phenomenological thinking.

In spite of incipient and open conflicts and in spite of his growing distance from phenomenology, Farber alone made the assembly of this core and the precipitation of their philosophical thoughts in PPR possible. For the refugee scholars, this again meant more than publication possibilities, reprints, and items for their publication records. It was the path back to the public world of international philosophy. If they regained a philosophical reputation in a period in which the cultural and philosophical traditions they represented seemed to be brutally stamped out forever on their home ground, it was so largely thanks to PPR. The activities around the journal remobilized them, even though at first *only* for the formidable task of placing phenomenology on the map of American philosophy.

What this meant concretely may be seen from the fact that four of the leading Central European contributors to PPR, between 1940 and 1949,[24] had one half or more of their philosophical papers published by Farber: Gurwitsch, six out of nine; Felix Kaufmann, eight out of sixteen; Schutz, six out of twelve; and Spiegelberg, five out of eight.[25] Of special interest is the fact that the first five papers by Gurwitsch and the first four by Schutz, written in the United States, were printed in PPR. Kaufmann and Schutz reached a balance only because they had easy access to *Social Research*, the journal for the Graduate Faculty of the New School. There can be little doubt that this early start in Farber's journal made it possible for the refugee scholars to find recognition in American philosophy. To pose only one question: Would Schutz have had contributions accepted in the *Review of Metaphysics* and the *Journal of Philosophy* without having gained his philosophical reputation through his contributions to PPR?

As mentioned earlier, the picture of the group around PPR changed considerably at the end of the forties. Volumes 10 to 20 (Fall 1949-Fall 1959) show a marketly different complexion. The editorial staff changed somewhat: In 1940, it counted seven refugee scholars; in 1949, six; and in 1959, five. But the contributions of the old refugee circle had been drastically reduced. Only three of the original twenty authors from their ranks were still published in Farber's journal. Altogether,

24. These four were the refugee thinkers who contributed most frequently to PPR.

25. In addition, Gurwitsch managed to have two of his papers published in France, and Schutz placed one in the British journal *Economica*. Spiegelberg, on his part, reported that he submitted two additional papers which, however, were eventually rejected.

refugee contributions amounted to ten articles in contrast to the fifty of the first period. Of Spiegelberg's eight articles, only one appeared in PPR; for Gurwitsch, the ratio was three out of seven. Only Schutz published as many as in the first period: six; however, his total output had gone up to nineteen.[26]

This drastic change expressed several developments. As a matter of policy, the attempts at inviting outstanding refugee scholars to write contributions had stopped. Both Farber's philosophical move away from phenomenology and his continuing firm grip on the editorial leadership of PPR had been accepted as irrevocable facts. But, in addition, the refugee scholars had developed firm roots in the United States and no longer needed the protective care of PPR; more or less, they stood by now quite solidly on the ground of their host country. And what is more, as the example of Spiegelberg, Gurwitsch, and Schutz shows, they now were published in various other countries: France, Germany, Holland, and Mexico. With regard to Europe, they began to retransfer their phenomenological knowledge, in part considerably enhanced by the "American experience," to the continent which had given birth to the phenomenological movement. This process, at least in the case of Gurwitsch and Schutz, has taken on considerable momentum after the death of both, thanks to the work of a few of their students who have gained key positions in the German academic system.[27]

V

It would be contrary to fact to claim that the revival of European phenomenology, after Hitler's defeat, was significantly due to the refugee group in the United States. The early return of Jean Wahl, however, must have sped up the recuperation of the existential-phenomenological movement in France, which came rather quickly and brought Merleau-Ponty's generation to the fore. In Germany, developments were slow and painful. The crisis of total defeat was accompanied by a spiritual

26. The comparatively low output of articles by Gurwitsch and Spiegelberg, at least in part, was due to their working on major studies during the second period of the journal.

27. I refer here to Thomas Luckmann at Constance University, who established the Sozialwissenschaftliche Archiv there, and to Richard Grathoff at Bielefeld University, who heads the Zentrum für interdisciplinäre Forschung. They and their collaborators at various German universities are responsible for a growing publication program of writings from the literary estate of both Alfred Schutz and Aron Gurwitsch. For the latter, significant credit is due also to Alexandre Métraux, the outstanding Swiss philosopher.

crisis, slower to be overcome than the economic ruin of the postwar period. The few remaining German students of Husserl, although re-enforced by a few "homecomers" from the United States (Helmut Kuhn and Alfred Metzger), found themselves in great isolation, especially from the new student generation. Five years after the war, Landgrebe and Fink had practically given up on the phenomenological movement in their country (see Spiegelberg, 1976, vol. 2: 596-97), and – at least in the case of Fink – eventually found their philosophical bearings in dimensions of considerable variance from their original phenomenological positions. The slow revival of phenomenology, in Germany, came only during the following decade. It, too, became largely the matter of a new generation. Insofar as its members were influenced by centers outside Germany, they owed their inspiration largely to the Husserl-Archives in Louvain, or rather to early German members of their staff who had returned to their own country. Most outstanding among them was the prominent Husserl student, Ludwig Landgrebe, who in 1956 gave the renewed German philosophical movement its first center: the Husserl-Archives in Cologne.[28]

The creation of the Louvain center, which initiated a new phase of phenomenology, occurred during that critical period in which the destruction of Husserl's literary estate seemed to be certain. The Belgian Franciscan priest, Herman Van Breda, undertook the transfer under dangerous conditions. He obtained far-reaching powers concerning the administration, transcription, and publication of the immense stock of Husserl's unpublished manuscripts and shorthand notes.[29] The spade-work for the cataloguing of this material was done by Fink and Landgrebe. During the war, the work was continued "underground" by Strasser and a few others. After Hitler's defeat, the Husserl-Archives came into the open; the actuarial work and the organization of Husserl research were intensified.[30] Thereby, one important precondition was

28. In its concreteness, this process was rather complex and involved a number of other phenomenologists of students and prewar adherents of Husserl who had remained in Europe. In addition, Heidegger's influence made itself felt. For a sketch of these complex developments, consult the third edition of Spiegelberg's study, *The Phenomenological Movements* (1982: 654-56).

29. After the war, Gerhart Husserl disagreed with Van Breda's interpretation of the contractual agreements of 1938. Their treatment is beyond the scope of the present paper. But it must be pointed out that this disagreement created considerable difficulties for the publication of further unpublished papers by Husserl in PPR.

30. It should take a considerable time to make the Husserl-Archives also into the center of the publication of both unpublished manuscripts of Husserl and new editions of his earlier published works (in the series, Husserliana), and later of the publication of phenomenological studies of living authors from various countries (the series, Phaenomenologica).

created for the reactivation of the phenomenological movement in Europe and its strengthening in the United States and elsewhere.

Farber had been in correspondence with Louvain already during the pre-preparatory period for the founding of IPS and PPR. This connection was cut off with the occupation of Belgium by Hitler's military forces.

Shortly before, Van Breda had not only welcomed the publication of the journal; he also promised to contribute to it small papers from Husserl's literary estate – at the rate of one per issue. In fact, two such papers appeared, one in each of the first two volumes. A third one was published in the volume, *Philosophical Essays in Memory of Edmund Husserl*, which Farber edited in 1940. Finally, it must be mentioned that Van Breda managed to send a larger collection of typed copies of a selection of the Husserl transcripts to Buffalo for safekeeping in case the Gestapo should seize and destroy the originals. Fortunately, the existence and quiet activities of the Husserl-Archives remained undetected.

The war over, Farber and his friends received the first news about the fate of Husserl's students who had spent the war years in Europe from Louvain. Malvine Husserl informed them of the survival of Fink, Landgrebe, and others, as well as that of Roman Ingarden in Poland. PPR published a first postwar article by Jean Wahl in 1946; it was written shortly after his return to his native country.

The difficult postwar situation and the starvation conditions, especially in occupied Germany, made impossible the quick resumption of philosophcial exchanges. Beyond this, the survivors among the German students of Husserl needed time to regain their intellectual bearings. As far as I know, none of the Central European phenomenologists in the United States tried to address them philosophically. For years, the overriding concern of and for them was physical survival. But the eventual recovery of Germany and Austria seems not to have led to the renewal of closer philosophical contacts – in contrast to the scholarly relations with a number of French philosophers, which were quickly resumed without difficulties.[31]

Of considerable potential significance was the establishment of connections with the Husserl-Archives in Louvain. Van Breda accounted for his activities and the plans for their continuation in two reports which, in 1947, appeared in PPR. The Americans were unable to mobilize American grants for the Archives, as Van Breda had hoped,

31. From 1946 to 1949, six contributions of three French thinkers (Berger, Koyré, and Wahl) were published in PPR. The first two contributions from Central and East European students of Husserl, which I could identify, appeared only in 1957 and 1958 (Strasser and Ingarden).

but Farber promised his full support in securing library subscriptions to all of the planned publications of the Archives and, most of all, proper publicity campaigns for them. Arrangements for the publication of further Husserl manuscripts in PPR were made; but, through no particular fault from either side, this agreement ran into difficulties.[32]

During the first four years after the war, the contacts between the American group and Louvain were not intense and did not assume an "official" character. In part, they occurred on a personal basis. As far as these contacts were meant to find ways of collaboration between the editorial group of PPR – which simultaneously appeared as the representative of IPS – and the directorate of the Louvain Archives, a close collaboration developed between Farber and Schutz. Both consulted and informed each other whenever one of them was to address himself to "Louvain" and when he had received a response, or else when he was addressed by Van Breda and prepared his answer. The existing evidence is strong enough for me to assert that, with regard to the working out of the concrete steps toward the forming and enactment of a "policy" toward "Louvain," it was the joint product of Farber and Schutz. This goes not only for the postwar period up to 1949 but also for the following decade which, in 1957, brought the culmination of these policies in the formalization of the "official" relationships between the Americans and the Europeans.[33]

The effectiveness of this collaboration hinged largely on a convenient division of labor. Farber, essentially, confined himself to writing letters to Louvain,[34] while Schutz assumed the personal contacts with Van Breda and other phenomenologists in Europe. This was possible because his business obligations included practically annual trips to Europe. Thus, he managed to visit the Husserl-Archives in Louvain as early as 1946. And he repeated these visits as often as he could.[35]

32. See note 29.

33. To be specific: This formalization concerned the relationship between the IPS – which, for all practical purposes, was completely inactive – and the European Branch of the Phenomenological Society – just in the process of formation. The latter, too, seems have been shortlived.

34. This correspondence was well underway before the end of 1945. In confirmation, I can point to a letter which Farber wrote to Schutz in December of this year. In it, he reported that he had asked Van Breda for the addresses of a few German phenomenologists, notably Fink and Landgrebe, in order to gain their participation in a "proposed phenomenological symposium" – most likely in the form of articles for a special issue of PPR. Further, he reported that he had encouraged Van Breda to proceed with the preparation of a microfilm edition of Husserl's literary estate, in spite of the expectation of objections on the part of Gerhart Husserl.

35. Needless to say, Schutz's visists to the Husserl-Archives were not merely devoted to discussions of the relationship between "Buffalo" and "Louvain." His overriding interests were scholarly. In particular, he was ardently interested in those

Of course, the pattern of this division of labor was not exclusive. In 1949, Farber finally managed to mobilize the funds for a trip to Europe. He visited Louvain and negotiated an agreement on some matters with Van Breda. Again, he informed Schutz that he had promised to support an application for support of Van Breda's publication plans, even though he himself was in favor of a larger committee (including Fink and Landgrebe) who would take charge of the whole publication program. He came home with bitter feelings against Van Breda, whom he suspected wanted to use phenomenology in a clever pursuit of winning converts to the Roman Catholic Church.

Schutz did not share such notions; he saw the issue in the usual political terms of two parties juggling for position in order to gain a maximum of influence – here, on the international phenomenological movement.[36]

Farber's visit to Louvain took place in 1949, that is, at the end of the first period of the rather intangible IPS and the very tangible journal, PPR. It is a fitting mark of the turning point into the second period, a period in which attempts were made to formalize the relationship between Buffalo and Louvain. However, the exposition of these attempts lies beyond the scope of the present paper.

VI

In Europe, the fifties saw the establishment of stronger ties among phenomenologists of various countries and the crystallization of Van Breda's long-range plans. In 1951 a first international conference of European phenomenologists convened in Brussels. The contacts between Louvain and Buffalo now gained an official character, the character of preliminary negotiations about a formal agreement between the American group and Louvain. When Schutz planned to visit the Husserl-Archives[37] in the summer of 1953, Farber wrote to him,

---

unpublished manuscripts in which Husserl had dealt further with the "problem of intersubjectivity." Further, I have to add that Schutz was not the only although by far the most important first-hand reporter about the people at, and the plans and policies of, the Husserl-Archives in Louvain. Occasionally, during the later years, Farber received such reports from other visitors to the Archives, so from Spiegelberg and Gurwitsch.

36. In the various direct negotiations, which were conducted between 1953 to 1957, Farber left matters in the hands and the judgment of Schutz. It has been suggested to me that this may have been a wise decision, leading eventually to friendly agreements, to friendly mutual tolerance in the relationships between the two centers of organized influences upon the phenomenological movement. With enough intransigence on either side, the negotiations might well have ended in hostilities and a damaging split to the detriment of the international phenomenological movement.

37. Schutz mailed a detailed report about this visit to Farber. No copy of it was found in Schutz's files.

"I hope you will speak your mind in any way you see fit for our interests." This seemed to be both an assertion of a "we and they" opposition and a statement of plenipotentiary powerş for Schutz. Facing Louvain, Farber invoked the primogeniture of the International Phenomenological Society,[38] and Van Breda gained his strength from his exclusive control of the Husserl-Archives and the growing financial support he was able to mobilize for his undertakings. There were letters exchanged and, in 1954, Van Breda spent a few hours in talks with Farber in Buffalo. Farber explained his agreement with Van Breda's major plans: (1) depositing copies (possibly microfilms) of Husserl's manuscripts at three centers in the United States: Harvard, St. Louis, and Buffalo;[39] (2) organizing international Husserl colloquia which were to convene in various European countries; and (3) publishing the series *Phaenomenologica*; it was to bring various studies of living phenomenologists from any country. In turn, Van Breda did not object to the publication, in the United States, of what Farber called the publications of the International Phenomenological Society.

Point 3 of this agreement is puzzling in that, officially, no series of *Publications of the International Phenomenological Society* existed or came into being later. Farber had easy access to a series called *University of Buffalo Publications in Philosophy*. It had been started under the label *Monographs in Philosophy*, and its first volume had been Farber's dissertation. In 1950 Faber edited a volume, *Philosophic Thought in France and America*, as part of the Buffalo series. A year later, he was named editor of the series *American Lectures in Philosophy* for the publishing house of C. C. Thomas. The series, a quite successfull undertaking, was not devoted to the specific promotion of phenomenological studies, but Farber made definite efforts to induce men like Schutz to contribute to it.

When Farber, in his correspondence with both Van Breda and Schutz, spoke up to 1957 of the "Publications of the International Phenomenological Society," he had in mind such publications as his *Foundation of Phenomenology*, which, appearing in various publishing houses, would be unofficially adopted by the society.

After having been informed by Farber about his talks with Van Breda, Schutz offered the only possible comment: A "tolerant pluralism" has to be accepted on both sides. "Of course, we are free to do

38. At this time, one of the founding members of the IPS (Spiegelberg) turned to Farber for factual information on the society, concerning membership criteria, principles and goals, and the working of its council. Farber assumed that the questioner himself knew the answers, and did not reply. But Spiegelberg was puzzled; his inquiry reflected his concern for an organization which seemed to exist only by fiat of its president.

39. According to my information, no such deposits were made at the time.

everything we want to do, but in order to achieve this result, we have to grant him also full freedom of action." Personally, he added, he preferred "this state of affairs to any kind of agreement." Farber concurred fully with him.

It seems that matters rested on this note until 1956, when a new European Husserl conference took place in Krefeld. At this colloquium, plans for an European association of phenomenologists were announced. In the following year, representatives from Belgium, France, Germany, Holland, Poland, and Yugoslavia met with Van Breda as chairman in order to deliberate the concrete steps to be taken toward the execution of this plan. The delegates met in Paris, in conjunction with the Husserl colloquium at the abbey of Royaumont. Farber, of course, had been properly informed; since Schutz was a speaker at the colloquium, he delegated him to represent the IPS. Thus, as Schutz said in his later report to Farber, he "was invited as representative of the USA mother society." Since the two phenomenologists from Poland and Yugoslavia explained that anyone in their countries would be prevented from joining a society based in the United States, Van Breda suggested that the planned society be called Société Internationale de Phénoménologie, Branche Européenne, that it not be incorporated, and that it enter into a loose federation with the American society.

He also had in his hands the "constitution" of the IPS and mentioned that the Europeans would not be able to live up to all its provisions. However, this could not have become an issue. As Farber had explained to Schutz six weeks before the Paris meeting (letter of April 13, 1957): This constitution was a document "which we circulated at the beginning of our organization. But that document was never ratified."[40]

In Paris, Van Breda assumed that it is understood that, in the planned federation, the European and the American organizations should have equal rights, to which Schutz agreed; and he suggested that Americans add to the name of their oganization the specification: American Branch. Cairns, Farber, and Schutz later agreed to table this suggestion indefinitely. On the other hand, Farber had no objections to accept Van Breda "ex officio" as "member of our board," that is, as representative of the European Branch.

After the Paris conference, Van Breda mailed "materials" and a letter to the Americans, concerning the decisions and plans of the meeting.

40. Neither Schutz's nor Spiegelberg's files contain any document which was labelled "Constitution of the IPS" or bears any resemblance to an organizational constitution. As far as the "unwritten constitution" is concerned – the ways in which it actually functions – I have some evidence that it originated in verbal agreements made between Farber and one or two of his closest collaborators at the time.

Farber answered with a note of good will. The rest is silence.[41]

Toward the end of the exchanges between Farber and Schutz about the position to take toward the organizational plans of Van Breda, Schutz mentioned that Cairns was possibly right with his remark that "we should not confuse membership in our Society with subscribers to our journal." It seems that, now, he himself had second thoughts about the reality of the society which he had represented at the Paris meeting. He explained to Farber: "Of course, we were very wise to avoid any red tape and legal niceties" concerning membership in the society. But, he added, "now we are faced perhaps with a legal question, although of no importance whatsoever. I naver saw a subscription form for our journal. Does it mention membership in the society?" An answer by Farber is not on record. However, the next volume of the journal (PPR 19, 1958-1959) bore the usual additional note after the listing of the editorial staff. As ever, it began with the declaration: "This journal is the official organ of the International Phenomenological Society." But, after the announcement of the subscription rates, it carried, for the first time, the explanation that individual subscriptions "entitle the subscriber to membership in the International Phenomenological Society."

This account, to stress once more, is based on necessarily incomplete sources. To the degree to which it can be trusted, it reveals Farber's role vis-à-vis the revigorated European phenomenological movement and its centers. At least since 1949, it was characterized by reluctance rather than wholehearted support and initiative. It seems that, in his contact with Van Breda, he was ill at ease. He did not shun him, but was largely satisfied with letting a few of the Europeans around PPR make and maintain the contacts.

In contrast to these official and organizational negotiations and their formal results, the relevant philosophical contacts and exchanges occurred on a personal basis. They were carried out by some of the most distinguished refugee phenomenologists. Thus, Gurwitsch's lectures at the Freie Universität in Berlin and his courses at the University of Cologne (1958-1959) were "American contributions" to European phenomenology at their best. In the same manner, Schutz's earlier paper at the Royaumont Husserl Colloquium (in 1957), "The Problem of Transcendental Intersubjectivity in Husserl," contributed significantly to the international Husserl critique. Significantly, it appeared first both in German and in an English translation.

41. The silence, most of all, is that of my sources. In the Farber-Schutz correspondence at my disposal is a time gap of eleven months between the exchange about the Paris meeting and the next letter. In the Spring of 1982, I had the occasion to ask two leading members of the Deutsche Gesellschaft für phänomenologische Forschung (founded in 1971). They were unable to give me any information about Van Breda's attempt of 1957 to get an Inter-European phenomenological society going. Steps are underway to procure the needed information.

Farber, as I have made clear, had no philosophical responsibility for the work of men like Gurwitsch and Schutz; but at least Schutz never forgot that it had been Farber who had set him out on the path to his contributions to the advancement of phenomenological thinking on the American continent. He had done this, simply, be creating organizational and publishing possibilities he otherwise would hardly have been able to find. He was too much convinced of the pragmatic character of man's existence in the world of practical life to have denied the importance of such external conditions and opportunities. However, while bowing to the *pragmatic* predominance of the external conditions of a thinker's existence in a given "natural and cultural setting," he was unable to accept Farber's conception of the *philosophical* priority of this setting.

These remarks have a broader significance. They point to the inherent tension between man's mundane existence and his efforts to transcend them, and they point to the dialectic between life-world and philosophy. Maybe my pedestrian and episodic exposition of the relationships between Farber, the editor of PPR and the president of the IPS, and the refugee phenomenologists, the pure thinkers and exponents of a philosophical cause, will gain more than historical significance if seen as a case study of this dialectical tension between the so-called hard facts of life in the ordinary world and the "evidence" of philosophical reflection in the world of the spirit.

REFERENCES

Published Materials

Cho, Kah Kyung

1982 "Marvin Farber (1901-1980) in memoriam. Sein Leben und Wirken für die Phänomenologie in USA." *Phänomenologische Forschungen* 12, Freiburg 1982: 145-72.

Farber, Marvin

1928 *Phenomenology as a Method and as a Philosophical Discipline*. University of Buffalo Studies, vol. 6. June 1928.

1940 (Editor) *Philosophical Essays in Memory of Edmund Husserl*. Cambridge, Mass.: Harvard University Press.

1943 *The Foundation of Phenomenology: Edmund Husserl and the Quest for a Rigorous Science of Philosophy*. Cambridge, Mass.: Harvard University Press.

1945 "Remarks about the Phenomenological Program," *Philosophy and Phenomenological Research* 6: 1-10.

1947 "Aspekte der Philosophie in USA von 1940 bis 1946," *Zeitschrift für philosophische Forschung* 2: 396-402.

1949 "Experience and Subjectivism." Pp. 591-632 in Roy Wood Sellars, V. J. McGill, and Marvin Farber (editors), *Philosophy for the Future: The Quest of Modern Materialism*. New York: Macmillan.

1950 (Editor) *Philosophic Thought in France and the United States: Essays Representing Major Trends in Contemporary French and American Philosophy*. University of Buffalo Publications in Philosophy.

1951 "Experience and Transcendence," *Philosophy and Phenomenological Research* 12: 1-23.

Spiegelberg, Herbert

1976 *The phenomenological Movement: A Historical Introduction.* 2 vols. Second edition. The Hague: Nijhoff.

1981 The same. Third edition.

Van Breda, Herman

1947 "The Husserl Archives in Louvain," *Philosophy and Phenomenological Research*, 7: 487-491.

1948 "Communications, Notes, and News from the Husserl Archives." *Philosophy and Phenomenological Research*, 8: 302-305.

1959 "Le sauvetage de l'héritage Husserlien et la fondation des Archives-Husserl." Pp. 1-42 in H.L. Van Breda and J. Taminiaux (eds.), *Husserl et la Pensée Moderne*. The Hague: Nijhoff.

From Philosophy and Phenomenological Research

Vols. 1-20: (1940-41 to 1959-60) Listings of editorial staff.

Same: Tables of Contents

Vol. 1-7, 9 (1940-41 to 1949-50): Lists of Members: International Phenomenological Society.

1940 Vol. 1, p. 126: "International Phenomenological Society: Foundation Meeting."

Unpublished Sources

Harry P. Reeder

Undated: Handwritten *Discursive Index* to the selected correspondence of Felix Kaufmann. Composed for the Centre for Advanced Research in Phenomenology at Wilfred Laurier University, Waterloo, Ont.

Alfred Schutz

Unpublished correspondence with Marvin Farber, Aron Gurwitsch, Helmut Kuhn, Fritz Machlup, Herbert Spiegelberg, Herman Van Breda.

Herbert Spiegelberg

Unpublished correspondence with Marvin Farber

Letters to HRW: 1/10/82, 2/10/82, 2/28/82

Richard H. Williams

Letter to HRW: 1/17/82

CONTRIBUTORS

Apel, Karl-Otto
Professor of Philosophy, Johann Wolfgang Goethe University, Frankfurt.
Honorary Member of the International Institute of Philosophy.
Publications: *Analytic Philosophy of Language and the 'Geisteswissenschaften'* (1967); *Die 'Erklären/Verstehen'-Kontroverse in transzendental-pragmatischer Sicht* (1979. An English translation is under preparation by MIT Press); *Toward a Transformation of Philosophy* (1980); *Charles S. Peirce: From Pragmatism to Pragmaticism* (1981).

Carr, David Tredway
Professor of Philosophy, University of Ottawa (Ph.D. Yale 1966).
Co-editor, *Dialogues in Phenomenology*.
Publications: (ed. & transl.) Husserl's *Crisis of European Sciences and the Transcendental Phenomenology* (1970); *Phenomenology and the Problem of History* (1974).

Chisholm, Roderick Milton
Andrew W. Mellon Professor of Humanities, Brown University (Ph.D. Harvard 1942).
President, American Philosophical Association (Eastern Division 1968); President, The Metaphysical Association of America (1972-73); Editor, *Philosophy and Phenomenological Research*.
Publications: *Perceiving: A Philosophical Study* (1957); (ed.) *Realism and the Background of Phenomenology* (1961); *Theory of Knowledge* (1966).

Cho, Kah Kyung
Professor of Philosophy, State University of New York at Buffalo (Ph.D. Heidelberg 1957).
Member, Editorial Board, *Philosophy and Phenomenological Research*;

Member, Editorial Board, *Husserl Studies.*
Publications: *Philosophy of Existence* (1961, 1969); (ed.) *Philosophy and Science in Phenomenological Perspective* (1984).

Dillon, Martin Conboy
Professor of Philosophy, State University of New York at Binghamton (Ph.D. Yale 1969).
Publications: "Sartre on the Phenomenal Body and Merleau-Ponty's Critique" (1974); "Merleau-Ponty and the Psychogenesis of the Self" (1978); "Love, Death and Creation" (1981).

Dufrenne, Mikel
Professor of Philosophy (Emeritus), University of Paris at Nanterre.
President, Société d'Esthétique; Co-Director, *Revue d'Esthétique.*
Publications: *The Phenomenology of Aesthetic Experience* (1953, English transl. 1973); *Language and Philosophy* (1968); *Le Poétique* (1963, 1972^2).

Edie, James M.
Professor of Philosophy, Northwestern University (Ph.D. Louvain 1958).
Secretary, Society for Phenomenology and Existential Philosophy (1962-1968).
Publications: *Invitation to Phenomenology* (1965); *Phenomenology in America* (1967); *Speaking and Meaning: The Phenomenology of Language* (1976).

Frings, Manfred Servatius
Professor of Philosophy, DePaul University, Chicago (Ph.D. Cologne 1953). Editor, Complete Works of Max Scheler.
Publications: *Max Scheler* (1965); *Person und Dasein: Zur Frage der Ontologie des Werseins* (1969); *Zur Phänomenologie der Lebensgemeinschaft: Ein Versuch mit Max Scheler* (1971).

Harris, Henry Silton
Professor of Philosophy and Humanities, Glendon College, York University (Educated at Oxford, Ph.D. University of Illinois 1954).
Member, Editorial Board, *Philosophy and Phenomenological Research.*
Publications: *The Social Philosophy of Giovanni Gentile* (1960); *Hegel's Development I: Toward the Sunlight* (1972); *Hegel's Development II: Night Thoughts* (1983).

Ihde, Don
Professor of Philosophy, State University of New York at Stony Brook

(Ph.D. Boston 1964). Fulbright Research Fellow, University of Paris.
Publications: *Hermeneutic Philosophy: The Philosophy of Paul Ricœur* (1971); *Sense and Significance* (1973); *Listening and Voice: A Phenomenology of Sound* (1976); *Technics and Praxis* (1979); *Existential Technics* (1983).

Mays, Wolfe
Director, Human Sciences Seminar at the Institute of Advanced Studies, Manchester Polytechnic. Editor, Journal of the British Society for Phenomenology.
Publications: *The Philosophy of Whitehead* (1969); *Arthur Koestler* (1973); Whitehead's Philosophy of Science and Metaphysics (1977); (Co-author) *Les liaisons analytiques et synthétiques dans les comportments du sujet* (1957); (Co-author) *Epistémologie génétique et recherche psychologique* (1957).

Mohanty, Jitendra N.
Professor of Philosophy, University of Oklahoma (Ph.D. Göttingen 1954). Served as President of the Indian Philosophical Association. Member, Editorial Board, *Philosophy and Phenomenological Research*; Co-editor, *Husserl Studies.*
Publications: *Edmund Husserl's Theory of Meaning* (1964); *Phenomenology and Ontology* (1971); *The Concept of Intentionality* (1972); *Husserl and Frege* (1982).

Orth, Ernst Wolfgang
Professor of Philosophy, University of Trier (Ph.D. Mainz 1965).
Editor, *Phänomenologische Forschungen*; President, German Society for Phenomenological Research; Secretary, Allgemeine Gesellschaft für Philosophie in Deutschland.
Publications: *Bedeutung, Sinn, Gegenstand, Studien zur Sprachphilosophie Edmund Husserls und Richard Hönigswalds* (1967); "Von der Ideologie zur Ideologiekritik" (1979); "Über Interesse" (1982).

Rotenstreich, Nathan
Ahad Ha'am Professor of Philosophy, Hebrew University of Jerusalem (Ph.D. Jerusalem 1938). Member, Israel Academy of Sciences, and Humanities. Visiting Professor, Harvard University (1980).
Publications: *Experience and Its Systematization: Studies in Kant* (1965); Basic Problems of Marx's Philosophy (1965); *Theory and Practice: An Essay on Human Intentionalities* (1977); *Practice and Realization: Studies in Kant* (1979).

Sallis, John Cleveland
Professor of Philosophy, Loyola University, Chicago (Ph.D. Tulane 1964).
Served as Director of Collegium Phaenomenologicum in Italy: Editor, *Research in Phenomenology.*
Publications: *The Gathering of Reason* (1980); (ed.) *Radical Phenomenology* (1978); (ed.) *Heraclitean Fragments* (1980).

Ströker, Elisabeth
Professor of Philosophy, University of Cologne (Ph.D. Bonn; Habilitation Hamburg).
Director, Husserl Archives at Cologne; Member, Editorial Board, *Phaenomenologica.*
Publications: *Philosophische Untersuchungen zum Raum* (1965, 1977) (English translation under preparation); *Denkwege der Chemie* (1967); *Wissenschaftstheorie als Herausforderung* (1976); *Theorienwandel in der Wissenschaftsgeschichte* (1982).

Wagner, Helmut R.
Research Professor of Sociology, Hobert and William Smith Colleges (Ph.D. in Sociology, New School for Social Research). Taught at New School for Social Research and Bucknell University.
Publications: *Psychology of Consciousness and the Sociology of the Life-World* (1983); (ed.) *Alfred Schutz on Phenomenology and Social Relations*; (ed.) A. Schutz, *Life Forms and Meaning Structure.*

INDEX OF SUBJECTS

INDEX OF NAMES

Made in the USA
Las Vegas, NV
14 November 2024

11637456R00155